CHILDREN

£18·9?

Children: Rights and Childhood is widely regarded as the first book to offer a detailed philosophical examination of children's rights. Drawing on a wide variety of sources from law and literature to politics and psychology, David Archard provides a clear and accessible introduction to a topic that has assumed increasing relevance since the book's first publication. Divided clearly into three parts, it covers key topics such as:

- John Locke's writings on children
- Philippe Ariès's *Centuries of Childhood*
- key texts on children's liberation and rights
- a child's right to vote and to sexual choice
- the rights of parents and the state over children
- defining and understanding child abuse.

The second edition has been fully revised and updated including a new preface, a new chapter on children's moral and legal rights, taking into account the United Nations Convention on the Rights of the Child and a new chapter on children under the law, taking changes in European law into account.

David Archard is Professor of Philosophy and Public Policy at Lancaster University. He is author of *Sexual Consent* and co-editor of *The Moral and Political Status of Children*.

CHILDREN

Rights and childhood

Second Edition

David Archard

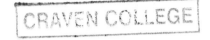

Routledge
Taylor & Francis Group

LONDON AND NEW YORK

First published 1993
by Routledge
2 Park Square, Milton Park, Abingdon, Oxon OX14 4RN

Simultaneously published in the USA and Canada
by Routledge
270 Madison Ave, New York, NY 10016

Reprinted 1995, 1998, 2002, 2003, 2007

Second edition published 2004

Routledge is an imprint of the Taylor & Francis Groups an informa business

© 1993, 2004 David Archard

Typeset in Sabon and Frutiger by
Keystroke, Jacaranda Lodge, Wolverhampton
Printed and bound in Great Britain by
MPG Books Ltd, Bodmin

British Library Cataloguing in Publication Data
A catalogue record for this book is available from the British Library

Library of Congress Cataloging in Publication Data
Archard, David.
Children : rights and childhood / David Archard.—2nd ed.
p. cm.
1. Children—History. 2. Children's rights—History. 3. Family policy—History.
I. Title.
HQ767 .87 .A73 2004
305.23—dc22
2004003946

ISBN 10: 0–415–30583–7 (hbk)
ISBN 10: 0–415–30584–5 (pbk)

ISBN 13: 978-0–415–30583–9 (hbk)
ISBN 13: 0–415–30584–6 (pbk)

FOR MY MOTHER

CONTENTS

CONTENTS

ACKNOWLEDGEMENTS

This book started life in discussions with Bernarde Lynn about her work with sexually abused children. My thanks to her for her ideas and her encouragement. Those discussions gave birth to a paper given at Bristol University and I thank those present for their criticisms. The paper was published in the *Journal of Applied Philosophy* (1990) and I learnt much from published criticism of it by Mary Midgley, and from correspondence about it with Mark Fisher.

Jonathan Rée suggested I speak about children to a *Radical Philosophy* conference, and then that the talk become a book. My thanks to him for the suggestion and subsequent help, especially his careful and conscientious editing of my text.

Part of the book was given as a paper to a Manchester University Political Theory Conference, and I thank those present for their criticisms. Special thanks are due to Hillel Steiner for making me think harder about the 'proprietarian' argument.

In fond memory of my own childhood this book is dedicated with much love to my mother.

PREFACE TO SECOND EDITION

I am grateful to Tony Bruce at Routledge for inviting me to write a second edition of this book for a number of reasons. Since the book was first published a great deal more philosophical work on children and their rights has been published. The second edition takes account of this new work. Second, any talk of children's rights must take account, as the first edition did not, of the United Nations Convention on the Rights of the Child (CRC). I have thus been able in this new edition of the book to write an entirely new chapter on the legal and moral rights of children. Third, I am no longer convinced of the defensibility of a view I gave prominence to in the first edition, namely that every child has the right to the best possible upbringing. No such right exists in the CRC and I am not now persuaded it should. I speak instead in this edition of every child's right to a minimally decent upbringing. Fourth, I have been able to add a chapter on the important topic, neglected in the first edition, of children under the law. The book has been extensively revised throughout with two entirely new chapters.

Since the publication of the original edition I have had the opportunity to discuss my ideas on children with a large number of people and at many different academic occasions. I am extremely grateful to all of these people. However, I would like to give special thanks to the following individuals for their help, advice and comments in various respects and at different times: Margaret Coady, Tony Coady, Karl Hanson, Michael King, Hugh LaFollette, Matthew Liao, Colin Macleod, Thomas Pogge, Tom Sorell and Hillel Steiner.

For seven years up until 2003 I was a member of the Dundee Children's Panel. The Scottish Children's Hearing System is briefly discussed in this new edition. I wish to say here that I greatly esteem the system and learned a huge amount about children, the law and society from my experiences on the Panel. I owe a debt of thanks to all those who serve the system, especially my fellow Panel members and the Reporters.

My partner, Bernarde, is due as always my heartfelt thanks for her help, encouragement and advice. The fact that these thanks are repeatedly given does not make them any the less deeply or sincerely felt.

1

JOHN LOCKE'S CHILDREN

John Locke (1632–1704) is one of the most important and influential figures in the history of English-speaking philosophy. He is a progenitor of the empiricist and analytic tradition of philosophy, and widely regarded as the 'father of English liberalism'. He did not write a philosophical treatise on childhood, although he did write *Some Thoughts Concerning Education* (1693)[1] which recommends the appropriate education for a young gentleman. These recommendations are surprisingly modern and liberal, permitting *Some Thoughts* to be viewed, along with Rousseau's *Émile* (1762),[2] as the earliest manifesto for a 'child-centred' education. Indeed the fact that he may be placed at the beginning of a long tradition of thought about the best way to bring up children fully justifies the euphonic sub-title of Christina Hardyment's *Dream Babies: Childcare from Locke to Spock*.[3]

Locke also wrote about children in other works devoted to the origins of civil government and the foundations of knowledge. He is thus typical of most philosophers in that his account of childhood has to be extracted from scattered remarks, and is not to be found explicitly and systematically expressed in a single work. Moreover, what Locke has to say about children in one context does not always sit easily with what he has to say about them in another. These tensions are due to writing about children from different perspectives. In this respect Locke's is fairly typical of much contemporary philosophical writing on childhood. Locke writes of children as the recipients of an ideal upbringing, citizens in the making, fledgling but imperfect reasoners and blank sheets filled by experience. It is not easy to be all these things simultaneously. Similarly, modern writers seem often to demand of their 'children' that they be different things, according to the aspect under which they are being regarded.

Consequently, Locke is an illustrious representative of anglophone philosophy both in general and in its thinking about childhood. Locke's philosophical children are good ones to start with, not least because their problems

1

are abiding ones. Before I explore these problems in greater depth, let me sketch the various circumstances in which Locke wrote about children, how these different accounts roughly hang together and where difficulties begin to arise for a consistent overall theory of childhood.

In *An Essay Concerning Human Understanding* (1689),[4] Locke supplied the first full-blown, forceful and persuasive defence of an empiricist theory of mind and knowledge. Such a theory holds that all human knowledge derives from a single source, experience. Famously, Locke denied that any knowledge is inborn. Young children display no awareness of those ideas, theorems or propositions which other philosophers had claimed to be innate. If knowledge is acquired from experience then it is acquired gradually. Humans *become* knowledgeable users of reason. Since childhood is a stage in the developmental process whose end is adulthood, children would seem to be imperfect, incomplete versions of their adult selves. The *Essay* is usefully supplemented by the posthumously published *Of the Conduct of the Understanding* (1697)[5] in which Locke offers a guide for the proper use of reason in the acquisition of truth in every area of human knowledge, scientific and moral.

In the first of his *Two Treatises of Government* (1698),[6] Locke criticised Robert Filmer's Tory, patriarchal account of political authority as bequeathed by God to Adam, and thence to his descendants, the kings. In the second *Treatise* Locke defended his own view of civil government as founded upon, and limited by, the freely given consent of rational individuals. While Locke believed that political power should not be thought of as parental, he readily conceded that parents should have power over their children. Children, for Locke, do not yet possess the rights of adult citizens.

In *Some Thoughts Concerning Education* (1693), Locke published letters he had written to his friend Edward Clarke on how best to educate the latter's young son. The advice ranges from diet, through discussion of punishment for misconduct, to a suggested programme of studies. Throughout, Locke appears to insist that the child has needs and interests which should be recognised for what they are, and that a child should be reasoned with, not simply beaten or coerced into conformity with the rules of required behaviour. The principal aim of education was to produce a virtuous person, and the essence of virtue was the subjection of one's character and appetites to rational self-control. To that end the child must eventually come to recognise, and be able to govern his behaviour in accordance with, reason.

What do these various accounts share? They have in common a view of children as not yet fully rational, only coming to be such as adults. It is to the achievement of reason that education is devoted; it is the acquiring of it, and of knowledge, that characterises human development from birth to

2

maturity; and it is the absence of reason that disqualifies children from citizenship, and at the same time warrants their subjection to their parents. But even this briefest of sketches indicates where there are going to be problems. Here are some of the more obvious ones: is reason, if not actual knowledge, an inborn capacity, and, if not, is it something that is acquired in the normal course of human development or must it be learnt? If children do not possess rationality to some degree, how can an education which appeals to their reason have any effect? If children have some rationality then why should they not enjoy a proportionate freedom? If the authority of civil government rests on the consent of the governed, then why should not parental authority require the consent of the children? Correlatively, if the latter is 'natural' rather than artificially founded by independent wills, then why should not the former be of a similar character? If the extent of legitimate political power is limited by the rights of the governed and the proper ends of government then should not parental authority be constrained by the rights of children and the due purposes of parenting? I will explore these various difficulties by considering two broad problem areas: 'coming to reason' and 'parental power'.

COMING TO REASON

Locke's theory of civil government and parental authority seems to presume that children lack what adult human beings possess. Children, says Locke, are 'travellers newly arrived in a strange country, of which they know nothing' (*Thoughts*, §120). What makes them 'strangers' in our 'country' is their lack of both knowledge and moral sense. 'Reason' covers both aspects of what must be acquired if they are to become full members of our 'country'. Children must be educated and brought to reason. A guiding thread in Locke's view of this process is his emphasis upon the acquisition of *powers* rather than discrete items of knowledge or fixed principles. The acquisition of powers is best achieved, indeed may be perfected, through their exercise and practice. By this means the possibilities are great indeed: 'We are born with faculties and powers capable of almost any thing, such at least as would carry us farther than can easily be imagined: but it is only the exercise of those powers, which gives us ability and skill in any thing, and leads us towards perfection' (*Conduct*, §2).

With regard to how human beings acquire knowledge, Locke's empiricism holds, famously, that the human mind may, at birth, be presumed to be a 'white Paper, void of all Characters, without any Ideas' (*Essay*, II.i.§2). It is experience alone which stocks the mind with its ideas, experience being both direct sensory awareness of the world and reflective awareness of the mind's own operations. Human knowledge comprises ideas which are directly furnished by experience and what can further be learnt by reasoning on and about these ideas.

Now, why should a child not be thought capable of being the equal of an adult in respect of knowledge and rationality? Locke's answer – though it is nowhere clearly stated – seems to be that both knowledge and rationality are incremental. In the first place, Locke does not hold to the simple thesis that a new-born infant's mind is completely empty. He admits to the possibility of pre-natal experiences, and accepts that a child has inborn dispositions – for instance, to seek pleasure and avoid pain. Locke is mainly concerned to deny the strong innatist claim that a child is born with knowledge of such ideas, propositions or principles as '2 + 2 = 4' or 'God exists'. He wanted to distinguish between 'natural tendencies imprinted on the Minds of Man', which he granted, and 'innate' 'Principles of Knowledge' which he rejected (*Essay*, I.iii.§3).

In the *Essay* Locke suggests that the child's first experiences are almost exclusively sensory, reflection upon the inward workings of the mind being a later development. Locke's reasoning is simple enough. A child, new to the world, is deluged with impressions of what surrounds her; she has no time for introspection. But with the progressive acquisition of ideas, the mind becomes increasingly 'awake'; it 'thinks more, the more it has matter to think on' (*Essay*, II.I.§22). In similar vein, Locke asserts that 'the use of Reason becomes daily more visible, as these Materials, that give it Employment, increase' (*Essay*, I.ii.§15). This might imply that a child's mind is the equal of an adult's; it is only that it is initially distracted from the business of introspection by the overwhelming acquisition of ideas from outside, ideas which it needs anyway in order to have something to think about. Thus, although Locke says that it is 'In time [that] the Mind comes to reflect on its own Operations, about the Ideas got by Sensation', he also says, within a line or two of this, that the mind is 'fitted' to gain experience from either sensation or reflection upon its workings as 'the first Capacity of Human Intellect' (*Essay*, II.I.§24).

Moreover, it is not just the faculty of introspection which Locke thinks inborn; God has given humans 'a Mind that can Reason without being instructed in Methods of Syllogising: The Understanding is not taught to reason by these Rules; it has a native Faculty to perceive the Coherence, or Incoherence of its Ideas' (*Essay*, IV.xvii.§4). The adult does not differ significantly from the child in basic cognitive abilities; he just has more time in which to reflect and more material on which to reflect. The adult's reason is that of the child's come 'awake', and made 'visible'.

In his *Thoughts*, however, Locke is more circumspect. Here he tempers his recommendation to treat children as rational creatures with the observation that such treatment should be relative to the child's particular capacities. And these, Locke thinks, increase with age. It is not just that children broaden the range of their experiences and thus have more to reason about; it is that their abilities to reason grow as they mature. The younger they are, the more the reasons appealed to by their teachers must be immediate, obvious and 'level to their thoughts'. 'Nobody', Locke asserts, 'can think a boy of three or seven years should be argued with as a grown man' (*Thoughts*, §81). Since, as we shall see, Locke thought that parental authority was grounded in a child's lack of reason, it follows that the exercise of the former should be proportionate to the degree of the latter: as children 'grow up to the use of reason' 'the rigour of government' may be 'gently relaxed' (*Thoughts*, §41).

The use of reason is then for Locke a faculty which is both inborn, 'native', and one that develops through a combination of natural maturation and educational encouragement. This helps to explain his apparent ambivalence on an issue which was beginning to assume prominence in contemporary debate – the relative contributions to character of nature and nurture. The *Thoughts* contains telling quotations for both sides of the argument. On the one hand, Locke declares that 'nine parts of ten (of all men) are what they are . . . by their education' (*Thoughts*, §1), and, echoing the Essay, that young children should be considered 'only as white paper or wax to be moulded and fashioned as one pleases' (*Thoughts*, §217); on the other hand, he insists that 'God hath stamped certain characters upon men's minds, which, like their shapes, may perhaps be a little mended but can hardly be totally altered and transformed into the contrary' (*Thoughts*, §66).

It would seem consistent with the essential supposition of empiricism – that all knowledge comes from experience – to hold that a child's mind is completely formed by her upbringing. Indeed Locke would probably think this to be true with respect to the ideational content of a mind. His apparently contrary comments about inflexible character refer to behavioural dispositions, temperamental traits such as temerity, laziness or love of power. Locke certainly thinks that character in this sense is inborn and relatively unmalleable. It is worth noting in passing, as most commentators do, that Locke does not subscribe to any naive belief in the inherent innocence or goodness of the child. His comments on the readily observable cruelty of young people are down to earth and perceptive. However, Locke did believe that a child, whatever his initial nature might be, could be brought up in the way of virtue, by being taught to subjugate his congenital dispositions to the dictates of reason.

The education in virtue is both possible and necessary. It is possible inasmuch as Locke believes that children can be taught moral rectitude. Virtue is 'natural' since it lies within the powers of man, but it is not independent of education and socialisation. It has to be taught. The education is necessary because children must become adult citizens living by the laws of nature. That means subordinating passions and desires to reason: 'the great Principle and Foundation of all Virtue and Worth, is placed in this, That a Man is able to deny himself his own Desires, cross his own Inclinations, and purely follow what Reason directs as best, tho' the appetite lean the other way' (*Thoughts*, §38).

These same inclinations and desires can, however, be used by the educator to mould the child. One should try to bring a child to moral maturity by working with and not against the grain of her nature. This nature, like that of the adult she will become, has the 'same Passions, the same Desires' (*Thoughts*, §41). Locke thought that a child was best educated by being put into situations which discouraged the exercise of the bad character traits and kept away from situations which encouraged them. This helps to explain Locke's noted insistence upon the educational value of habit. For Locke, the essence of moral education was the practice and cultivation of the powers of moral reason, not the learning by rote of fixed moral principles: 'Children are not to be taught by Rules. . . . What you think necessary for them to do, settle in them by an indispensable practice' (*Thoughts*, §66).

His distaste for the teaching of 'rules' leads him to insist that 'well principling' consists in giving the young mind 'that freedom, that disposition, and those habits that may enable him to attain any part of knowledge he shall apply himself to' (*Conduct*, §12). Indeed, Locke argues against 'instilling a reverence and veneration for certain dogmas' (*Conduct*, §12) and argues instead for 'a variety and freedom of thinking'. This is to be encouraged for supplying 'an increase of the powers and activity of the mind, not as an enlargement of its possessions' (*Conduct*, §19). Interestingly, this emphasis upon 'freedom' and the criticism of any reverence for principles alarmed Thomas Reid and other Scottish Enlightenment thinkers who were otherwise deeply sympathetic to Locke's ideas.[7]

Locke's emphasis upon habits of good behaviour under the governance of a child's natural inclinations does not lead him to a simple-minded use of stick and carrot. Indeed, he offers a principled objection to corporal punishment (even if he tolerates its use as a last resort). Locke feared that the use of beatings would only strengthen a child's natural predilection to seek pleasure and avoid pain. At the same time it would lead the child to associate the forbidden action with the displeasure suffered rather than recognise the reason for its being forbidden. In both respects the punishment promotes a natural disposition at the expense of an exercise of reason.

There may be an interesting ambivalence here. Locke could be asserting that children, though able to see what is rational to do, are overwhelmed by their non-rational inclinations. They are weak-willed. They must be induced and cajoled into that rational mastery of their desires which is the mark of adult virtue. This is why parents must choose for their children, since the latter are not yet capable of choosing rationally for themselves. On the other hand, Locke can seem to suggest that a child is like Aristotle's slave, one who 'participates in reason to the extent of apprehending it in others, though destitute of it himself'.[8] Children cannot do what is rational because they cannot yet see what is rational. However, they can see that their adult parents are rational, and this grounds their obligation to accept parental commands until the time when they become rational. At the same time, for Locke, the onus is upon parents to display, both in their commands and in their own behaviour, that rationality which is distinctive of their adulthood. Children must come to respect, and even revere, the reason which their parents' conduct exemplifies.

It can be seen then that Locke's thoughts about the coming to adult reason of a child are nuanced and far from straightforward. Children have reason as a 'native', 'first' capacity, but this faculty must be cognitively awakened and brought into use, once experience of the world has stocked the mind with ideas to think about; children 'understand [reason] as early as they do language' (*Thoughts*, §81), but their use of it to govern their behaviour must be encouraged lest they mature into creatures of mere natural proclivities; or perhaps they can understand reason only as that which they lack but adults have. Children are born, in some sense, with or to reason; they develop through the normal course of nature into fully rational adults, and yet may be 'moulded' into exercisers of reason.

The acquisition of reason is a gradual process; its possession is not an all-or-nothing affair. Humans may differ from other animals in being rational, but no such sharp dividing line distinguishes young from old. Although it is a part of the natural, and normal, process of psychological development and maturation that a child should become a fully rational adult, it is not inevitable and it is subject to some significant environmental control. 'Adulthood' is to be thought of as a state of mind rather than a question of age. Adulthood and full rationality are normally associated with one another, but childhood cannot accurately be characterised as the complete absence of reason. A child is born with reason; it is age, as Locke says, which brings its exercise. Significantly, for Locke the exercise of reason qualifies an individual for the exercise of freedom.

PARENTAL POWER

According to a simple model of parental power, parents have absolute authority over their children, who have no rights. A major principle of Roman law was that of *patria potestas*. The father as head of the family, paterfamilias, had the absolute power of life and death over his son, the latter being released from this state only by his father's death or by manumission. One might modify this model by insisting that children acquire the rights of adults, and are discharged from the power of their parents, when they themselves reach adulthood. Thomas Hobbes accorded parents total and absolute dominion over their children. Locke's views are notably more liberal, gesturing towards what might be seen as a modern theory of justified parenthood. Locke denies that political power proper is patriarchal, but he also denies that parental power has the same sort of foundations as civil government. Locke's recognition of this asymmetry between the two kinds of authority is important for modern discussions of parent–child relations. Of equal significance is his silence on the proper relationship between the two authorities.

Locke's important legacy to political theory is his insistence that legitimate political authority is founded upon the freely given consent of those individuals over whom authority is exercised. Human beings, in a state of nature, enjoy a freedom subject to the laws of nature and are, 'as Creatures of the same species and rank', entitled to equality of recognition. It is only by means of consent, their contracted agreement, that they quit this state for 'the bonds of Civil Society'. The rights – to life, liberty and estate – enjoyed in the state of nature are not given up with the creation of the state; it is only the power to enforce and protect these rights which is transferred from individuals to government. Civil government retains its legitimacy only in so far as it continues to secure and protect these rights.

For Locke, it is adult humans who make the contract, and enjoy under civil government the protection of their rights. Children are neither parties to the contract nor rights-holding citizens of the government thereby agreed to. Nevertheless, Locke does not think children lack all rights, and, whilst he believes that some measure of parental power is warranted, he does not think parents have absolute dominion over their offspring of the kind attributed by his Tory adversary Sir Robert Filmer to the first father, Adam.

For Locke, children are not born *in* the full state of equality enjoyed by their parents, but they are born *to* it (*Treatises*, II.vi.§55). Consequently, parents have 'a sort of Rule and Jurisdiction' over their children, albeit a temporally restricted one. Children are weak, vulnerable and incapable of providing for their own maintenance. They also lack reason and thus

8

cannot truly act freely. Locke holds that freedom requires action in accordance with the law of reason, and whoever lacks reason thereby lacks the means to be free. Moreover, for a person to be given liberty before acquiring reason is 'to thrust him out amongst Brutes, and abandon him to a state as wretched, and as much beneath that of a Man, as theirs' (*Treatises*, II.vi.§63). Locke concedes that a lack of reason is not exclusive to children; there are adults – 'innocents' and 'madmen' – who remain in the state that naturally defines childhood.

The condition of children – incapable of supporting themselves and of acting for their best interests – justifies parents in acting on behalf of their children, but it also constitutes such tutelage as a duty. Indeed, the power that parents have to bring up their children derives from this obligation to care for those who cannot care for themselves. Where does this duty come from? Locke is unclear whether it simply arises out of the brute natural fact that children are born to parents, or is grounded upon an antecedent right that the children themselves possess. He is certainly clear that children do have a right 'not only to a bare Subsistance but to the conveniences and comforts of Life, as far as the conditions of their Parents can afford it' (*Treatises*, I.I.§89).

But why should a duty to care for those whose condition requires it automatically and naturally fall upon their begetters? Although Locke appears to assume that it is in virtue of being parents that such an obligation is incurred, he does not, correlatively, think that anyone has rights over a child simply on account of being his parent. Indeed, he is explicit that a parent's power does not 'belong to the Father by any peculiar right of Nature, but only as he is Guardian' (*Treatises*, II.vi.§65). A foster parent who cared adequately for his or her charges would have, in virtue of fulfilling the parental obligation and in respect of the children, the same rights as any natural parent.

Locke specifically rejects the view that natural parents enjoy rights over their children because they *own* them. He famously defended the labour theory of property acquisition, whereby an individual justly owns that on which he has laboured, which 'he hath mixed his Labour with, and joined to it something that is his own' (*Treatises*, II.v.§27). Yet he denies that parents own their offspring in virtue of having produced them.

Locke thus needs to show that there is some relevant difference between the process whereby children are produced and other processes of labouring which ground entitlements to own the result. If he cannot, then it follows from his own argument that children *are*, as a result of being conceived by and born to particular parents, these parents' property; if, on the other hand, he insists that children are not owned by their parents then he must abandon the labour theory as defective. But, as Robert Nozick has pointed out, Locke's attempt to display that difference is singularly unconvincing.[9] He appears to argue both that no one can own what is really the creation of God, and that no one can own something the design or process of manufacture of which is, in the last analysis, beyond their ken and control (*Treatises*, I.vi.§52–4). Whilst it is true that, on these conditions, a child cannot be owned by anyone, it is also true that very few other things can be owned either.

Hidden between these unsatisfactory arguments is the far more productive suggestion that what is different about the production of a child is that it is the bringing into being of a human life. Now what matters is not that human life is ultimately God's gift, nor that its creation is a mystery to us, but that to be or have a human life is to be in possession of rights to continued life and liberty. The latter right clearly trumps any prospective right on the part of others to own one. For Locke, human beings have a right to own things in virtue of owning their own persons and thus their own labour; this foundational right of self-ownership could not be foregone in the case of children just because they require other human beings in order to be brought into existence.[10]

Not only does Locke reject the idea that parents own their children; he also finds cruel and barbarous the associated idea that parents might dispose of their children as they see fit. Filmer thought Adam had absolute dominion over his children, including the power of life and death, and such a power, *patria potestas*, was granted to the father under ancient Roman law. Locke deemed such a claim contrary to reason and nature. He was convinced that parents are naturally disposed to act in the interests of their children, that they are bound to them by natural ties of affection and would more likely neglect their own good than not care for their offspring (*Treatises*, I.vi.§56; II.vi.§63, §67).

This inbuilt parental propensity to promote a child's good serves a further useful purpose in Locke's argument. The limits of a parent's power are, in one respect, given simply by the duration of the state of minority. When a child comes of age she must enjoy the same rights and freedoms as any other adult, including her parents. But beyond the need to satisfy the obligation to care for the child, and respecting the child's right to life and liberty, Locke does not clearly specify the constraints on legitimate parental authority. A parent has powers of 'commanding and chastising', but Locke does not say what their limits are. He only repeats that nature has equipped humans with a 'tenderness', 'care' and 'affection' toward their offspring which would not countenance any abuse of their powers.

On Locke's account, then, the brute natural fact of being someone's progenitor does not give one any special rights over the other, though it does seem to explain why the duty of caring for the other falls to one, and it does entail the further brute natural fact that one will fulfil one's duty in an appropriately self-denying fashion. But does Locke think that government should enforce these duties? And what is the proper balance between the authority of a state to protect the most vulnerable members of society and the authority of a parent to 'command and chastise' its own children?

For Locke, rights possessed in the state of nature are preserved in the passage to government. The state cannot legitimately alienate, abrogate or abridge what are, properly, natural rights. Now, whereas Locke sees a child's rights as natural, he is not prepared to concede that there is any right, as of nature, possessed by a parent in respect of her children. Seemingly then, the scope of the state's warranted authority in relation to the family is constrained only by respect for the child's interests – a view which, if it was Locke's, is a strikingly modern one. Locke is understandably anxious to rebut any suggestion that there are some forms of authority which are natural, rather than artificially created by contract. His target is Filmer's patriarchal notions, and doctrines of natural 'dominion and sovereignty'. But the compass of his critique is such that it cannot help but take in the putative power of a parent.

Independently of these general considerations, Locke does specifically reject the idea that a natural parent has such a right over his children as can be alienated or transferred. It may only be 'forfeited' as a consequence of dereliction of parental duty. A foster parent can acquire a parental right only in consequence of acting as a dutiful parent should, and not as the bequest of an allegedly rightful owner. Locke imagines the case of a neglectful natural father giving over his child to another man who is equally neglectful and who transfers the child in turn to a third man. This last rears and cherishes the child as his own. Locke is explicit that parental power over the child cannot be at the disposal of some title-holder. They are gained or lost solely to the extent that 'the office and care of a father' is or is not adequately discharged (*Treatises*, I.ix.§100).

For Locke, then, parental power is not natural, though normally it is assumed by natural parents. It is derived from and constrained by the natural right of children to be cared for and protected. Its warrant is the temporally bounded state of natural incapacity which defines childhood. Otherwise, the terms of its justified exercise are circumscribed by no more than the rights of the child and a confidence in the natural benevolence of parents.

CONCLUSION

Locke exemplifies a philosophical tradition of understanding children in a mixture of epistemological, educational and political terms. The problem is how these various ways of thinking about children may consistently be combined with one another. Sometimes the joins tend to show. This is true of Locke, as it is of others who think about children in these different ways. His relevance to contemporary debates on the subject can be indicated by reviewing the problems his account raises and doing so in the light of that debate. I shall consider seven such problems.

First, there is the problem of how to dovetail a psychological account of human development, or an epistemological account of the acquisition of knowledge, with the establishment of criteria whose possession guarantees a certain moral, political and juridical status. Maturation is gradual and it would appear absurd to insist otherwise. However, the granting of rights would seem to be an all-or-nothing affair. In terms of becoming a reasoner, or knowledgeable, the passage from childhood into adulthood is continuous and cumulative. In terms of acquiring citizenship, the same passage is discontinuous and abrupt. Locke is sensitive to, and demands that the educator also be sensitive to, the steady growth of a child into moral and cognitive maturity. Yet at the same time he thinks that the adult quits parental authority, inherits property and becomes a citizen at a stroke.

It is not just that the two stories of the passage into adulthood are inconsistent. It is also that the narrative of acquired politico-juridical status seems insensitive to the facts that the other narrative can tell. A young person just below the age of majority is less like an infant and more like an adult. Yet its legal status remains that of the former. I will review these issues further when I look, in chapters 4 and 9, at the rights a child may possess and the child at law.

The second problem is that the notion of childhood can be parasitic on that of adulthood, in that a child is principally understood as lacking that which defines an adult, for instance reason or physical independence. Locke tends to favour this view. Although he is alert to the particular character of childhood, he sees it in general terms as a stage on the way to a terminus, adulthood, and the maturation of human powers. Against this way of thinking is a recognition, implicit in modern educational ideals, that the child has a distinctive and special set of characteristics, needs and interests. The child is not so much an adult which is yet to be, as something different from the adult which requires acknowledgement as such. This is 'the child in the child', as Jean-Jacques Rousseau expressed it. The former picture derives much of its strength from an understanding of adulthood as a state which is accomplished absolutely, once and for all, when childhood, its contrary, is transcended. Childhood on this view is merely the preparation for that which definitively leaves it behind. I will explore these issues further in the next chapter.

Third, if we do think in terms of rights we should, it seems, believe that children have at least as many rights as things which are not even adult human beings. Children could not surely have a lesser moral status than animals. Locke departs from the Hobbesian view that children are under the absolute and unconditional dominion of their parents. Yet he does not specify what forms of protection of their interests children are entitled to rather than what they might simply expect given the natural disposition of parents to care for their own. In the modern debate, the language of rights has been crucial in securing adequate protection for children. This language is especially important for opening up the possibility of moving beyond the mere safeguarding of children's welfare to their empowerment as the guardians of their own lives. Those who are critical of the idea that children do have rights do not think that this discharges adults from certain fundamental responsibilities to care for children. This will be further explored in chapters 5 and 8.

The fourth problem arises from the fact that, as Locke noted, abandoning a child to the exercise of a liberty before he has acquired the reason to guide him is a cruel barbarism; it is 'to thrust him out amongst Brutes' (*Treatises*, II.xv.§63). Yet a favoured presumption of moral thinking is that paternalism is an odious tyranny. To deny an individual her freedom in the name of her own good is deeply to wrong her. It needs to be shown that adult humans deserve their freedom as much as children merit its denial. Locke sketches a view which is now very influential, namely that denying a child his freedom must be done with the end of bringing him to a state of maturity wherein he can exercise his own freedom. The power of guardians is 'nothing but that, which Parents have over their Children, to govern them for the Childrens good, till they come to the use of Reason' (*Treatises*, II.xv.§170). I shall call such a view the 'caretaking thesis' and critically examine it in chapter 5.

Fifth, it seems reasonable to concede a certain power or authority to parents, that they may bring up children in the way they think appropriate. It further seems plausible to believe that this power is closely related to an obligation on the parents' part to care for their children and rear them to the point when they can act and decide for themselves. How the putative power and duty are related is less clear. Some have argued that the duty to care is primary and others that parents have no rights, only this duty to discharge. The role of the state in recognising the powers and enforcing the duties of parents needs to be clarified. Locke characterises the parents' power as nothing but that to govern for the child's good. He is less clear on how that

13

power is to be exercised and how that duty is to be acquitted beyond trusting to the natural benevolence of guardians. For his part he does not appear to see the state as having any clear role in enforcing parental duties to care for the child and to constrain the exercise of parental powers. The rights of parents will be treated in chapters 10 and 12, and the role of the state in chapter 11.

A sixth problem arises from a different kind of relationship between state and family. This has to do with the sources of their respective legitimacy or authority. Filmer, to criticism of whom Locke devoted the first *Treatise*, thought that all authority was patriarchal. The power of the monarch is that of the father over his offspring, bequeathed originally to Adam by God and thence by patrilinear descent to kings. The dilemma of patriarchalism is that 'if kings are fathers, fathers cannot be patriarchs. If fathers are patriarchs at home, kings cannot be patriarchs on their thrones'.[11] Locke avoided this problem by construing the authority of the civil magistrate or ruler as deriving from the freely given consent of his subjects. Yet he also insists that the authority of a parent over his child cannot rest in the same kind of way on the child's consent. However, if a parent's authority is somehow natural – and does not arise from a voluntary commitment on the child's part – why should not political authority be thought of as also natural? Conversely, if political authority requires the consent of those subject to it, why shouldn't a child's consent be required for the exercise of parental authority?

Hobbes solved the problem by welding together voluntarism and patri- archalism, seeing parental power as absolute and natural, yet exercised with the child's tacit consent.[12] Locke simply declared that 'the Power of a Magistrate over a Subject, may be distinguished from that of a Father over his Children' (*Treatises*, I.v.§2). The problem of political obligation – of finding a warrant for the rule of government over its citizens – remains; as does that of justifying a parent's 'rule' over her children. Locke simply asserts that the two kinds of rule are different without explaining why.

The seventh and final problem concerns the weight and significance of certain brute natural facts. Locke thinks that God 'has in all the parts of the Creation taken a particular care to propagate and continue the several species of Creatures, and make Individuals act so strongly to this end, that they sometimes neglect their own private good for it, and seem to forget that general Rule which Nature teaches all things of self Preservation, and the Preservation of their Young, as the strongest Principle in them over rules the Constitution of their particular Natures' (*Treatises*, I.vi.§56; see also II.vi.§63). However, as it would be naive to refuse to acknowledge that many natural parents abuse their children, so it would be obtuse to deny that very many others display an extraordinary self-sacrificial love for theirs. At the very least it is ingenuous to trust, as Locke does, to such natural affection as the sole guarantee of a child's welfare.

Locke does not think that parents own their children and are free to dispose of them as they would of any of their property. He seems to think that parental title is or is not held according to whether the duties of the office are properly discharged. However, to think that parents have *no* special claim over their own children – that is, one stronger than any other adults who would be equally good guardians – is counterintuitive. It is also wrong to discount the evidence of the very special love that a parent feels for her own child. The problem we face is how far natural facts should be accommodated within a defensible theory of parental rights without either naively assuming too much or blithely disregarding the obvious.

Locke should not be condemned for bequeathing these kinds of problems. Indeed, that they endure in contemporary debate shows just how clear-headed and prescient a philosopher of childhood he was. Now that philosophical discussion of childhood and children's rights is more common that it was some years ago, it is worth returning to Locke, as to other figures in the history of philosophy, for the fresh, and sometimes very bright, light they can shed on this discussion. To that discussion itself the rest of the book is devoted.

Part I

CHILDHOOD

Childhood is unknown. Starting from the false idea one has of it, the farther one goes, the more one loses one's way.

Jean-Jacques Rousseau, Preface,
Émile or On Education (1762)

2

THE CONCEPT OF CHILDHOOD

THE ARIÈS THESIS

The end of the seventeenth century, when John Locke wrote, occupies a pivotal point, according to an extremely influential work on the history of childhood. The work in question is *L'Enfant et la vie familiale sous l'ancien régime* (1960) by Philippe Ariès, translated into English as *Centuries of Childhood* (1962).[1] Its key claim is that it was not until the late seventeenth century that the 'concept of childhood' began to emerge.

Ariès's book has had an extraordinary impact, firstly upon the discipline of social history but also in many other areas. It was the first general historical study of childhood. It was published at a singularly apposite moment when there were both political and intellectual pressures to appreciate and defend the particular character of childhood. Its claim to be the first text in the field may be seen as illuminating its own general thesis, namely that only in modern times could an adequate understanding of childhood be achieved. Its being first has also given it an apparently authoritative stature, so that it has not always been easy for subsequent commentators to separate an acknowledgement of its pioneering status from a critical evaluation of its content. This is not only true in social history. Discussions of childhood in social, moral, legal and political theory are often prefaced with a resumé of Ariès's thesis presented as a fundamental and universally acknowledged truth. 'As Ariès has shown' is a familiar opening phrase.

Ariès summarises the argument of Part One of his book in admirably clear and concise terms:

> In medieval society the idea of childhood did not exist; this is not to suggest that children were neglected, forsaken or despised. The idea of childhood is not to be confused with affection for children: it corresponds to an awareness of the particular nature of childhood,

that particular nature which distinguishes the child from the adult, even the young adult. In medieval society, this awareness was lacking.[2]

The awareness of childhood which medieval society lacks is present in contemporary society. Although Ariès's chronology is rather vague and imprecise, it seems that he thinks of the fifteenth, sixteenth and seventeenth centuries, especially the last, as the crucial periods in an observable transition from traditional to present-day thinking about children. For Ariès, the unawareness of the particular nature of children showed itself in the following characteristic behaviour. Although infants, that is, those under seven, were recognised as fragile and vulnerable creatures, their parents were on the whole indifferent to them, and treated their death with casualness. This can be attributed to the high rates of infant mortality then prevalent. After the age of seven the child was simply regarded as another, albeit smaller, adult. It was not in any way distinguished as having the particular nature of a child.

Ariès's evidence for his thesis is taken from a number of disparate sources. In paintings children were portrayed only as miniature scaled-down adults, with no representative appreciation of their particular and distinctive attributes. Children were dressed in reduced versions of the clothes worn by adults. The games that children played were also played by adults, and children were not excluded from playing games, such as those of chance, which we might now think of as exclusively adult. Finally, Ariès uses the diary of Henri IV's doctor, Heroard. This records in detail the childhood of Louis XIII and is apparent evidence that a child at that time was not seen as meriting protection from the sexually immodest language and actions of adults.

In our time, the separate nature of the child is recognised. This finds expression in the literal and metaphorical separation of the child's world from that of adults. Children have different games and clothes from those of adults. They are kept apart from the adult world of work, and enjoy forms of play which are distinctively different from those of adults. They inhabit a world that is sexually innocent where the adult world is knowing. They learn about themselves and their surroundings in the separate space that formal education provides at a distance from the adult world.

There are two ambiguities in this thesis. First, Ariès's thesis, strictly construed, has been conflated with a separate claim associated with other historians of childhood such as Lloyd de Mause and Lawrence Stone. This is that children in the past were the systematic victims of cruel treatment and abuse which nevertheless was not perceived as other than normal or natural. Correlatively, parental attitudes towards their children were marked by formality, distance and cold indifference. Incidentally, the 'cruelty thesis' is almost as much of an orthodoxy as Ariès's own theory. Yet it can be and has been disputed.[3] Ariès does not in fact claim that children in the past were cruelly treated as a matter of course. At most he asserts that children simply 'did not count' for adults. Indeed, he defines one attitude towards children developed after 1700 in the wake of a recognition of the concept of childhood as involving an increased moral solicitude about children. This resulted in their subjection to a rigid and puritanical discipline. Nevertheless there are reasons why, on Ariès's understanding of what it is for a society to have a concept of childhood, a society lacking one should be thought disposed to the habitual ill-treatment of its children. I will return to this point later.

The second difficulty with the Ariès thesis is terminological. The French word which Ariès actually uses, and which is translated as 'concept', is *sentiment*, rather than *idée* or *concept*. *Sentiment* connotes both 'awareness' and 'feeling'. A society which has a *sentiment* of childhood is both conscious of children as a distinct group and possessed of a certain attitude towards them as a group. Ariès allows the term its double meaning even though, in the quoted summary of his view, he seems explicitly to deny that being aware of children implies being affectionate towards them.

However, the use of a term weaker than 'concept' does have further implications which may or may not straightforwardly serve Ariès's thesis. In the first place, such a usage helps to avoid the suggestion that a society with an 'awareness' of the 'particular nature' of children has it in an explicit, abstract, theoretical and formal way, by for instance publishing treatises upon childhood or agreeing a fixed definition of the term. A society and an individual can demonstrate its possession of a 'concept' of something, in this weak sense, merely by behaving towards that thing in distinctive ways.

Even so, something more is indicated by speaking of 'childhood' rather than simply 'children'. The former is an abstract noun which denotes the state of being or the stage at which one is a child. Its use dictates a certain formal and sophisticated grasp of what and when it is to be a child, one that abstracts from the particularities of individual children. It is thus likely to be informed, at some level, by theory. A society could have an 'awareness' of the 'particular nature' of *children* without possessing a 'concept' of *childhood*. Ariès's thesis derives some plausibility at least from the fact that there did develop, from about the sixteenth century onwards, a more elaborate, explicitly stated and abstract appreciation of what is involved in being a child. This involved, centrally, the progressive articulation of theories of human development, which I will consider in the next chapter. But, as we shall see, it does not follow that, prior to or in the absence of such theories, society lacked an 'awareness' that children differ from adults.

21

Having noted these two difficulties in stating the Ariès thesis, I can now turn to an assessment of its central claim. Criticism has taken two basic forms – disputing its evidential warrant and charging that it is irredeemably value-laden. I shall deal with these in turn. First, critics have disputed Ariès's evidence, both suggesting alternative interpretations of the same facts and offering evidence against the thesis. For example, it can be shown that his iconographic argument presumes that art is straightforwardly realistic in its representation of social facts. It ignores the extent to which the changes in paintings are due to general developments in art rather than simply altered attitudes to the subjects of the pictures. Again, whilst dressing children differently from adults probably indicates that they are regarded as different, failing to dress differently does not indicate that they are *not* seen as different. There are also plausible, straightforward explanations of why children, without being thereby seen as no different from adults, might be dressed in 'adult' clothes. Heroard's diary is a single document telling the story of an exceptional child, the heir to the throne. There is no reason to think the upbringing of Louis XIII representative. Contrary to Ariès's claims, there is evidence from legal documents, medical writings and church chronicles for the view that the child's 'particular nature' *was* recognised in the Middle Ages.

Apart from the weakness of its evidential basis, Ariès's thesis is also notable for its inconsistencies. For instance, a development of the modern predisposition to be concerned about infants predates any significant decline in the high infant mortality rate which he holds responsible for parental indifference. The thesis is chronologically imprecise. It presumes that the conspicuous and explicit statements of a society's values may be taken as reliable guides to its actual practices and behaviour. The emergence of an educational system and the preeminence of the family are presented as following from a society's having a 'concept of childhood'. Yet these developments are also seen as the preconditions for the acquisition of the concept.

But it is the second form of criticism of Ariès's thesis which is most damning and also the most relevant to the concerns of this chapter. This is that his thesis is value-laden. Specifically, Ariès is criticised for what has been called his *presentism*, that is his predisposition to interpret the past in the light of present-day attitudes, assumptions and concerns. It is important to distinguish the two aspects of this presentism. The first is simply, and without any moral presumptions, to regard as notably absent from past societies what happens to be present in contemporary society. From the standpoint of our age, which understands the difference between children and adults in a specific manner, Ariès judges that the past lacked a concept of childhood. In fact what the past lacked was *our* concept of childhood. Previous society did not fail to think of children as different from adults; it merely thought about the difference in different ways from ours. Ariès claims to disclose an absence in the past where he should only have found a dissimilar presence.

The second aspect of his presentism involves an assumption that the modern concept of childhood is right in that it correctly grasps the nature of children and so leads to morally appropriate behaviour towards them. It is evident that, for Ariès, the two aspects of presentism are necessarily linked. For he thinks that to recognise, as we now do, the nature of childhood automatically conduces to a certain moral sensibility regarding children. To see what children are really like means treating them properly.

However, it is important to keep the two aspects of presentism separate. It is possible to accept that childhood is now recognised in a way that it was not in the past, but fail to agree that this constitutes a form of moral progress. For example, one notable defender of children's liberation, Daniel Farson, concurs with Ariès's claim that the concept of childhood is exclusively modern. But where Ariès would speak of a belated recognition, Farson disparagingly speaks of an 'invention'. Where Ariès talks merely of separating the worlds of adult and child, Farson uses the term 'segregation' and deploys all its connotations of enforced and unnatural exclusion.[4]

Again, conflating the two aspects of Ariès's presentism obscures the question of whether children were cruelly treated in the past. Ariès does not in fact believe that children were the victims of habitual ill-treatment, but it is easy to see why he might be thought to. For if the modern recognition of what childhood amounts to is presumed to entail a certain moral disposition towards children, then a society lacking such a recognition might be assumed to treat its children immorally. But all that can be said is that previous societies had different moral views from ours as to how children should be brought up. The idea that we in the present know better than those in the past may be a dangerous prejudice.

There is a related point. It is essential to distinguish the question of what would count as cruel treatment of any human from that of what counts as cruel treatment specifically of children. We could agree, for instance, that torturing a human of whatever age is barbaric and immoral. And perhaps torturing a child is especially immoral because she is a smaller and frailer human being; or it may be especially immoral just because she is a child. Similarly, some might see the setting to work of children as cruel but only because of a theory concerning what is morally appropriate behaviour towards children as such. Any such theory is contentious. Ariès thinks the modern child rightly excluded from the adult world of work. Defenders of children's liberation and many non-Western cultures disagree. To speak confidently of cruelty towards children in the past may thus presuppose the truth of a general moral outlook and a particular theory about children.

To summarise thus far: Ariès understands by the 'concept' of childhood a peculiarly modern awareness of what distinguishes children from adults. This is manifested in morally appropriate forms of treatment, chiefly a certain separation of the worlds of child and adult. Previous societies, on Ariès's account, lacked this concept of childhood, and whilst it does not follow that they treated children badly it is natural to think they were disposed to do so. In reply it can be argued that the evidence fails to show that previous societies lacked a concept of childhood. At most it shows they lacked our concept. To conclude that this means they lacked any is to be guilty of interpreting the past in terms of the present. And to think the past morally inferior to the present is a further unwarranted presumption. For we can say of previous societies only that they treated their children in ways of which *we* disapprove whilst having to acknowledge that, for some critics, our ways are not obviously superior.

An analogy might helpfully complement this summary. One can easily imagine someone arguing that the past lacked a concept of 'madness', meaning only that previous societies, whilst clearly distinguishing between and treating differently the sane and the insane, failed to hold a specifically modern theory of what madness is and how it should be treated. Indeed, it might be argued that past understandings of madness were more humane than our own.

A NOTE ON 'MODERNITY'

Careful use of terms such as 'the present', 'our age' and 'now' cannot really disguise the fact that Ariès is urging a thesis about 'modernity'. He seeks to contrast a distinctively modern awareness of childhood with a premodern neglect. Now this may appear to present a difficulty. The associated terms 'modern', 'modernity' and 'modernism' are presently the subject of intense and complex debate. To simplify greatly, the 'modern' age has conventionally been understood to mean the industrial and capitalist era. It has also been characterised as one of more or less universal human progress not simply in economic and social terms, but also intellectually and culturally. 'Modernity' is thus associated with the triumph of scientific and rational enquiry over 'traditional' obscurantism. To a large extent the contrast between 'modern' and 'traditional' has also been taken as coextensive with one between Western and non-Western modes of social organisation and thought.

Beginning in literature and the arts, the second half of the last century witnessed an increasing scepticism about and critique of the alleged achievements of modernity. This has extended in more recent years to a sustained attack upon modern intellectual certitude and its philosophical foundations. Some now prefer to speak of 'postmodernity'.

Ariès subscribes to the historical understanding of 'modernity' as the culmination of a long and painful passage to moral enlightenment. He thus shares the modernist understanding of the present as the end and highest goal of History. I have given reasons to doubt this assumption, at least so far as it concerns the allegedly superior present understanding of childhood and children. 'Modern' can have a relatively uncontentious descriptive usage simply as referring to the most recent period of human history. Nothing beyond this needs to be taken as implied by its use. One can therefore speak of the modern conception of childhood and mean only that we now think of children in ways that differ interestingly from those of the past.

One bias should be made explicit. 'Modern' and cognate terms are elliptical; they generally mean 'modern Western' (and indeed Northern). And where this use has commendatory connotations there is a clear danger of ethnocentrism. However, I will often try to contrast our present understanding of children and childhood with those of non-Western cultures. It is thus to be hoped that my discussion runs no risk of an implicit partisanship.

A NOTE ON SOCIAL CONSTRUCTIONISM

Clearly indebted to the work of Ariès but also showing sympathies with broader theoretical views, some have argued that childhood is a 'social construction'. This view has been highly influential in the emerging discipline of the sociology of childhood. The claim draws upon indisputable facts but is ambiguous and, on certain readings, false, or at least highly exaggerated. The facts that are beyond dispute attest to the variability in the understanding of childhood across different historical periods and different cultures. The claim turns on a contrast between the biological or natural on the one hand and the social or cultural on the other. The former is the domain of the immutable and the given, the latter that of the variable and the artefactual. Whereas immaturity belongs to the first, childhood lies within the second. Thus the underdevelopment of children is a biological given, a brute fact of human existence. However, childhood is not a natural phenomenon. Rather, it is a socially constructed category, a mode of understanding these facts. Childhood, in short, is a 'social construct'.

The contrast being drawn here bears useful comparison with that between 'sex' and 'gender', a distinction of central importance to feminist theory. The early theorists of second-wave feminism argued that men and women differ in their 'sex', which is biological, and their 'gender', which is socially

25

constructed. Further, they argued that whereas biological differences are immutable across history and societies, gender differences are open to change. This latter claim alone is extremely important in providing feminist practice with emancipatory potential. In more recent feminist writings the 'sex–gender' distinction has been subjected to critical scrutiny. The resultant debate has been about 'essentialism'. The forms of scepticism articulated in respect of the 'sex–gender' distinction are highly relevant to social constructionism about childhood.

In the first place, it would be a mistake to view biology or the natural as a sphere of immutable facts. The physical differences between adults and children – just like those between men and women – are theoretically constructed. They represent the articulated claims of particular scientific discourses. In this way they are poorly defined as merely brute facts of the given. Second, biological facts are not immutable over time and across cultures. The physical differences between men and women have changed. In similar fashion, children are less immature now than they were in previous times. For instance, the average age of the onset of puberty in both boys and girls has steadily, if slowly, declined in Western societies over the last hundred years. Importantly, society has played a causal role in these changes. The construction of immaturity – that is of a child's physical nature relative to adults – is and has been very much a matter of real social, political, geographical and economic factors.

Third, there is a danger of relying on an unhelpful and distorting mutual exclusivity of nature and society. 'Childhood is not a biological phenomenon but a social construction,' it will be said. But it is surely both. Childhood is a period of immaturity understood in a particular way. A child is a young human being the facts of whose youth are interpreted differently across different societies and different historical periods. What is the concept of 'childhood'? Clearly it is not the concept of some kind of object whose physical or metaphysical status is unambiguous, a concept whose correct application to the object is simply and entirely fixed by the features of the object. This would be true of the concept of a physical object like 'a chestnut tree' or 'copper'. The concept of 'childhood', by contrast, does place a grid over objects. It does not simply carve nature at her joints or follow the physical world's given boundaries. It is, in this respect, like many other concepts. In these cases the facts do not exhaustively determine the application of the concept. The concept interprets these facts in certain ways. 'Childhood' is contrasted with 'adulthood'. Where and how we draw the line is not determined solely by facts of age or immaturity. These facts must be interpreted in certain ways. Nevertheless, this shows 'childhood' to be a categorisation that mixes empirical facts with an interpretation of these facts. It does not show 'childhood' to be an exclusively constructed or social concept any more than it is an exclusively biological one.

The further danger of this oversimplifying exclusivism is idealism. Childhood, it will be alleged, does not exist save in the space of cultural constructions. That is, it does not exist in any real or material sense. In this vein one author writes that 'it is quite possible for a culture to exist without children'.[5] Taken literally the bold assertion is false. All societies – save the last – have children. Every society does not have to understand what it is to be a child in the same way as the others. Some, though likely very few if any, may lack any concept of children as a distinct subset of their members. But the absence of the concept does not mean the literal or physical non-existence of those the concept picks out. Social constructionism in respect of childhood is thus in danger of overstating an important but essentially simple point, namely that we can and do understand childhood in different ways. This point can be better expressed if we make a distinction between 'concepts' and 'conceptions'.

CONCEPTS AND CONCEPTIONS

A useful way of restating the basic criticism of the Ariès thesis and also allowing us to see what may be involved in different ways of thinking about childhood requires the introduction of an important distinction. In his book *A Theory of Justice* Rawls employs with respect to 'justice' a distinction between a 'concept' and a 'conception'. His purpose in making the distinction is to render consistent the claim that 'justice' has an uncontroversial and commonly agreed sense with a recognition that different and perhaps incompatible principles of justice are defended. It is Rawls's contention that there is a single concept of 'justice' which can be 'specified by the role which these different sets of principles, these different conceptions, have in common'.[6] It is a requirement of the *concept* of justice that distinctions between individuals not be made arbitrarily, and that the different claims individuals make to a division of social benefits be adjudicated properly. It is the function of a *conception* of justice as a set of rules or principles to specify such a non-arbitrary and proper allocation of these benefits.

Something similar can be said of 'childhood'. The *concept* of childhood requires that children be distinguishable from adults in respect of some unspecified set of attributes. A *conception* of childhood is a specification of those attributes. In simple terms, to have a concept of 'childhood' is to recognise that children differ interestingly from adults; to have a conception of childhood is to have a view of what those interesting differences are.

27

I have the concept of childhood if, in my behaviour towards children and the way I talk about them, I display a clear recognition that they are at a distinct and interestingly different stage of their lives from adults. I have a particular conception of childhood in so far as my treatment of children and discourse concerning them reveals a particular view of what specifically distinguishes children from adults.

We can ask of any linguistic community, past and present, 'Does it have a concept of childhood?' Indeed we can ask this of other concepts and we may conclude that a given community does not or did not have a particular concept. A familiar exercise in the history of ideas is a rehearsal of the reasons to doubt a society's secure possession of a concept central to the discourses and practices of other societies, especially our own. Did the ancient Greeks, for instance, understand the notion of a 'right'? There is no reason – to repeat the essential criticism of Ariès – to think that premodern societies lacked the concept of childhood. This is so even if we acknowledge both that these societies employed very different conceptions of childhood and that it is not impossible, even if very unlikely, that a society should have no concept of childhood at all.

One point about the Rawlsian distinction ought to be made. Rawls's intention was to defend a particular conception of justice as the correct one. A correct conception of justice is a morally defensible view of what justice requires. Moreover, for Rawls a conception of justice is a matter of political choice. Those principles – famously in his case the two principles of justice as fairness – which give expression to the correct conception of justice can and should be adopted as regulatory of the major institutions of our society. In the case of childhood, it may make sense to speak of one conception as the morally defensible view of what childhood is. However, it is probably more accurate to say that there are better or worse ways to treat children, and that some ways of thinking about childhood are more conducive than others to the better modes of treatment. Nevertheless we should recognise – as already noted in the dispute between a child liberationist like Farson and Ariès – that whether or not the modern conception of childhood is a moral achievement or a regressive invention is open to serious dispute. Moreover, it is certainly the case that whereas a conception of justice is open to collective adoption, how we as a society conceive of children is the result of factors – historical, cultural, economic and social – that are largely beyond our control.

How does this distinction between 'concept' and 'conception' help in the case of Ariès? He, as we saw, spoke of a *sentiment* of childhood as an 'awareness of the *particular nature* of childhood' (emphasis added). If what is meant by 'particular nature' is only a recognition that something significant serves to distinguish children from adults, then Ariès is talking about having the concept of childhood. In so far as Ariès is alluding to or implying what the 'particular nature' actually is, he is speaking about a conception of childhood. The criticism of Ariès is that he understands 'particular nature' in this latter way.

However, it does seem clear that, at a minimum, childhood has to be understood in terms of *age* and that, in the normal course of events, children grow up into adults. That children are younger than adults is not all that separates them. This much is clear from the fact that we do customarily also make distinctions within adulthood between, for instance, 'middle age' and 'old age'. But these distinctions have none of the force of that between 'childhood' and 'adulthood'. Being young is associated with, indeed may well be held responsible for, other distinguishing attributes. Still, at the very least, children are young human beings.

Thus the concept of 'childhood' is necessarily linked to that of 'adulthood'. Being a child is the opposite of being an adult, and vice versa. This is not of course to imply that one state is better than the other. As we shall see later, there has been a tendency to see childhood only as the absence of adulthood. And even where there is due recognition of childhood's own specific qualities, there may be a belief that its loss and the gaining of adult status represents a distinct improvement. Against this current of thought there have always been those who celebrate childhood against adulthood, seeing in the passage from the first to the second an irretrievable loss. The point is that it is our specific conceptions of childhood which will determine how it is judged against adulthood. Indeed it may well be our judgments as to what matters in being an adult that explain why we have the particular conception of childhood we do.

With the distinction between 'concept' and 'conception' in place it is possible to restate the fundamental criticism of Ariès's thesis. It is that he personally favours a modern conception of childhood. This conception is now widely embraced but was signally absent from past societies. The modern conception amounts to a specification of what is seen to be the particular and separate nature of the child and one which warrants its proper separation from the adult world. What cannot be sustained, however, is Ariès's key claim that past societies lacked the concept of childhood. They merely possessed a different conception. What underpins Ariès's thesis is the presumption that having the concept of childhood means having the modern conception of childhood. Put another way, this presumption is the belief that if you see children as different from adults you must do so in the ways that we now customarily do.

A NOTE ON ROUSSEAU

Rousseau is widely credited with pioneering a modern view of childhood. In fact, he can be taken as doing two things. He proclaims the necessity of having the concept of childhood and he defends the merits of his own particular conception. In the first place he defends the intelligibility and value of having the concept of childhood, that is, of recognising the child as a child. He criticises those 'seeking the man in the child without thinking of what he is before being a man', insisting that 'childhood has its (place) in the order of human life. The man must be considered in the man, and the child in the child' (*Émile*, pp. 34 and 80). But Rousseau also has a particular conception of the child, that is, a view of what does actually constitute the proper place of the child in the order of human life. Famously, he is credited with thinking of the child as a moral innocent, close to Nature and deserving a freedom to express herself, a being who is standardly corrupted by social convention. Thus Rousseau demands that education recognise the identity and peculiar nature of the child. This entails seeing children both as children, that is not as adults, and as having certain qualities in virtue of being children.

This much is orthodoxy. Rousseau's role in inaugurating a child-centred view of education – one that is central to progressive pedagogy – is widely acknowledged. The first words of Book I of *Émile* – 'Everything is good as it leaves the hands of the Author of things; everything degenerates in the hands of man' (*Émile*, p. 37) – seem to celebrate a naturally good asocial humanity. In the orthodox interpretation of Rousseau, education should be the undirected, free and spontaneous development of a naturally good child. Interpreted in this fashion, Rousseau stands in marked contrast to Locke's teacher or guardian, the deliberate cultivator into reason and social virtue of the apprentice adult. Yet things are slightly more complicated. It is true that Rousseau does honour the special nature of childhood and insists that education should be directed to the 'child in the child'. But although man is naturally good he must live within society and Rousseau's problem – in *Émile* at least – is that of transforming a human so that he can be good in our society as it is.

In the orthodox view of Rousseau, he is seen as an anti-educationalist who preaches 'negative education': 'Take the opposite of the practised path, and you will almost always do well' (*Émile*, p. 94). Yet Rousseau does not seek not to teach anything. Rather, he wants to match the mode and content of any education to the proper stages of a child's development. It is not simply a matter of what one teaches but of when one teaches certain matters. From the orthodox perspective, Rousseau is seen as anti-educationalist in the sense of commending an unconstrained freedom to learn, leaving the child to his own devices. But in fact Rousseau prescribes a highly structured and even manipulative form of teaching one's pupil: 'Let him always believe he is the master, and let it always be you who are. There is no subjection so perfect as that which keeps the appearance of freedom' (*Émile*, p. 120).

From the orthodox point of view, Rousseau celebrates asocial nature as such. The opening words of Book I are cited in this context. But Rousseau does not trust to the pure endogenous development of the child. The pedagogue is, as much as in Locke, a guide and former of the child. Moreover, nature as such is not liberating. Rather, man must learn submission to the rule of necessity, though not of course to the wills of other men. The orthodox view of Rousseau sees him as radically non-instrumental in his approach to education, which should have intrinsic value and not be geared to the realities of life. Yet Rousseau continually emphasises the importance of acquiring practical skills and the utility of what is learnt.

It is important to complicate and correct the orthodox interpretation of Rousseau, both because the contrast with Locke is otherwise overdrawn and also because the author of *Émile* is at some distance from the Rousseau celebrated in progressive, child-centred pedagogy. Yet we cannot appreciate the modern conception of childhood without acknowledging Rousseau's central role in directing our attention to 'the child in the child'.

CONCEPTIONS OF CHILDHOOD

The distinction between a concept of and conceptions of childhood should be clear enough. There are also good reasons for thinking that all societies at all times have had the concept of childhood. But there have been different conceptions of childhood. These have made different claims about the extent of childhood (how long it lasts), its nature (precisely what qualities distinguish the child from the adult) and its significance (how important these differences are held to be). I want now to spell out the respects in which conceptions of childhood may differ and to hint at the underlying judgments which may explain why they do differ. There are at least three basic respects in which conceptions of childhood can differ. These are its *boundaries*, its *dimensions* and its *divisions*.

The *boundary* of childhood is the point at which it is deemed to end. There is also a question of when childhood begins. But, to all intents and purposes, this is the same as the question of when a human person comes into existence. Whilst this is a very important issue for many traditional philosophical disputes, over the morality of abortion for instance, it is not strictly pertinent to this discussion. We are concerned here with how we may distinguish

31

childhood from adulthood, and for this distinction what matters is the point at which childhood ends. A conception may not fix a firm upper limit and thus leave it vague when exactly a child becomes an adult. However, very many cultures do have an age of majority and there are reasons why they should. The existence of a legal system can be of crucial importance, not least since it requires the attribution of legal responsibility for one's actions to a specified class of persons. If, as seems reasonable, children cannot be thought of as legal agents in the same way as adults, then it is up to the law to draw the required distinction.

Again, a society may have formal practices or a division of roles and responsibilities that amount to the setting of a boundary. There may even be rites of passage or initiation ceremonies which celebrate the end of childhood and beginning of adulthood. These are likely to be associated with permission to marry, departure from the parental home or assumption of the responsibility to provide for oneself. The fact that different conceptions of childhood have different boundaries is relevant to a criticism of Ariès. A distinction can be made between failing to mark any difference between children and adults, and marking it in the wrong place. Non-modern societies can be accused of failing to recognise that children are different from adults or of failing, whilst marking *some* difference, to include as children those young persons that 'we' do. For Ariès, a 10-year-old is, standardly and unproblematically, a 'child'. However, some contemporary non-Western cultures conduct their initiation rituals marking entry into adulthood close to the time of puberty. For these, childhood ends at 8–10 for girls and 10–12 for boys. Ariès might claim that such cultures lack a concept of childhood. But it is clear that all he would be entitled to say is that they have a different conception of it.

The second respect in which conceptions of childhood may differ is their *dimensions*. As discussion of Locke's views illustrated, childhood may be understood from a number of different angles. This means that there are several vantage points from which to detect a difference between children and adults. These include the moral or juridical perspective from which persons may be judged incapable, in virtue of age, of being responsible for their deeds; an epistemological or metaphysical viewpoint from which persons, in virtue of their immaturity, are seen as lacking in adult reason or knowledge; and a political angle from which young humans are thought unable to contribute towards and participate in the running of the community.

These are dimensions which matter to us and play a crucial role in the modern conception of childhood. But there are others. For instance, there is the point marked by puberty at which a human is able to procreate; or the period when individuals are capable in practice of independently sustaining themselves. Now it is not obvious that a person who is a child, juridically or epistemologically, is also a child from the point of view of reproductive capacity or self-sufficiency. In other words, the various dimensions of 'childhood' need not converge in defining one consistent and agreed period of human life. Now there are various ways of dealing with this problem. An unsatisfactory one would be to accept that a person enjoys different childhoods of different lengths according to the aspect under which childhood is regarded. One might, for instance, be said to cease to be an asexual child even whilst one is not yet a legal adult.

On the other hand, a particular conception of childhood may treat the various dimensions *as if* they were consistent one with another. This can mean that the point at which a given conception deems childhood to end has a notional or virtual status. The end of childhood under one or several of its aspects is simply assumed to be the end under all the others. It can also mean that the boundary of childhood is 'borrowed' from the terms of one dimension and applied to another. For instance, the law might select as an upper limit to childhood an age whose significance is non-legal. It is, by way of illustration, an interesting thought that the age of majority may possibly originally have been fixed in the Middle Ages by the capacity of a young boy to bear arms. As armour became more elaborate and heavier in the twelfth century so the strength required to wear it increased. Consequently the time at which armed service could be performed got later, and the age of majority was set correspondingly higher.[7]

Of course it is most probable that a conception of childhood legislates as to what are the significant respects in which children and adults differ. It is on the basis of these that a relatively clear boundary to childhood is indicated. The selection of significant differences depends upon broad value-judgments. If, as John Locke and many others have believed, rationality is the distinctive and unique attribute of the human species, then it would be natural to see the acquisition of reason as the key criterion of maturation. On the other hand, the basis upon which childhood is seen essentially to differ from adulthood may be no more than a reflection of prevailing social priorities. In a society where sustaining and reproducing life is of overriding importance the ability to work and bear offspring is a strikingly obvious mark of maturity.

The third respect in which conceptions of childhood can differ is their *divisions*. A human being's early years, that period from birth to adulthood, can be sub-divided into a number of different periods, and the category of 'childhood' can bear different relations to these. Nearly all cultures recognise a very early period of infancy, characterised as one of extreme vulnerability and dependence upon adult care. Our culture acknowledges the significance of these first couple of years, though, as we saw, Ariès takes infancy, on the modern conception, to extend from birth to about the age of seven. Non-Western cultures attach a great deal of significance to weaning, not least because this normally tends to occur during the next pregnancy of the mother. It thus marks a point at which the young infant is about to be replaced as the object of close maternal attention. Some cultures deem the acquisition of speech to be a key point of transition. Interestingly, Roman law at the time of Justinian specified three age-periods of childhood: *infantia*, when children were incapable of speech, *tutela impuberes*, when, prior to puberty, children required a tutor, and *cura minoris*, when, after puberty, young persons had not yet reached their majority and required the care of a guardian.

A key period for the modern conception of childhood is 'adolescence'. Indeed Ariès argues that this period was first recognised in the nineteenth century. Critics have disputed his claim by pointing to earlier acknowledgements of 'youth', an age of apprenticeship for the roles required of adulthood. However, there is reason to view our characterisation of adolescence, with all its attendant psychological qualities and social significance, as a peculiarly modern construct. Certainly the widespread use of the term, and the fact that it is regarded as appropriate for scientific study, can be attributed to the influential work early in the last century of G. S. Hall.

The fact that there are terms such as 'infancy' and 'adolescence' with which to think about a person's early years bears on conceptions of childhood as follows. Childhood may be understood in two distinct ways. On a broad understanding, childhood is a comprehensive term for the stage extending from birth to adulthood. Infancy, adolescence and whatever other terms may be available to a culture constitute sub-divisions of that period. On a narrow rendering of the term, childhood is the stage after infancy but before adolescence. The 'child' proper is sandwiched between the helpless infant and the young person on the threshold of their majority.

This is an appropriate moment to take a slight detour and consider the peculiar and distinctive role played in the modern conception of childhood by what could be called the 'middle-aged child', that is one roughly from ages 6 to 12. As we saw, Ariès takes infancy to last until around 7. The ages 5–7 constitute a significant watershed in two modern influential theories of development. Piaget takes this to mark the acquisition of a qualitatively higher cognitive competence, namely concrete operational thinking. For Freud, the time from 5 or 6 to the onset of puberty is the 'latency period' characterised, for boys at least, by the dissolution of infantile sexuality originating in the crisis of the Oedipus complex and occasioning significant repression. According to both theorists, the child at this time begins to think about himself and his world in important new ways.

34

At the other end of the child's 'middle age', the 12-year-old is on the threshold of her preparation for adulthood. She is at or close to puberty and may more properly be described as a 'young person' than as a child. Now we saw that Ariès concedes premodernity to have recognised the 'particular nature' of infancy, separating her world from that of adults. If 'young persons' in non-modern societies are performing adult roles, Ariès's complaint is unlikely to be forceful since our society's adolescents tend also to be recognised as on the edge of and acting in anticipation of their own adulthood. However, non-modern conceptions of childhood tend to set their boundaries early by Ariès's terms, that is around 7–10. Or at least, 'children' of that age will be assuming some adult responsibilities such as work, or will even have undergone initiation rites. Thus Ariès's criticism of non-modern conceptions of childhood is that they leave out the 'middle-aged child'. To have the modern conception of childhood is to see the post-infantile and pre-adolescent of 7 to 12 years as a child.

To summarise, any conception of childhood will vary according to the ways in which its boundaries are set, its dimensions ordered and its divisions managed. This will determine how a culture thinks about the extent, nature and significance of childhood. The adoption of one conception rather than another will reflect prevailing general beliefs, assumptions and priorities. Is what matters to a society that a human can speak, distinguish good from evil, exercise reason, learn and acquire knowledge, fend for itself, procreate, participate in running the society or work alongside its other members? Whatever conception is adopted, it will be subject to difficulties or tensions which show themselves in tendencies to incoherence or ambiguity, and which undermine its practical utility. These difficulties arise from the ways in which the dimensions, boundaries and divisions of conceptions of childhood interrelate. For instance, do the dimensions in respect of which childhood is said to differ from adulthood have the same force for all of its divisions? An adolescent is clearly not as incapable in relation to adults as an infant is. Or again, do the various dimensions indicate a single boundary or several boundaries to childhood? The 12-year-old who is deemed a political child in virtue of being thought incapable of voting in elections can procreate and is to that extent a sexual adult.

These kinds of difficulties affect conceptions. They do not undermine the concept of childhood in the same way. All cultures appear to have known that children are importantly different from adults. But we cannot with confidence claim to know what these differences actually are, and what limits they set to childhood. To have that mistaken confidence is probably a result of making the ill-judged leap from concept to conception without noticing. It is certainly this blind leap which Ariès makes. However, to be aware of the gap between concept and conception is at the same time to realise that there can be and are different conceptions of childhood, and that these different conceptions imply different general values, priorities and assumptions. After all, the way we see the difference between children and adults owes everything to what concerns us about being adults in an adult world.

3

THE MODERN CONCEPTION
OF CHILDHOOD

Ariès may be wrong to think that it is only modern society which has a concept of childhood; he may be right to believe that there is a distinctively modern conception of 'the particular nature of the child'. Nevertheless this conception is not necessarily a clear and consistent one. There are different, indeed contradictory, contemporary views about childhood. Again, our conception of the child has been to a considerable degree infused with what are essentially myths, or imaginative projections, deriving from a mixture of cultural and ideological sources. The result is that it is sometimes hard to separate the modern conception proper from what is in fact a symbolic ideal of childhood.

SEPARATENESS

Ariès is at least right to observe that the most important feature of the way in which the modern age conceives of children is as meriting separation from the world of adults. The particular nature of children is separate; it clearly and distinctly sets them apart from adults. Children neither work nor play alongside adults; they do not participate in the adult world of law and politics. Their world is innocent where the adult one is knowing; and so on. We now insist upon a sharp distinction between the behaviour demanded of children and that expected of adults; what is thought appropriate treatment of children is distinct from that of adults. There is a marked division of roles and responsibilities.

Other cultures possess the concept of childhood and so recognise a difference between children and adults. But they see children as differing from adults in a far less dramatic and obvious fashion than is implied by the modern conception. One index of this is understandings of work and play. The modern conception construes the child as someone who plays; work is the polar opposite of play, and something only adults engage in. Non-Western societies may not see work and play as such obvious contraries; nor will they think children clearly exempt from the responsibility to contribute to their own and the community's subsistence. This is not to say that the tasks expected of children will not be suited to their size and capabilities. Many societies standardly require their children to execute simple jobs from an early age, such as looking after infants, fetching water and fuel or tending a herd. Cheyenne Indians used to present a boy at birth with a toy bow, and thereafter replaced it with usable bows appropriate to his size. As he grew up the boy learnt to shoot animals on a scale of increasing size and difficulty. Each capture was duly prepared and eaten by the family with as much seriousness as a buffalo killed by the father. The boy's eventual killing of a buffalo was the final step into adulthood. But, as the example neatly illustrates, there was no single radical leap from childish play to adult work.[1]

The question of children and labour is an interesting one, and it has been given a particular pre-eminence by Article 32 of the United Nations Convention of the Rights of the Child (hereafter referred to as the CRC and discussed in much greater detail in chapter 4) that accords the child the right 'to be protected from economic exploitation and from performing any work that is likely to be hazardous or to interfere with the child's education, or to be harmful to the child's health or physical, mental, spiritual, moral or social development'.[2] A background prevalent assumption is that any problem of child labour is restricted to the underdeveloped economies. In the developed North, it is presumed, children only engage in appropriate 'children's work', such as, most classically, newspaper delivering for an addition to their pocket money. However, things are not so simple. First, child employment *is* a problem in developed countries, though largely one that remains unseen. Studies in the United Kingdom, for instance, regularly highlight the problem: school-age children working long hours, children employed in a range of adult jobs, and children employed under the minimum working age.

Second, and more importantly, the view that there is a simple and obvious problem of child labour is a distortion of the truth. It is being increasingly recognised that there are a large variety of contexts in which children work, and these can have a different significance and set of consequences for the child. Crucially, children themselves can, and frequently do, view their work as valuable – by, for example, giving them self-respect or allowing them to make a meaningful contribution to their families' resources. Appeal to the CRC in support of the idea that children may not work at all should be tempered by the recognition that Article 32 speaks specifically of exploitative and hazardous work.[3]

It is clear that we not only think of the child as a radically separate being from the adult: we have a theoretically well-formed idea as to what this separateness consists of. The past century has seen a systematic exploration of childhood from the perspective of psychology, biology, educational theory and sociology. The dominant notion has been of childhood as a 'stage' in the development of a human being, and the influence of this approach will be considered in due course. But it is important to note how extensive and sophisticated is the knowledge that we in the twentieth century can claim to have of the child's nature, and how this knowledge turns on an appreciation of childhood as an abstraction from the particularities of individual children. What the present age knows all about is what it is to be at the stage of and in the state of childhood.

For us, childhood is a stage or state of incompetence relative to adulthood. The ideal adult is equipped with certain cognitive capacities, is rational, physically independent and autonomous, has a sense of identity, and is conscious of her beliefs and desires, and thus able to make informed free choices for which she can be held personally responsible. It is on account of these dispositions that an adult is thought able to work for her living, be accountable at law for her actions, make sexual choices and help to choose the government of the community. It is because the child lacks these adult dispositions that he may not participate in this adult world.

Childhood is defined as that which lacks the capacities, skills and powers of adulthood. To be a child is to be not yet an adult. Adulthood is something which is gained, and although there may be losses in leaving childhood behind, what is lost tends to be construed as that which could never possibly serve the adult in an adult world. If childhood has virtues they are such only because of their very inappropriateness to adult life. They show up not what is lacking in the adult but what, unfortunately, is bad about the real world to which the adult is well adapted. It is good to be an innocent in an innocent world; it is a matter for regret, but not self-condemnation, that one cannot be an innocent in our world.

The significance of childhood for our time is more pronounced than for previous societies. It is seen as meriting a clear separation of adult and child worlds. The extent of childhood for the modern age is also longer than that of past times, and a peculiar prominence is accorded to the 'middle-aged child', aged between 6 and 12. In our periodisation of childhood it is almost as if the child proper was that which is no longer an infant but not yet a young person.

The modern view of childhood is of an extended stage before and below adulthood, demanding its own distinct world. This view is deeply embedded in our culture's practices and institutions; it underpins our differential attribution of rights and responsibilities to, respectively, children and adults. It would be all too easy to think that the child's habitation of a separate world

39

reflects his possession of a separate nature. If children and adults do have distinct sets of characteristics then they should be fitted for different kinds of life. It can be salutary to turn this claim on its head. A child may be possessed of a separate nature because he is set apart, brought up to act and think of himself as different from the adult. It is the separation of worlds that explains the separateness of natures, and not the latter which justifies the former.

The apt analogy is provided by J. S. Mill's critique of arguments supporting the maintenance of women's continued subordination to men. To those who charged that women's inequality is a natural fact, Mill had a double reply. What appears natural may only be what is customary: 'So true is it that unnatural generally means only uncustomary, and that everything which is usual appears natural. The subjection of women to men being a universal custom, any departure from it quite naturally appears unnatural.' Further, what is customary may only be an artificial product untrue to the real nature of women: 'They have always hitherto been kept, as far as regards spontaneous development, in so unnatural a state, that their nature cannot but have been greatly distorted and disguised.'[4] Mill's counter-argument may be applied with equal force to the case of children in relation to adults.

The modern view of childhood is of a separate state or stage. The sources of this view are both scientific and cultural, and I will examine each in turn.

THE DEVELOPMENTAL MODEL: CHILDHOOD AS A 'STAGE'

It was in the second half of the nineteenth century that 'childhood' became the object of serious scientific investigation. The science in question was psychology, and childhood was principally conceived as a stage in human development. The first published developmental study of a child was Tiedemann's account of three years in his own son's behavioural progress. It appeared in 1787. There were earlier records. Heroard's journal of the young Louis XIII dates from the beginning of the seventeenth century, and, as we saw, played a prominent role in Ariès's thesis. But it was not published until 1868, and then in edited form. Similarly, Pestalozzi's diarised record of his son's education and behaviour was published only in abridged form after Pestalozzi's death in 1827.

The origins of child psychology proper are conventionally held to be the publication of two texts, Wilhelm Preyer's *Die Seele des Kindes* (1882) and G. S. Hall's article, 'Contents of Children's Minds' (1883). More pertinently, though, 1877 saw the publication of Charles Darwin's 'A Biographical Sketch of the Infant' in *Mind*.[5] The importance of Darwin's contribution is as follows:

he saw the significance of childhood in a broader evolutionary context, and it is this which has been so influential in subsequent child-psychological theory. It was natural for Darwin to think that a study of the early development in humans of cognitive, motor and communicative skills, as well as the expression of emotions, bore an intimate relation to the evolutionary thesis, namely that there is a developmental continuity between humans and lower animals. The beginnings of the individual human life should shed light on the beginnings of human life in general; the descent of man might be read in the ascent to adulthood.

An explicit formulation of the relationship between the development of the individual and that of the species, Darwinian in spirit and employed by Darwin himself, was made by Ernst Haeckel. His 'biogenetic law', which can be briefly summarised as 'ontogeny is the short and rapid recapitulation of phylogeny', was embraced by many late-nineteenth-century evolutionary thinkers. The law claims that the development of an individual human from embryo to adult (ontogeny) reiterates the complete development of the species or race (phylogeny). The recapitulation was taken by Haeckel and many others to be literal. For instance, the earliest stages of embryological development are said to reveal the animal ancestry of humans. Haeckel used illustrations to show that, at the outset of their development, human and various animal foetuses are similar in form. The individual human is believed literally to develop out of an animality which is at the origin of its own species' evolution. Again, the child is said to inherit and display preserved phylogenetic memories and instincts which are only lost as she grows up.

In this strict form the biogenetic law is widely discredited. Nevertheless, it had a tremendous influence on much psychological theory, notably that of Sigmund Freud, who took it very seriously indeed. Interestingly, a version of the biogenetic law seems, even now, to be widely accepted. This holds ontogeny to be parallel to, isomorphic with, phylogeny. The development of the child into an adult mirrors, without literally reproducing, the progress of humanity as a whole. The child is seen as the analogue of the 'primitive' human or pre-human animal. To make this clearer I need to spell out all the assumptions of the developmental model. These can be summarised under the three headings of teleology, necessity and endogeneity.

In the first place, the developmental model is teleological; that is, it presupposes an end or *telos* to be reached. From the developmental perspective, we view the child's progress as an approach toward a terminus which is the state of adulthood. Development is construed normatively in a double sense. Maturity is that which, in the normal course of events, is reached, and it is a valued achievement. Adulthood represents an ideal end-state. Children are understood as 'becoming', a stage, rather than as 'being', a state.[6] A child

41

is an 'unfinished' adult, and the finished being is normatively defined. The respects in which adulthood is a norm will depend upon the developmental theory in question. Perhaps the two most influential theories are those of Jean Piaget and Sigmund Freud. For Freud, the normal adult is one whose sexual desire is genital in aim and heterosexual in its object. For Piaget, the state of adult maturity is defined in logico-scientific terms as the capacity for formal operational, that is, abstract and hypothetical, thinking.

Especially for Freud, abnormal outcomes, such as sexually deviant adults, are to be explained by anomalies in the developmental process. These are failures to surmount particular crises, such as the Oedipus complex. The direction of development is given then by an implicit ideal of the normal adult, successful maturity, and departures from this ideal can be traced back to false steps in the development itself. The development is a unilinear progression, and its progressive nature is given not just by the ideal nature of its ultimate end. There is also the fact that the move from each stage of the development to the succeeding one represents a passage from the simpler to the more complex, whereby the later stage includes and comprehends the earlier one as a component reintegrated at a higher level. For this reason, each succeeding stage is not merely a quantitative increment but a qualitative improvement upon the earlier. Adulthood is not more of what childhood has less of; it is of a different and higher order. And this qualitative progression applies not just to the passage from childhood into adulthood, but also to the various stages within childhood.

The apex of the developmental sequence is an ideal of adulthood which mirrors a general cultural or species norm. The growth into maturity of a child runs parallel to the social evolution of humanity. There is a nice example of this parallelism in the work of Lawrence Kohlberg. He researched the development of moral judgment and character in young people and claimed to discover an invariant number of stages in this process. These run from an initial concern with avoidance of punishment, through respect for authority, up to morality proper, that is, acting from conscience and in accord with ethical principles. Now Kohlberg takes the final stages to be a recognition of that universal morality which distinguishes modern civilised Western society from any other. He claims that the highest stages of moral development are absent in pre-literate and semi-literate societies; he is also happy to find a close parallel between his own developmental stages and the alleged stages in the moral evolution of cultures argued for by a social evolutionist like L. T. Hobhouse.[7]

The second important feature of the developmental model is its necessity. Development is the inevitable unfolding and bringing into being of a *telos* implicit within the child. Each stage must be gone through and is a necessary precondition of progress to the next. This necessary connectedness of the developmental stages supports the idea of the development as continuous. Although each successive stage represents a qualitative improvement, there are no abrupt breaks in the progress from child to adult. The necessity of the development also explains its cultural invariance. All humans must pass through the designated stages. Piaget's and Freud's theories are both supposed to apply to any child whatsoever.

The third and final feature of any developmental model is its endogeneity. The development is self-propelled: it derives its motive force from structures, functions and processes which are rooted within the child's nature. This nature – and here again the Darwinian influence is clear – is normally conceived of as genetically inherited and biologically fixed. There is thus a measure of fatalism about any developmental model. At the same time this stress on the inner, biologically rooted momentum of development explains a frequent criticism of both Piaget's and Freud's theories, namely their comparative neglect of the influence of social context. The environment tends to be viewed only as the occasion for and scene of personal change. Of course both Piaget and Freud, the first especially and explicitly, talk about interaction between the child and his surroundings. But it is the inbuilt structures of the former which are doing the primary work and driving the development forward. It is in adapting to and transforming her own nature against her surroundings that a child progresses.

A developmental account proper may be distinguished from the theory of human maturation attributable to the empiricism represented by John Locke. The latter sees the child as a *tabula rasa*, a blank and empty nature which is shaped by the environment. Experience fills the child's mind; maturation is a cumulative aggregation of facts, abilities and dispositions.

This distinction between a developmental and an empiricist account of maturation cuts across two familiar debates. The first is that between innatists and their empiricist opponents. Historically, the philosophical argument was between those, such as Plato or Descartes, who maintained that the mind possesses from birth an innate knowledge of certain fundamental ideas or propositions (such as the existence of God or truths of mathematics and logic), and those, such as Locke, who held all ideas to be derived from experience. In the context of developmental theory, however, what is held to be innate are not so much specific contents, ideas or truths, as structures or predispositions. An empiricist account of development which offers no explanation of the mechanisms whereby experience is assimilated and transformed, along standard and universal lines, into knowledge is an impoverished one. But, to the extent that such an account requires the inheritance of inborn structures and functions, it is not obviously an anti-innatist one.

43

The second familiar debate concerns the relative influence of nature and nurture upon an individual's character. It might seem that the empiricist account ought to be correlated with the view that an individual's personality is a product of the environment. Correspondingly, a developmental account would conduce to the contrary understanding of personality as due to genetic inheritance. However, it should be remembered that Locke, the archetypal empiricist, held a child's temperament or character to be inborn and, to that extent, relatively unmalleable. On the other hand, the developmental theorist is committed only to the view that it is a genetically transmitted nature which equips individuals to adapt themselves to their environment, not that this nature determines the entire outcome of their development.

Let me summarise the influence of the developmental model upon the modern conception of childhood. Childhood is seen principally as a stage on the road to adulthood, which has a normative status. Childhood in relation to adulthood mirrors the primitive in relation to the civilised and the modern, the primate in relation to the properly human. This development is an inevitable and invariant process driven by a biologically rooted structure which the child inherits. This, however, is not to say that the child learns nothing from experience, nor that the mature adult is entirely uninfluenced by the surroundings in which she grew up.

'CHILDHOOD' AND 'ADULTHOOD'

If childhood is a stage, it is a stage on the way to adulthood. Adulthood is not a stage. It is the culmination and goal of development, and thus what brings to an end the sequence of stages. To that extent childhood is the 'not-yet-ness' of adulthood. In the modern conception childhood is not quite what philosophers would call a 'privative' term. This is one whose definition is given by the absence of those properties which constitute its contrary. Health, for instance, can be defined as the lack of failures and abnormalities in an organism's standard functioning. Childhood could similarly be understood simply as the absence of adult qualities.

On the modern view, childhood has its own characteristic needs and interests, and these have a value of their own. The modern conception of childhood can claim to be child-centred, to consider 'the child in the child' as Rousseau expressed it. Yet Rousseau said this because he thought that childhood had its place in the order of human life. In this order adulthood remained primary. The needs and interests of childhood and the value accorded them are relative to those of adulthood. Childhood remains that which is not adulthood, which is prior to and a preparation for it. There is no suggestion that childhood has an equal or even superior status to adulthood in the order of human life.

The developmental model conceives of adulthood as an achieved state. When one ceases to be a child, one has become an adult. Yet this is not the only way of understanding adulthood. There are two possible conceptions of what it is to be an adult. In one, which is arguably Western, adulthood is a state; in the other, which is arguably oriental, it is a process.[8] Adulthood as a state is seen as accomplished absolutely, once and for all, when childhood, its contrary, is left behind. The adult is an individual who has grown up and achieved maturity. Adulthood is defined by the possession of properties which clearly and distinctly separate it from childhood. In the normal course of events the acquisition of these properties follows an invariant developmental process. Maturity is both a desired end-state and a description of physical age; chronological and qualitative progress coincide.

Adulthood as a process is a continual becoming, a never-completed maturing. It is not a plateau of age but the asymptote of life's developmental curve. The individual can become more and more of an adult, but there is no guarantee that ageing automatically brings with it maturity as understood normatively. Childhood is not necessarily left behind forever when one grows older; its characteristics may be retained to lesser or greater degree in later years. To that extent childhood is construed not so much as an actual period of one's life, but more as a metaphorical immaturity which can be present to some extent throughout a lifetime.

The modern Western conception is of adulthood as a state of being, and childhood is correspondingly clearly defined against, and set apart from and below, adulthood. But when adulthood is viewed as a becoming there can be no obvious line of division between it and childhood. And if adulthood is a never-realised goal towards which one is forever maturing, childhood is not obviously an inferior stage which is left behind at once and completely. In sum, the former view of adulthood reinforces the sense of childhood as separate, and as being a necessarily surpassed stage in normal human development towards better and higher things.

THE RELIGIOUS AND LITERARY IDEAL: CHILDHOOD AS 'INNOCENCE'

From Christianity we inherit a confused, even contradictory, image of childhood, which has contributed immeasurably to the contemporary conception. The Christian image is defined by familiar ideals and their polar opposites. In the first instance, children are seen as nearest to God, whilst adults, correlatively, are furthest from Him. Children have a purity which derives from their having arrived only recently in the world. They are Nature which Society corrupts. Growing up is an inevitable degeneration, a growing away from an original perfection.

This is clearly understood in moral terms. The child is without fault or sin, innocent of evil. Innocent and angel are synonyms for baby; one is guiltless as a child. Indeed, following the terms of the biogenetic law, the child mirrors the original state of grace enjoyed by humanity in the beginning. The child is Adam or Eve before the Fall. The adult who wishes to be pure and saved must thus rediscover the state of childhood. Matthew reports Christ as saying, 'Except ye be converted and become as little children, ye shall not enter into the kingdom of heaven' (XVIII.3), which is echoed in Mark, 'Suffer the little children to come unto me, and forbid them not: for of such is the kingdom of God' (X.14). Yet the prelapsarian condition is an artless one. Its purity is that of ignorance. The innocent do not sin because they do not know how to. The child cannot be tempted because she has no understanding of wrongdoing. Thus, the innocence of the child is, in an important sense, an empty one.

Set against this vision of moral purity is the view of the child as inheriting the inherent sinfulness of man. The child is born with Original Sin. Seventeenth- and eighteenth-century Puritanism, especially in its Calvinist form, conceived children as essentially prone to a badness which only a rigid disciplinary upbringing could correct. Following the advice of Proverbs, XXIX.15, 'The rod and reproof gives wisdom; but a child left to himself bringeth his mother to shame', the Puritan parent sought to break the child's will and instil a moral disposition against the grain of nature. This evangelist sentiment is admirably summarised by Hannah More:

> Is it not a fundamental error to consider children as innocent beings, whose little weaknesses may perhaps want some correction, rather than as beings who bring into the world a corrupt nature and evil disposition, which it should be the great end of education to rectify?[9]

This fundamental difference of outlook – the child as original innocent or as originally sinful – is echoed in both literature and theory. On the one hand there is an ideal of the child as born good but corrupted by human society. 'God makes all things good: man meddles with them and they become evil', said Aphra Behn in 1688, echoed, in remarkably similar language, in the opening words of Rousseau's *Émile*, 'Everything is good as it leaves the hands of the Author of things; everything degenerates in the hands of man'.[10] On the other hand, there is the view of children as vicious, requiring society's education and constraints to secure proper behaviour. William Golding's *Lord of the Flies* is, without doubt, the classic literary representation of children as brutes within a thin veneer of educated civility. To paraphrase Rousseau in inverted form, 'everything is bad as it leaves the hands of the Author of things; everything can only be improved in the hands of man'. Without these efforts man returns to his original, and evil, nature.

There is a further dichotomous view of childhood which may in part be attributed to Christianity. The child is possessed of a wonderful preternatural wisdom, a natural untaught and intuitive insight into the way of things. 'Out of the mouths of babes and sucklings' come fundamental truths that cannot be seen by adults, corrupted and blinded as they are by formal education. In many respects the alleged wisdom of children is intended as a reproof to bookishness and mere erudition; it is a celebration of primitive knowing against scholarly knowledgeableness, and serves a certain anti-intellectualism. However, against this there is also a clear Christian view of the child as lacking knowledge. Wisdom is learned in the process of growing to maturity. This outlook finds its clearest expression in St Paul's famous words, 'When I was a child, I spake as a child, I understood as a child, I thought as a child; but when I became a man, I put away childish things' (I Corinthians, XIII.11).

English literature echoes a principal feature of the Christian image of childhood, namely its innocence before the world.[11] It is only after 1790 that the child is a serious subject for English literature, and it is the work of the Romantics, especially Blake and Wordsworth, which chiefly celebrates the original innocence of childhood. The child's state is seen as one of spontaneous wonderment and joy before Nature; the child displays an unforced and instinctive sensibility and imagination. Opposed to these qualities and capacities is the corrupted adult condition in which religion, desiccated rationalism and utilitarianism predominate. Childhood represents humanity's original imaginative enthusiasm for the world; the passage into adulthood is the extinction of that enthusiasm by the straitening forces of social convention and tradition. In Wordsworth there is the further sense of nostalgia for that lost innocence, a regret that maturity brings knowledge but leaves behind a joyful imagination and intuition. Wordsworth also endorses an organic view of human development, wherein childhood is the 'seed-time' of the 'soul'. Seeing the child as 'father of the man', Wordsworth sought a form of growth whereby the qualities of childhood might be integrated and preserved within the nature of the mature individual.

After the Romantics the celebration of childhood innocence deteriorated through the Victorian era into mere sentimentality. The child's innocence, frailty and vulnerability were exploited in order to expose and highlight the particular inhumanities of nineteenth-century society. In Dickens above all the child is the sentimentalised victim of corrupt times and a brutal environment. Nostalgia and a regretful sense of loss deteriorate into mere escapism. Childhood is a lost dream world, cut off and detached from adult reality. It is a world which never existed but to which the adult can imaginatively flee from the pressures and responsibilities of maturity. The twentieth century rediscovered a more realistic literary image of childhood – explored from within, no longer conceived as pure and innocent and recognised for its decisive influence on the adult character.

The fact remains that the English literary exploration of childhood is no more than two centuries old, and this exploration has, in many ways, been an exploitation of childhood as a symbol for what is deemed to be missing from and degenerate about adulthood. The adult writer views the child as that which they can no longer be, but whose attributes may shame their alleged maturity. Nevertheless, in both literature and religion the child's 'innocence' is an unreal one. It is that of a being which does no evil because he knows none. The wisdom of the child is the opposite of knowledge. Having learnt nothing she may see more simply and directly. The child who recognises that the Emperor is wearing no clothes does not see the need for a tactical blindness. But he does not fear power because he does not see what power is. He does not defer to status because he does not understand what status implies. The child is not fitted to survive in our world, but sometimes his incompetent innocence reminds us how corrupt is our own fitness for this world.

In this context, J. M. Barrie's famous play, *Peter Pan*, stands out.[12] Written in 1904, it looks away from the sentiment of the previous century and towards the realities of the new one. Wrongly invoked – and often by adults who would be children – as a magical tale of childhood innocence preserved, it is in fact a social satire written for adults that most emphatically does not celebrate the possibility of eternal youth. Peter is, as the play's subtitle indicates, a 'Boy Who Would Not Grow Up' and he inhabits a literally impossible world, 'Never Land'. It is one where children can play forever but is also one without memory or knowledge of sex and death. Life proper – one lived in full adult knowledge – is, like death, no more for Peter than an 'awfully big adventure'. His refusal to grow up is wilful and pointless. For the play's author, the evasion of memory, time and death is not an affirmation but a denial of life. It is Wendy who lives in reality and who, in Barrie's 'afterthought' of a play 'When Wendy Grew Up', becomes a mother herself. In that play Peter cannot even remember his own previous adventures, and his eternal youthfulness compares poorly with Wendy's mature realism. For Barrie childhood has its place, but it is one we do and must leave behind. He thus does not articulate the literary orthodoxy that the adult world is an impoverished one when set besides the lost wonders of childhood.

A brief word is in order about the relationship between the child's 'innocence' and her or his sexuality. Freud is conventionally credited with persuading us that children are libidinous creatures whose polymorphous and perverse sexuality must be channelled and constricted in appropriate ways to make civilisation possible. Yet the idea that before Freud children were viewed as sexless creatures is contestable. Michel Foucault in particular has argued that it is wrong to think children's sex had previously been passed over in silence. Indeed, he claims the institutional discourse of eighteenth-century educational establishments to have presumed the existence of a precocious and active children's sexuality.[13]

Nevertheless, the assumption that we are now readily prepared to see children in sexual terms is misleading. Childhood is in fact most often represented as a period of asexual innocence. The sexual abuse of children is seen as horrific precisely because it robs children of the innocence that is naturally and rightfully theirs. A premature education in the facts of life is viewed with suspicion for similar reasons, namely that it might corrupt children with inappropriate 'adult' knowledge.

Such thinking can be dangerous. The supposed sexual innocence of children is largely contradicted by the known facts. Yet talk of innocence serves ideologically to hinder the empowerment of children through aware-ness and knowledge. For such knowledge is maligned as preternatural and improper. Most worryingly, innocence itself can be a sexualised notion as applied to children. It connotes a purity, virginity, freshness and immaculate-ness which excites by the possibilities of possession and defilement. The child as innocent is in danger of being the idealised woman of a certain male sexual desire – hairless, vulnerable, weak, dependent and uncorrupted.[14] In sum the ideology of 'innocence' may not protect children from sex. It may only expose them to a sexuality in the face of which such innocence is debilitating.

The modern conception of childhood is neither a simple nor a straight-forwardly coherent one, since it is constituted by different theoretical understandings and cultural representations. The conception is a very modern one inasmuch as literature has treated of childhood for only two hundred years, and science one hundred. Both, in essence, see the child as having a separate nature and inhabiting a separate world. Developmental science views childhood as a stage on the road to adulthood, and the nature of the child as impelling her to the achievement of the adult capacities and dispositions she lacks. Literature rues the passage from child to adult precisely because the latter cannot see things and himself as he once did if he is to survive in an adult world. If this is a degeneration it is only because the world is itself degenerate. In sum, the modern child is an innocent incompetent who is not but must become the adult. The 'must' conveys both the necessity of human development and the ideal character of maturity. In our culture this outlook determines the proper place of the child as one who cannot enjoy the rights and responsibilities of the adult. In the Part II, I will examine in more detail the arguments for and against the separate moral, political and legal status of the child.

Part II

CHILDREN'S RIGHTS

The feebleness of infancy demands a continual protection. Everything must be done for an imperfect being, which as yet does nothing for itself.

Jeremy Bentham, *Theory of Legislation* (1840)

The issue of self-determination is at the heart of children's liberation. It is, in fact, the only issue, a definition of the entire concept.

Richard Farson, *Birthrights* (1974)

4

CHILDREN'S RIGHTS

MORAL AND LEGAL

Part II of this book deals with the rights of children. I defer until Part III discussion of the related questions of what rights parents might have over children, and of how the state should act to balance the rights of children and those of their parents. The chapters in this part address the following issues. In this chapter I look at the question of whether children have rights and, if so, which ones. I do so in the terms of an important distinction between moral and legal rights. In chapter 5 I compare the liberationist case, as the most passionate and radical defence of the most extensive rights for children, with a liberal 'caretaking' view, which would deny children the rights liberationists regard as central to their liberation. In chapter 6 I examine in more detail what is seen as central to the case for and against children's rights, namely the charge that drawing a line is arbitrary and that children are incapable of possessing and exercising rights. In chapter 7 I look at some examples of putative children's rights, namely a child's rights to vote and to exercise sexual choice. In chapter 8 I examine the case, made on a number of grounds, against giving children any rights at all. In chapter 9 I look at the child's legal status, since not everything that needs to be said about the child in law is exhausted by talk of their legal rights.

MORAL RIGHTS

We can draw a fundamental distinction between rights that persons have under law – sometimes called their 'positive' rights – and rights that they have morally. Obviously, this is not a distinction between two sets of rights. One and the same right can be both a moral and a legal right. Rather, it is a distinction in how rights are understood. That I have a moral right does not mean that I have this right under the law, although of course it provides strong support for the claim that I should have. Historically, demands for legal rights have been driven by the view that what persons are morally entitled to they should also be legally entitled to. Conversely, what is recognised as a right by the law need not be a moral right.

It is, normally, a matter of fact whether or not a right is legally recognised. Most obviously and centrally, such rights are listed in charters, covenants or bills of rights. Occasionally, however, courts can discover legal rights that are nowhere so explicitly stated. This was the case in America with the right of privacy which was found 'between the lines' of the Bill of Rights. Determining whether or not there is a moral right is not a factual matter. Rather, it is a question of moral argument as to whether or not individuals ought to have the right in question. Hence when we ask whether or not children have rights we can answer in one of two ways – either by pointing to the facts of the law or by considering the weight of moral reasons for and against. I want initially to consider the case in respect of children for moral rights.

However, there is a background concern that affects the attribution of both moral and legal rights. The worry is that according more rights – whether this is increasing the number of rights possessed by a given set of persons or enlarging the group who possesses rights – is a bad thing. It is thought to be bad because the more rights there are the less value they can have. A much invoked metaphor in this context is that of 'rights inflation'. If rights are thought of as a currency then their value – their legal or moral 'purchasing power' – is diminished if too much of the currency is produced, if there are too many rights. The relevance to the case of children is obvious. However, the concern about inflation is not of itself a reason not to give children rights. At most it provides a cautionary note about the possible effects of extending rights to include children as their possessors. If children ought to have rights then they ought to have them.

One good reason for not giving children rights is that they do not qualify as possible holders of rights. To understand this claim it is necessary to look at what it is to be a rights-holder and, in consequence, at what it is to hold a right. According to what is known as the will or choice theory, a right is the protected exercise of a choice. According to the competing 'interest' theory, a right is the protection of an important interest. On the will theory it would seem that only those capable of exercising choice can have rights, whereas on the interest theory anyone who has important interests can have rights. If, as many will argue, children are incapable of exercising choice then, according to the will theory at least, they do not have rights.

For some, this implication of the will theory is sufficient to show that it is false. Since children obviously do have rights, the will theory cannot have it right about rights. In this sense children are a 'test case' of the correctness

54

of the competing theories of rights.[1] However, a will theorist can respond that just because children lack the capacity to exercise choice it does not follow that they lack rights. They can still have rights, but the choices which these rights protect are exercised not by them but by their representatives.[2] These proxies choose for the children as they themselves would choose if capable of doing so. This, of course, leaves to be answered questions of who these representatives are and of how they can determine what a child would choose for herself if able to choose.

Yet a theorist of rights who insists that children do not have rights can immediately add that it does not follow that we, as adults, do not have any duties towards children. We should not – by way of a parallel – ill-treat animals, but it need not follow from acceptance of this obligation that animals have rights against us. Not everything that morally we must do can be specified in terms of rights and their associated duties. However, if children can have rights then the next question that needs answering is, 'Which rights do children have?' Do they, for instance, have all the rights that adults have or only some? Do they have rights as children that adults do not have?

Saying that a child has special rights in virtue of being a child is, in one sense, not problematic. Special rights are given to identifiable groups of human beings in recognition of their distinctive status or social role. Thus we do not see anything particularly troubling in the idea that women have rights that men do not – reproductive rights for instance. Or that prisoners and students have rights that non-prisoners and non-students, respectively, do not have: to have visitors at specified times and to borrow books from the university library. The problem with the idea of specifically children's rights, if there is one, lies in the manner in which children, and of course childhood, are thereby represented. So what rights might children have just because of their status as children?

Joel Feinberg has distinguished between A-rights, the rights that adults alone have, A–C rights, the rights that both adults and children have, and C-rights, the rights that children alone possess.[3] Many of those who talk about children's rights think that the A-rights include, most centrally, the liberty rights but that A–C rights do not. At most they encompass welfare rights. Liberty rights are rights to exercise one's freedom – of speech, religion, the vote, etc. – whereas welfare right are rights that protect important elements of one's well-being – one's health, or opportunity to work, for example.

The distinction between liberty and welfare rights is a distinction between rights in respect of their content: what they are rights to. It is not the same as the distinction between the will and interest theories of rights, which are theories of what it is to hold a right. On either theory it is left open what rights children, if they can have rights, do have. Thus an interest theorist could argue that children do have rights because they do have interests of sufficient importance to be protected by rights, but maintain that these interests do not include the exercise of liberty of religion. Hence those who think that the A–C rights do not include the liberty rights are inclined to argue that children lack the capacity to make the kinds of choices that would warrant attributing to them an interest in doing so. I shall further discuss this crucial question of a child's incompetence in chapter 6.

C-rights can be viewed from two perspectives: as possessed by children in so far as they are children, or as possessed by children in so far as they will develop into adults. In this latter sense the rights are possessed by the future adult the child will eventually and normally, turn into. Feinberg calls them 'A-rights-in-trust'. In very similar terms John Eekelaar calls them a child's 'developmental rights'.[4] If, for instance, there is a right to healthcare the child might be said to have this because it is good for the child to be healthy and flourishing, sound of mind and body. But you might also think that a healthy child will develop, all being well, into a healthy adult. It is the future adult who has the right when a child to be healthy. I am thus glad that I was properly cared for as a child so that I could grow up into the hale and hearty person I now am. We could of course think that the child has the right both in her own right as a child and in the person of her future self. However, these are two very different ways to think of the same right.

So, to summarise, moral rights are possessed and exercised by children if, according to the will theory, they can make choices or, according to the interest theory, they have interests of sufficient importance. It may be that children have some rights only insofar as they are children, though these rights may also be thought of as protecting the future adults the children will become. Children may share some rights with adults, although it is normally thought that they do not share the liberty rights because they are not competent to make the choices that adults can.

LEGAL RIGHTS

Independently of whether or not children ought morally to have rights, the law can give children rights. That it can and that it does so does not of course settle the issue of whether children ought to have these rights. Law and morality do not always perfectly coincide. Perhaps it is a fundamental mistake legally to give children that to which they are not morally entitled. Nevertheless, giving children legal rights will make a huge difference to how we think about them. It is hard to see children as moral incompetents if our laws, consistently and persistently, do not. Moreover, children may exploit the status they are given at law to display or to acquire the competence they putatively lack.

How do children get rights at law? International charters or conventions that may or may not have binding effect on domestic law can give children rights. One in particular has been very important in this role. Or children can be given rights through the laws of particular jurisdictions. What sorts of legal rights do children acquire? The law – domestic or international – may declare that children have special rights – rights that adults lack and that are accorded to children in virtue of their status as children. Of course, as already noted, even groups of adults, such as women prisoners, can be given special rights. However, the case of children is different. All (or most) children become adults, whereas women do not (normally) develop into men and very many adults will never be prisoners. Moreover, it is arguable that the rights possessed by some groups of adults are the rights they have as adults *and* as the members of the group. By contrast, children may have special rights precisely inasmuch as they are not adults. It is in consequence important to be clear what it is about children, what their claimed status is, that merits the ascription to them of the special rights denied to adults.

The law may give children special rights. Or it may simply give children all the rights that adults have. More cautiously, it may declare that children have some of the most basic or central rights that adults have. For instance, in its momentous decision, *In re Gault* [1967], the American Supreme Court determined that the Fourteenth Amendment, which affords all citizens of the United States the equal protection of its laws, is not for adults alone. Thus children are entitled to the very same fundamental legal protection as adults. In this particular case a 15-year-old had been denied that protection by being deprived of his liberties without the due process of law constitutionally guaranteed to adults. The issue was not whether the child, Jerry Gault, should have appeared before an adult rather than a juvenile court. It was whether his actual appearance before a juvenile court satisfied the requirements of due process assured to an adult appearing before an adult court. The Supreme Court thought that it did not but that it should have.

The decision gave American children the legal status of persons entitled, just as adults are, to protection by the Bill of Rights and by at least one fundamental constitutional amendment. Indeed, in another judgment around the same time, *Tinker* [1969], the Supreme Court affirmed that school students are 'persons' possessed of the fundamental rights afforded to adult citizens under the Constitution. However, it is noteworthy that the children in both of these two decisions – *Gault* and *Tinker* – were young persons rather than infants. For it is not clear the Supreme Court would extend to the very young the basic liberties – such as that of speech or religion – listed as constitutional rights.

THE UNITED NATIONS CONVENTION ON THE RIGHTS OF THE CHILD

Some legal instruments do see children as fundamentally different from adults, but nevertheless – indeed because of that very fact – as entitled to the possession of basic rights. The United Nations Convention on the Rights of the Child (CRC) is just such an instrument. This is an extremely important document, for reasons to be shortly discussed. Nevertheless, its existence and its influence do not settle the issue of what rights children should have – both morally and at law. There are other charters of children's rights, and some of these give children rights that are not included in the CRC. For instance, and controversially, a child's right to love is not a CRC right but it is one guaranteed by Declaration of the Rights of the Child in Israel (1979) and the Children's Charter, Japan (1951).

Yet the CRC is an unavoidable starting point for any discussion of the legal rights of children. This is not simply because it is the most ratified instrument of international law and thus exerts considerable and pervasive influence over how we must think, practically and juridically, about the rights of children. Over 190 countries have ratified the CRC, only the United States and Somalia failing to do so, although they have signalled their intention to ratify by formally signing the Convention. It is also because the CRC codifies a recognisable canon of thought about the rights of children. The rights given to children in the CRC are the rights that we – at least the 'we' of Western liberal democratic post-Enlightenment societies – now think it important to give to children. The CRC gives children rights to, *inter alia*, freedom of expression, association, thought, conscience and religion, protection against abuse and violence, enjoyment of the highest attainable standard of health, education, rest and leisure, protection from economic exploitation and hazardous work.

The CRC is important in the following respect. It represents children as the subjects of rights. Children are recognised in a major international covenant as moral and legal subjects possessed of fundamental entitlements. They are acknowledged as having agency and as having a voice that must be listened to. This is no mean achievement. The CRC has also generated further international commitments and agreements in respect of children's rights in key areas. There is, for instance, the Optional Protocol on the rights of the children involved in armed conflict which entered into force in 2002, binding those states which have ratified it. There is also the Optional Protocol on the sale of children, child prostitution, and child pornography which entered into force in 2002. Over 60 states have ratified both Protocols.

However, the practical and legal impact of the CRC is at present limited. In the first place, the world-wide systematic abuse of children's rights continues. Many children are compelled to labour under extremely difficult conditions, often as bonded labourers or in forced prostitution. Refugee and asylum-seeking children are often separated from their families. Children globally endure terrible abuse. Street children in Latin America are killed or tortured by the police. Children – especially in Africa – as young as 7 or 8 are recruited or kidnapped to serve as soldiers in military forces, engaging in violent conflict. Orphaned and abandoned children under the state's 'care' and control are often subject to abuse and maltreatment, housed in institutions where they suffer cruelty and neglect. Many thousands of children world-wide are denied a basic education or, within schools, are discriminated against or suffer corporal punishment.

In the second place, the CRC has not yet had a significant impact upon domestic legislation. Or it has not had an impact commensurate with its significance as a codification of children's rights. States ratifying the Convention are required to bring their national legislation into lines with its provisions. They are also accountable for their actions in respect of children, required to report on the Convention's implementation to a central monitoring agency, the Committee on the Rights of the Child. Yet it is widely recognised that many signatory states pay no more than lip service to the Convention. States have failed to submit annual reports on time, and, as noted above, the widespread abuse of children continues even in those states that have ratified the Convention. The CRC has not functioned, as has say the European Convention on Human Rights (ECHR) – now incorporated into United Kingdom domestic law under the Human Rights Act (HRA) – to shape, constrain and change the law of the ratifying nations.

One important reason it has not done so is the absence of an international court to which cases alleging breaches of the CRC could be brought. Prior to its incorporation into domestic law, cases under the ECHR could be brought by citizens of the United Kingdom to thethe European Court of Human Rights. Signatory states were and are bound by the final decisions of the Court. In the absence of any such court acting in respect of the CRC children, or their representatives, alleging breaches of the Convention have no obvious means of litigation. In consequence, it would thus be a major step forward for the ratifying states to incorporate the CRC within their own domestic law. It could then function directly and through the courts of the signatory states to protect the rights of children, as the HRA now functions to protect the rights of adults in the United Kingdom.

There is one further and extremely important point about the CRC. It acknowledges and affirms the difference of children. After all, if children were simply viewed as human beings, albeit smaller and younger human beings, then they would already have extensive rights under the existing international charters and covenants of human rights. The CRC gives rights to children only and in so far as they are children. Indeed the Preamble to the CRC specifically quotes from the previous Declaration of the Rights of the Child, stating that 'the child, by reason of his physical and mental immaturity, needs special safeguards and care, including appropriate legal protection, before as well as after birth'.

When people evaluate the rights children have within the CRC, they frequently identify a central tension. This is between the ascription to children of two very different kinds of rights. The distinction is often cited as one between participation and protection rights. To overstate the case the distinction operates as follows: one kind of right represents children as subjects or agents, capable of exercising for themselves certain fundamental powers. In this vein are rights such as that under Article 13 to freedom of expression or that under Article 15 to freedom of association and to freedom of peaceful assembly. The other kind of right represents children as patients or objects, potential victims of forms of harmful treatment. In this vein is, most centrally, the right of the child under Article 19 to be protected from all forms of physical or mental violence, injury or abuse, neglect or negligent treatment, maltreatment or exploitation; or Article 32 which accords the child the right to be protected from economic exploitation and from performing hazardous work.

This contrast of rights can be overstated. After all, adults, classically, are given both liberty and welfare rights. The latter – such as rights to health, housing, employment – are rights to be treated in certain ways, to receive certain goods. They are not rights that empower adults as agents to act in ways that they choose. Nevertheless, what is distinctive about the protection rights accorded to children is that they are not normally given to adults. Adults are not protected against exploitation, abuse, neglect or negligent treatment. They are not because of a strong anti-paternalist assumption that adults should be free to run the risks of being exploited or abused, so long as they are choosing voluntarily and in full awareness of the dangers. However, we tend to think that children are in need of forms of protection it is inappropriate to accord to adults.

Is this because we are paternalistic in respect of children? In fact, children may be thought to differ from adults in this context in two respects that need to be kept carefully apart. The first is that children suffer particular

– and especially serious – harms that adults do not suffer in being subjected to certain forms of treatment. Thus we believe, rightly, that a greater wrong is done to a child who suffers sexual abuse at the hands of an adult than is done to an adult who suffers non-consensual sex. The second is that children are prone to suffer these harms precisely because they are less capable than adults are of defending themselves against the relevant mistreatment. In this regard we think of children as vulnerable, dependent and defenceless. In short, children, first, suffer specific (and often greater) harms as children and, second, are more likely to suffer them because they are children.

We saw that the Preamble to the CRC states that 'the child, *by reason of* his physical and mental immaturity, needs special safeguards and care'. In very similar terms the Preamble of the African Charter of the Rights and Welfare of the Child recognises that 'the child, *due to* the needs of his physical and mental development requires particular care with regard to health, physical, mental, moral and social development' (emphasis in both cases added). A child requires protective rights on account of his status as a child. The 'because' or 'on account of' here has a double meaning. First, the rights are necessary to protect a child against harms that befall the child insofar (and possibly only insofar) as she is a child. Second, these rights impose duties on those entrusted with the care of children to ensure that the child does not suffer these harms. These duties must be imposed because children are simply incapable, or are markedly less capable than adults, of caring for themselves.

It is important to keep these two points separate. A child may suffer particular harms because she is a child but may not be, because she is a child, incapable of exercising the rights that protect her against these harms. The descriptive language used to characterise childhood – which speaks of vulnerability, dependence, weakness, defencelessness, etc. – can prejudice our understanding of children's protective rights. It tends to lead us to think that the very same factors that explain the wrongness of doing certain things to children also explain why children cannot protect themselves from these wrongs. This need not be so.

There are many things to say about the very many rights given to children by the CRC. Article 2 affirms the principle of non-discrimination of any kind and Article 6.1 accords to every child the 'inherent right to life'. However, two other articles in the CRC are worth commenting on. These underpin everything else that is said in the Convention. However, the import of each of the articles is far from clear and, moreover, they are in tension with one another. The two articles in question, first require the promotion of the child's best interests and, second, accord the child's views on matters affecting its interests a certain weight.

61

Article 3.1 of the CRC states that 'In all actions concerning children, whether undertaken by public or private social welfare institutions, courts of law, administrative authorities or legislative bodies, the best interests of the child shall be a primary consideration.' The key legislative instrument of the United Kingdom in respect of children, the 1989 Children Act, similarly states that the child's welfare shall be the paramount consideration. Neither the CRC nor the Children Act speaks of a right, only of a requirement. In addition, whereas the CRC says that the child's best interests shall be *a* primary consideration the Children Act says that the child's best interests shall be *the* paramount consideration. The distinction is one between the best interests being an important but not the only consideration and their being the most important consideration. The drafters of the CRC deliberately adopted the weaker formulation of the principle but did, nevertheless, generalise its scope to *all* actions concerning children.

The language of best interests is maximising. The principle says that agencies and individuals charged with the care of a child's interests must do the *best* by the child that they can. It says more than that they must simply do good for the child. As a simple example, consider determining whether a child should undergo a certain medical procedure which treats an identified problem. It might seem obvious that there is a 'best' choice: the child should have the operation. This is certainly better than not having the operation at all. But is it 'best'? Why shouldn't one think that the *best* for this child is to be operated on by the best qualified surgeon with the best ancillary medical staff in the best equipped hospital in the world, to receive the very best post-operative care, and so on?

Because it is a maximising principle, the best interests requirement seems unfeasibly demanding. Can it really plausibly be demanded that every public or private institution must do its best by every child? The difficulties of its maximising character aside, the principle is also very difficult to render as a set of determinate recommendations of policy and action. We normally know what does and does not benefit a child. There may be some difficulties here but they are not insuperable. However, it is hard, and some would argue impossibly hard, to know what, in any particular set of circumstances, is in fact the *best* thing to do for this child. There are simply too many complex variables: the number of options, the value of these options, and the probabilities of various outcomes being realised.[5] Perhaps this is overstating a problem that, after all, is not unique to the case of doing right by children.

However, there is yet another difficulty. What is best for a child is not a question that can be settled by an appeal to facts. It is a moral issue. Moreover, there are deep and abiding disagreements about the issue. In arguing about what is best for a child we appeal to fundamental ideals which are in dispute. Such disagreement is not of a kind that permits reconciliation or an eventual consensus. After all, and in the last analysis, we are trying to determine what the best life to lead is. Should we allow a child to be brought up in the religious faith of her parents, indeed to be educated in these religious beliefs at school and to the exclusion of non-religious and other religious values? This is certainly what the parents, and their fellow believers, would judge is best for the child. Or should we so educate the child that she is encouraged to challenge the values and beliefs of her community and parents? Should she be taught to have an open mind on all things, her own familial outlook included? This is certainly what, on a familiar classical liberal view, would be best for the child.

Acknowledging that there will be significant differences of opinion as to what is best for a child is not a concession to moral relativism. Certainly, some have argued that a best interests principle is subverted, or at least rendered deeply problematic, by the existence of deep and pervasive cultural disagreements.[6] However, the assertion that what is best for a child may be different in different cultural contexts is ambiguous. Moral philosophers are fond of pointing out that a single agreed general moral principle can be applied in different cultures to yield different moral judgments. For instance, two cultures may both seek to honour a principle such as 'Show appropriate respect for the dead'. But one culture finds the idea of cremation appalling (where the other does not) and thinks (what the other considers abhorrent) that consumption of the bodies of the dead is appropriate. There is here no deep-lying moral disagreement. In similar terms, two cultures may agree that all children have a right to an education, yet act in different ways to honour the right. These differences may be attributed to various factors, including for instance the ends that any education can serve in a culture.

On the other hand, cultures may disagree at the most fundamental level about what is best for children. If one culture thinks that all children should receive a general education and another believes that only boys, but not girls, should receive one then this is not a case of applying a single agreed principle to two different contexts. The disagreement is more basic. One culture does not think that every child has a right to an education. Moreover, there is a further point. Someone who asserts in the light of such fundamental moral disagreement that both cultures are morally right is affirming moral relativism: what culture A thinks best for *any* child is not what culture B thinks best for *any* child, and yet *both* A and B are right to think as they do. Sophisticated forms of moral relativism have been defended. But in the form instanced here it is ultimately incoherent. Moreover, such moral relativism is not required by nor does it support an attitude of tolerance to cultural differences.

63

For – as is frequently pointed out – there is a basic inconsistency in arguing both that moral principles are relative to context and that there is at least one universal moral principle – 'be tolerant of difference' – that is not.

The rights accorded to children by the CRC are universal in scope and the large number of signatories to the convention is a good indication of the general recognition that its rights do apply to all children wherever they live. Yet those who proclaim universal rights should always be sensitive to the differences between cultures (without endorsing each and every difference) and to the local realities of implementing rights. It is sometimes said of the CRC, for instance, that it merely codifies a Western, urban, middle-class ideal of childhood. If it is not practically possible for some societies – those which are predominantly rural and poor – to honour that ideal, then the criticism is well made. It is wrong for those who can easily implement laws to criticise those who cannot, or can do so only with great difficulty and at enormous cost. On the other hand, some non-Western cultures may not share the ideal in question. But that does not show that the ideal is erroneous and should not be universally implemented if possible. It shows only that there is moral disagreement. It does not show that all ideals are correct, any more than it shows that any one is. That is a matter for further argument. If there is an ideal of childhood to which some set of rights best gives expression then it ought, if it can, to be put into practice.

Besides Article 3.1 of the CRC which gives expression to the best interests principle the other crucial Article is 12.1. This states that, 'State parties shall assure to the child who is capable of forming his or her own views the right to express those views freely in all matters affecting the child, the view of the child being given due weight in accordance with the age and maturity of the child.' This Article, unlike 3.1, does speak of a right. It is also a right recognised in English law. Indeed, it is at the heart of the influential idea of 'Gillick competence'. This, following from the celebrated House of Lords case, allows that a minor with sufficient maturity shall have the right to determine, especially in respect of medical procedures, what shall or shall not be done to him.

As has been widely acknowledged, this right is a very important one. Some would see it as the most important right within the CRC. It represents the child as having a voice, and a voice that must be heard. Article 3.1 sees the child as having his own interests which need to be taken account of and indeed promoted. Article 12.1 gives each and every child a voice that demands to be heard. Both articles thus, in their different ways, characterise the child as a distinct and independent person. The child is not someone who has no identity of her own, to be regarded simply as a part of a family the voice of which is the parents. Nor is the child the property of her parents.

Crucially, Article 12.1 also sees the recognised entitlements of any child as relative to his actual capacities. In effect it says that the closer a child is to the status of adulthood the more seriously his views are to be taken. This allows the enforcement of the right to mark differences between children in terms of their abilities. It thus goes some way to meeting the criticism that a convention which defines the child as anyone below 18 is incapable of acknowledging that children mature from infantile incapacity to the proto- or almost achieved adulthood of young persons, and that children differ greatly in their abilities. Let me explain further.

Article 12.1 attaches two conditions to the right of a child to express her views on all matters affecting her. The first (the *capability* condition) is that the right is assured only to a child 'who is capable of forming his or her own views'. I shall adopt the crudest of subdivisions of childhood, speaking of the 'infant' as a child from birth to around 6, the 'child' proper as from 6 to around 12, and a 'young person' as anyone from 12 to 18. The important thing is not to accept these divisions nor their age-defined boundaries, but rather to accept that some such kind of division can be made. Then it seems reasonable to say that infants (or very young children) are not capable of forming their own views, whereas young persons most certainly are. Thus in the first instance the right enshrined in Article 12 is *not* assured to *all* children.

The second condition (the *weight* condition) attached to the right within Article 12.1 is that the views of children have a weight proportionate to their age and maturity. In fact we should drop the word 'age'. For what matters is not so much age as associated maturity. It is simply assumed that the older the child the more mature he is, and thus age may be taken as a reliable index of maturity. According a view more or less weight means in practice that the child's own view is more or less likely to determine the action or policy in respect of what happens to him. The more mature he is the more his own views of what should happen to him ought to determine what in fact will happen to him. This second condition on the right thus allows those entrusted with the care of children to recognise that children of different ages have different abilities to understand and to appreciate what is going on in their lives. Moreover, the import of the right is that such adult guardians are required to act on their recognition of this fact of differential ability.

In this way the attachment of both conditions to what is a central right goes a long way to acquitting the CRC of the simple charge that childhood is characterised within its terms as an undifferentiated, homogeneous condition. This is undoubtedly valuable, especially since Article 12.1 can be read as an overarching principle determining the manner in which all the other rights of the CRC are enforced. However, the import of Article 12.1 is limited.

The right to be heard is a valuable one both because there is a point to making one's views known *and* because making one's views known makes a difference. What is important is not just that one can speak (rather than be silenced) but that one is heard (rather than ignored). I want not just publicly to state my view but for it to be effective.

In Article 12.1 the crucial words are 'due' and 'may'. This is because the child's right to be heard on matters affecting her own interests is a substitute for a liberty right to make her own choices. The right to be heard is only the right to have an opportunity to influence the person who will otherwise choose for the child. The power to make those choices ultimately resides with someone other than the child. Indeed, the import of Article 3.1 is that someone other than the child is obligated to choose for the child in the light of what is best for her. Under Article 12.1 all that the child retains is the right to try to motivate or to persuade the adult to choose as the child herself would choose if allowed to. Although Article 3.1 is constrained by Article 12.1, adults still retain final authority over children. They do so in two respects. First, they are mandated to act in a child's best interests, and are the judge of what those interests are. Second, even when that requirement yields to the demand that the child's own views should be given weight, adults are the judge of what weight these views should be given.

How should we 'weight' a child's views? The Gillick judgment in England, and subsequent court decisions, have arguably employed a fairly stringent test of a child's maturity. The original decision held that a minor had the right to determine what shall happen if and when he, in the words of Lord Scarman, 'achieves a sufficient understanding and intelligence to enable him to understand fully what is proposed'.[7] This seems to imply that the child must both know the nature of the proposed act and appreciate its significance. Thus, for instance, a child must know that this act is one of sexual intercourse. Further, the child must understand that sex may result in pregnancy and appreciate the significance of such an outcome. 'Appreciation' presumably covers a grasp of what pregnancy would mean for anybody – if carried to term the birth of a child for whom one would, in the first instance, have responsibility, the burdens of childrearing, and so on. Scarman insisted that the child would need to have an appreciation of the 'moral and family' questions involved.

Under the law of contract an adult's consent is taken to be valid and is binding merely if he knows the nature of the act to which he is agreeing. He does not need to 'understand fully' what is involved in entering into the contract. Why should it be any different with a child? Is it not enough that a child knows the nature of the act? Moreover, there are many adults in very many contexts who do not display the maturity and understanding of what is involved in the making of a choice that the Gillick test requires of a child. Why should a child have to display a competence that some adults lack in general and very many lack on occasion?

The process whereby a child's views are 'weighted' according to his maturity can thus be stringent to varying degrees. The Gillick test of competence is very stringent. The key point is that the right enshrined in Article 12.1 is more or less concessive to children (and their views) depending on whether the weighting process is more or less demanding. Interpreting it in a way that is very favourable to children – giving great weight to their views – does not, however, remove the tension between it and Article 3.1. What is the tension in question?

In essence, Article 3.1 is paternalist and shares this feature with those articles which may be described as 'protectionist'. Article 3.1 requires those entrusted with the care of children to do what they, but not necessarily the child herself, judge is best for the child. By contrast, the tenor of Article 12.1 is anti-paternalist and shares this feature with those articles which may be described as 'participatory'. Article 12.1 requires those entrusted with the care and protection of children to take seriously (the more seriously the more mature the child) what the child wants to have happen. At the end of the day, what is judged to be best for the child may not be what the child views as for the best. The CRC does not specify a hierarchy of rights. Indeed, Article 4 requires states to take 'all appropriate measures' to implement the rights of the CRC, and 'the rights' may be taken to read as 'all the rights equally'. Nevertheless, Article 3.1 speaks of the best interests of the child being *a* primary, and not the paramount, consideration. Hence a child's best interests do not necessarily trump all other considerations, his own views included.

There is more to say about the relationship between Articles 3.1 and 12.1. First, a well-founded judgment that what the child says ought to happen is contrary to her best interests does not of itself show that the child lacks the maturity to decide for herself. This point illustrates a more general principle that constrains the operation of any defensible paternalism. The folly of a particular decision is at most evidence of incapacity to choose. It cannot and should not be taken to constitute that incapacity. It is the incapacity to choose and not the folly of any particular decision which justifies the paternalist in usurping that choice. For example, the child says she does not want to undergo a particular operation. Relevant adults – the medical personnel, her parents – judge that it is in her best interests that she does have the operation. The judgment the adults make supports but does not amount to the view that the child lacks sufficient maturity to decide for herself. The child is, in the adults' minds, making a bad choice, but she still may be capable of making her own choices. If she is, then she ought to be allowed to make the bad decision. After all, adults are thought generally capable of determining how to lead their own lives. But most adults occasionally make stupid decisions, and some adults repeatedly make stupid ones.

The second point to make about the relationship between the two articles is this. What a child says he thinks is in his best interests need not be in his best interests, and we would be failing in our obligations under Article 3.1 if we did not give some considerable weight to what we do judge to be in the child's best interests. However, two further comments are in order. First, what a child says he thinks is in his best interest does give us invaluable evidence as to what in fact is in its best interests. A child's views are an extremely important source of information about his desires, beliefs, hopes, anxieties, fears, attachments, and commitments.

Second, it cannot always be in a child's best interests to compel her to do what she does not herself think is in her best interests. An influential claim in contemporary political philosophy is expressed under the title of the 'endorsement constraint'. This holds that my life only goes better if it is led from the inside according to values that I endorse. It is on account of the endorsement constraint that many think paternalism is self-defeating. You cannot force a person to lead a life that is better (according to you), since if that person does not think it better it will not be worth leading. A similar claim will apply to children. Compelling children to do what you, but not they, think is for the best need not be for their best. This is so even if we think that children do not, like adults, lead their lives by values they can and do endorse. The point is that it can be counterproductive to make someone do what they do not want to do if what you are trying to achieve is make their life go better.

Take the case of a simple custody dispute. After their separation both parents claim that it would be better if their child lived with them, and, minimal access apart, neither of them will countenance shared childcare. In the face of such an irresolvable dispute a court must decide. It seeks the views of the child. The court must give these views a weight according to the child's age and maturity. But the court will find them invaluable evidence of what would in fact be best for the child. If the child says he would be happiest living with his father, is this not a strong indication that he might indeed be happier if this were the court's decision? Second, a court should take seriously the following thought. Acting on its judgment that it would be best for the child to live with the parent he has expressed a wish *not* to live with may be the worse outcome all things considered. Requiring the child to live with the parent he does not want to live with may not be in the child's best interests.

Whether or not a child has moral or legal rights, there is still the question of whether the child has all, or has only some, of the rights that adults have, or has at least some rights that adults do not have. In essence, the dispute examined in the next chapter is between those who see no difference in entitlements to rights between children and adults, and those who think that children have a special status in virtue of which they should lack rights of self-determination.

5

LIBERATION OR CARETAKING?

CHILDREN'S LIBERATION

The early 1970s saw a significant number of manifestos proclaiming the urgent need for children to be liberated. The two key texts are Richard Farson's *Birthrights* (1974) and John Holt's *Escape from Childhood* (1974).[1] The liberation of children was seen as forming an important part of a more general movement for the emancipation of humanity as a whole. Nevertheless, children were specifically represented as one of the major oppressed groups in Western society, alongside blacks, women and the proletariat. In *The Dialectic of Sex* (1970) Shulamith Firestone made explicit the link between the liberation of women and that of children, speaking of their respective oppressions as 'intertwined and mutually reinforcing'.[2] What was demanded on behalf of children ranged from Firestone's somewhat imprecise injunction to 'leave them alone' to the far more concrete insistence that they be given all the rights currently possessed by adults.

The roots of the children's liberation movement lay in the general ferment of the 1960s which sought new strategies of resistance to oppression within the Western industrialised nations. The 'new' was understood in relation to traditional, class-based Marxist analyses of capitalism. Feminist critiques of patriarchy assumed enormous importance and, in this context, the family was identified as an oppressive institution. But the family could be seen as oppressing not only women but children. Reinforcing the feminist case was the criticism by radical psychiatrists such as R. D. Laing of the nuclear family as the potential destroyer of young lives, familial 'love' being only veiled violence leading occasionally to madness.

A further current in the social critiques of the 1960s and 1970s was an anarcho-libertarian rejection of established authority. The school was perceived both as a central, paradigmatic institution of authority in its own right, and as the main means by which ideologies of deference to authority and hierarchy were transmitted to the young. Consequently, there were attempts to define and give actual practical expression to radical, alternative methods of schooling. The emphasis was on non-authoritarian, cooperative forms of education which allowed the child to give free expression to his own nature. The theoretical history of such child-centred education could be traced back to Rousseau, but the 1960s were particularly important in that the experiments of a number of progressive educationalists assumed emblematic importance during this decade. For instance, A. S. Neill's record of his work at Summerhill was published in 1968, and Michael Duane's radical headship of the London comprehensive school, Risinghill, lasted from 1960 to 1965.

There is a neat irony in all of this. The children's liberationists identified the nuclear family and school as the major sources of children's contemporary oppression. Yet it is the rise to prominence of just these two institutions which Ariès takes as confirmation of the awareness by modern society of the child's 'particular nature'. And, as we saw, Ariès favours the modern conception of childhood. It is not surprising then that Firestone, Farson and Holt should all commend Ariès's historical thesis, whilst refusing to share his endorsement of the modern view. Ariès is commended for having shown the conception of children as possessing a separate nature and meriting a separate world to be peculiarly modern. At the same time this separation is denigrated as 'segregation' by Farson and Firestone, whilst Holt speaks of an 'institution' of childhood which puts a 'great gulf or barrier' between young and old: 'what is both new and bad about modern childhood is that children are so cut off from the adult world.'[3] There is also a certain nostalgia for the past with its extended family, communal life and lack of distinction between the worlds of child and adult.

The basic claims of the children's liberationists are that the modern separation of the child's and adult's worlds is an unwarranted and oppressive discrimination; that this segregation is accompanied and reinforced by a false ideology of 'childishness'; and that children are entitled to all the rights and privileges possessed by adults. Farson and Holt draw a crucial distinction between the kinds of rights which can be accorded children. There are those rights which guarantee children certain forms of treatment such as, for instance, a minimum standard of health care, education and freedom from violence and cruelty. Crucially, these kinds of right do not require children to do anything. Rather, it is up to others to act so as to secure the appropriate conditions for children. On the other hand there are those rights which it is up to children themselves to exercise if they choose. The duties of others are defined as requirements not to prevent children from doing as these rights allow them. Key examples of such rights are those to vote, work or travel.

71

The core ideal common to these rights is that of self-determination or freedom. Children who possess them must be able to choose for themselves how to lead their own lives.

Child liberationists acknowledge that children may already have been given the first kind of rights. But, Farson argues, this is a way of protecting children, not protecting their rights. For it is consonant with a paternalist view of children as needing adults to secure their welfare. Indeed, it is precisely the alleged incapacity and vulnerability of children – their inability to look after themselves – which requires that they be given these sorts of rights. Child liberationists seek for children those rights, of the first kind, which require children to act and choose for themselves.

The crucial rights in question are those to vote, work, own property, choose one's guardian and make sexual choices. In short, children should have all those rights which adults currently possess. I will return later to some arguments for and against the attribution of particular rights to children. But it is worth briefly noting a few of the considerations urged by Holt and Farson in relation to the particular rights they commend. In respect to the right to work both argue the essential irrelevance of the facts of child exploitation in the nineteenth century. Such facts tell against not the validity of allowing children to work but rather the condition in which *anyone* had to work. The issue is not the exploitation of children, but of workers as such. Instead of seeking to protect children from the awfulness of adult labour, we should make that labour less awful for everyone.

Both argue for the right of children to the same protection of the law as is accorded adults. They claim that the law presently treats children worse than adults, not simply by denying them these rights but by imposing extra burdens upon them. For instance, it is maintained that children can be convicted of a crime for doing what, if done by an adult, would not be criminal. Moreover, children are badly mistreated in those penal institutions specifically designed to protect them as minors.

Both see the right to choose one's guardian, or the circumstances of one's upbringing, as requiring a plurality of home environments. As alternatives to natural parents, children should be able to choose amongst many options including secondary guardians, multi-family communes, child-exchange programmes and children's residences. A wide variety of childrearing practices is viewed as the necessary correlate of this particular right.

All adult rights are to be extended to *all* children. Holt speaks of the rights as to be held by someone of 'any' or 'whatever' age. Farson says the 'achievement of children's rights must apply to children of *all* ages, from birth to adulthood'.[4] They have two basic argumentative strategies to support this extreme position. The first is an appeal to the arbitrariness of age as a criterion

72

for the possession or non-possession of rights. The second is an attack upon what could be called the 'incompetence thesis', that is, the view that children are rightly disqualified from holding rights in virtue of their inabilities in certain relevant respects. I will consider these in turn.

An initially attractive and plausible claim is that age alone should not be the basis on which rights are awarded or withheld. Talk of society as unfairly divided along the lines of race, sex *and* age, or talk of 'ageism' as an evil to compare with sexism and racism, seems to reinforce the idea that distributing rights according to how old you are is as morally arbitrary as doing so according to the colour of one's skin. However, it is evident that society distinguishes between young and old on the basis not of age alone, but rather what it takes to be a significant correlation between age and possession of capacities relevant to the holding of rights. It is not that young people lack rights just because they are young, but that, being young, they are assumed insufficiently competent in the appropriate ways. Holt and Farson seem to recognise this. For, notwithstanding their rhetorical attack on age as an arbitrary standard, they concentrate their criticism on the incompetence thesis. This second line of argument comprises several strands, one disputing the validity and value of a competence standard, another seeking to show that children are not incompetent.

In some instances Holt and Farson argue that competence is not the issue. Farson, for instance, declares that children should have the vote not because they are as able as adults to make an intelligent informed electoral decision, but simply because they are members of society and affected by the decisions of its elected government. Elsewhere they argue that, even if competence is the issue, it is unfair to assume that it is always directly correlative with age. If a child cannot vote on account of being unable to make a rational choice, then an adult who is similarly incapable of doing so should also be electorally disqualified. Similarly, Holt argues that the right to drive should be conditional only on a proven display of the requisite skill and knowledge. What should matter is passing a test, not passing 17.

However, the main thrust of the child liberationist argument is that, even if a certain competence rightly remains the crucial criterion for the possession of adult rights, it is a mistake to judge children incompetent. In fact, Holt and Farson do not try to show that children are as competent as adults. Rather, they seek to expose the assumption that children are incompetent as a key ideological feature of the modern conception of childhood. Here there is a direct parallel with contemporaneous feminist writing. Feminists argue that the idea of women as necessarily fitted to occupy certain subordinate roles on account of their female nature is in fact a major element in patriarchal ideology. Weakness, dependence, emotionalism and illogicality are not the natural properties of women as a sex. Rather, they are attributable to the socially constituted category of femininity which endorses the continued oppression of women. Similarly, Holt and Farson seem to claim that 'childishness', connoting vulnerability, frailty and helplessness, is not a natural quality of children but rather an ideological construct which helps to support the denial of their proper rights. The innocence and incompetence of children is not a biological fact, but a projection onto young humans of our own adult needs. We want children to be helpless so that we can help them; we need them to be dependent so that we can exercise authority over them. 'Cute' is the archetypal adjective of this oppressive ideology. But it is a form of praise which barely conceals the condemnation of its object to subordinate and dependent status. The adult's concern to assist the helpless child in her development is as patronisingly offensive as the 'respect' a man might declare he had for the 'weaker sex'.

Moreover, it is a self-confirming ideology. Presumed incapable of making choices for themselves, children are denied the opportunity to show that they can. Analogously, J. S. Mill argued against the 'naturalness' of women's subjection by pointing both to the evidence of those societies in which women did not suffer an inferior status, and to the inculcation of inferiority within our own society. Child liberationists appeal to the anecdotal evidence of what children, even in our culture, can do if encouraged and permitted to express themselves. They also cite the precocity of children in the past.

I will assess the 'incompetence thesis' and the charge that age is an arbitrary criterion in the next chapter. Here I want to point to some immediate difficulties with the liberationist thesis. There are problems with any polemic, especially one designed to demolish a conventional wisdom. The central one is that rhetorical criticism of this kind is anxious to do as much damage as possible. To this end an argumentative scatter gun is employed, spraying the target from as many directions as possible. A concern to ensure that fire is steady and from a single source is unlikely. The premises of the child liberationist arguments are not obviously consistent one with another, nor well-founded. Sometimes the argument is that the considerations that warrant adults enjoying a right apply to children too. Elsewhere it is argued that children should have a right, just as adults do, but for reasons which have to do with their nature as children. Children should be given the vote because like adults they can make informed choices or are subject to the decisions of government. Yet children should be allowed to work because it is a way in which they can learn from adults and develop an understanding of the difference their actions make to the world.

Again, it may be plausible to suggest that modern childhood inhibits the precocious development of skills and independent action on the part of children. But it does not follow that even the prodigies of the past were the match of their guardians. It is one thing to underestimate the capacities of children, another to reckon them equal to those of adults. Herein lies the most obvious weakness of a strategy which does not so much positively establish the equal competence of children as negatively argue that their representation as relative incompetents is mere ideology.

Furthermore, the rhetoric of children's liberation trades on the ambiguity between a broad and a narrow understanding of childhood. It urges rights for a child of 'any' age whilst systematically representing the child as a young person who is no longer an infant. Farson thus sees nothing wrong with conceding the 'obvious incapacity' of a 2-month-old baby to administer its inherited property, nor the 'obvious inability' of a very young child to vote.[5] But at what age does such an 'obvious inability' become so obviously an ability which, being the equal of an adult, merits the reward of a full right? Finally, it is simply inconsistent to see self-determination as the fundamental right of all children, and yet, in the case of the very young, to speak of rights which are possessed but not exercised by their holders and which must thus be upheld by adult protectors. Obviously, very young children are less equal than others in their right to self-determination.

A modern liberationist, Howard Cohen, acknowledges that the propriety of according children rights turns on their capacity or lack of it. However, he allows that children may '*borrow*' the capacities of others to secure their entitlements.[6] Children could have agents or advisers who would ensure that their rights were exercised. In chapter 4 I noted that, in similar fashion, a will theorist of rights could make provision for representatives of a child who exercise her rights. However, there are a number of problems with this idea of an appointed proxy from whom the child borrows the competence to exercise her right. First, what are the criteria for selecting the adviser? Presumably a child who is incapable of choosing for herself is not competent to choose the best person to choose for her. Parents may claim to fit the bill, but the bare fact of parenthood does not of itself constitute a competence to choose for their children. Moreover, we saw in chapter 4 that what is in the best interests of a child can be contested. Similarly, the best person to choose for a child will be hotly disputed.

Second, what a child would choose if able to choose is not necessarily what is in his best interests. We saw that even competent adults make foolish choices. Moreover, what a child would choose if able to do so, that is if possessed of an adult competence to choose, is difficult to make precise sense of. It is hard to understand the idea of a hypothetical child-adult – an adult in virtue of *how* it makes a decision, but a child in virtue of *what* it has to make a decision about. Third, is the child bound to take the advice of his adviser? If he is, then it is hard to see how talk of 'borrowed' capacities differs interestingly from simple paternalism. The child has no choice and the adult chooses for him. If, on the other hand, the child is not bound by the adviser's advice then the child retains his right to choose for himself. He does not differ from an adult who can take or ignore the advice of other adults. Yet this sits oddly with the claim that a child does need to 'borrow' a capacity they somehow lack.

Child liberationists may say that children have the rights of self-determination only if they want to exercise them. Holt says, for instance, that the rights of self-determination should be 'made *available*' to any child 'who wants to make use of them'.[7] The implication is that rights are taken up only by those who are interested in them, and that the very young would simply lack such an interest. In the first place, Holt's talk of availability for use subject to demand is ambiguous. There is a difference between choosing to have a right, and choosing to exercise one that is possessed. It is entirely possible that someone should elect to take up a right which they prefer not to exercise. They might, for instance, wish to be enfranchised but never to vote. Equally, an individual could decide to have a right but ask someone else to decide how it is exercised. Indeed a child is a plausible example of someone who might want a caretaker to exercise its rights for it.

Second, it is likely that many children other than the very young would have no interest in exercising the rights on offer. Indeed Farson is honest enough to admit that 'children will be their own worst enemies in the movement for their liberation'.[8] Both Farson and Holt argue that children are presently the victims of the adult ideology of childish helplessness, and can be empowered only through the concession of rights currently denied them. There is something odd then about making the possession of these rights conditional upon an interest which is likely to be absent and which will be activated only by the very exercise of these rights. Should adults compel children to choose to have the rights of choice? Should children have no choice over whether they want to be choosers?

Third, an interest in exercising a right does not coincide with a competence to exercise it. It seems plain wrong to maintain that the very young should have a freedom right simply if and when they 'want to make use of it'. Should a 1-year-old be free to drink alcohol or experiment sexually with an adult if she 'wants'? It is implausible to suggest there would never be any cases of very young children wanting to do these things. And it is unsatisfactory to claim that a very young child is not in a position to know what she 'really' wants. For to stipulate that the 'want' must be properly informed and sensible if it is to count is only to introduce the notion of competent choice at another level. Instead of a child being deemed incapable simply of having the right, she is now likely to be judged incapable of expressing the desire that would qualify her to have the right that is available to her in principle.

THE CARETAKER THESIS

Farson says explicitly that:

> the issue of self-determination is at the heart of children's liberation. It is, in fact, the only issue, a definition of the entire concept. The acceptance of the child's right to self-determination is fundamental to all the rights to which children are entitled.[9]

It is appropriate then to look at the claim, diametrically opposed to the liberationist view, that children should not be seen as self-determining agents. This finds its most developed articulation in what I shall call the 'caretaker thesis' which is standardly defended within the context of liberal political philosophical presuppositions about autonomy and paternalism. The 'caretaker thesis' offers an account of why children should not be free to make autonomous decisions, and of how their caretakers should be guided in making decisions for them.

Obviously, there are other grounds on which children might be denied rights of self-determination. For instance, it has been argued that children are the property of their natural parents and have no rights at all, their treatment being at the sole discretion of their parental owners. Again, it should not be thought that all liberals subscribe to the 'caretaker thesis'. Some are sympathetic to the liberationist case, suspecting that children may be unfairly disqualified from enjoyment of important adult rights. However, the 'caretaker thesis' merits being counterposed to liberationism for the following reason. It denies to children only the rights, those of self-determination, whose refusal the liberationist sees as most central to their present alleged oppression; and it does so from within a general political philosophy that accords self-determination a central and much valued place. In this sense the 'caretaker thesis' thinks self-determination too important to be left to children.

A central and influential presumption of modern liberal political philosophy is that all adult human beings are capable of making rational, autonomous decisions. In view of this they should be left to lead their own lives as they see fit. The one constraint on this freedom is that its exercise should not interfere with a similar freedom for others. The reasoning behind this view, given classic expression in John Stuart Mill's *On Liberty*, is as follows: individuals are usually the best judges of what is in their interests and acting on the contrary presumption, that others may know better, is likely to lead to far worse outcomes.

Some adults, such as the brain-damaged and the seriously mentally disturbed, are permanently incapable of making rational, autonomous decisions. In their case other adults must make decisions on their behalf, and are justified in doing so. Normal adults may also make decisions that are not sensible in the required sense. The standard cases are acting in serious ignorance of the consequences of one's action and making decisions whilst clearly irrational, or what J. S. Mill delightfully calls 'in some state of excitement or absorption incompatible with the full use of the reflecting faculty'.[10] In these cases other adults would be entitled to make for us the decisions we would have made had we been aware of what we were doing and deciding rationally. Paternalism is making choices for other people. It is justified when people cannot make the choices they would make if they were rational and autonomous.

On the standard liberal analysis, children are in a state where adults may paternalistically choose for them. Children are thought to merit paternalism both because they have not yet developed the cognitive capacity to make intelligent decisions in the light of relevant information about themselves and the world, and because they are prone to emotional inconstancy such that their decisions are likely to be wild and variable. However, the case of children differs interestingly from the two other sorts of case where paternalism is supposed to be justified. Their state is permanent in that, unlike otherwise rational adults, they will not recover from their temporary ignorance or irrationality. Yet it is not permanent in that, unlike the mentally ill, children will grow out of their diminshed condition. In the normal course of events children will *become* rational, autonomous adults.

Adults may choose paternalistically for children as the latter would choose if they were adults. In the first instance the relevant adults will be the child's immediate caretakers, that is, most probably their parents. The 'caretaker thesis' not only argues that caretakers can choose for their children; it suggests *how* they should choose. A paternalist chooses for an adult as the latter would choose if competent to do so. An adult normally chooses in the light of what may reasonably be regarded as its own best interests. The case of a child presents an interesting difference. What a child chooses to do affects both his immediate and his future adult self. So the paternalist caretaker must choose what the child would choose if competent to make choices, and choose with regard to the interests of the adult the child will become. The caretaker, if you like, chooses for the child in the person of the adult which the child is not yet but will eventually be.

One way in which this line of thought has been expressed is by means of the notion of a 'trust'. In legal terms a trust is an arrangement made for a particular purpose whereby the owner of property, the truster, vests the rights of its administration in another, the trustee. The trustee must administer the property to the benefit of the truster. So the adult caretaker might be described as the trustee of the child's interests who acts to promote them until such time as the child is able to do so for herself. This is when the child herself becomes an adult and marks the termination of the trust. The purpose of the trust is to safeguard the future adult's interests, which the child is herself unable to do.[11]

Laura Purdy defends a version of the caretaker thesis which appeals directly to the consequences for both the adult and society as a whole of allowing children to make their own free choices. She believes that the possession by children of rights of self-determination is inconsistent with their maturation into adults who can lead worthwhile lives.[12] The argument is that adults must have acquired certain traits of character if they are to be able to lead valuable lives. For instance, one thing that matters to us when we are fully grown is being able to choose the goals that we will pursue in life and to make choices in the light of these goals. Locke thought children were born not in but to equality. Similarly, we could argue that children are not born free but will gain freedom as adults. However, they will only acquire freedom if they are denied it whilst still children. Giving children the liberty to make choices subverts their development into adults who can make choices. Locke thought that giving a child the same rights as an adult was very bad for the child. It was 'to thrust him out amongst Brutes, and abandon him to a state as wretched, and as much beneath that of a Man, as theirs'. In very similar fashion Purdy says that granting immature children equal rights is like releasing mental patients from state hospitals without means of care.[13] The additional claim is that it is also very bad for the adult the child will develop into. Further, a society composed of adults poorly able or unable to choose how to live their lives is not desirable.

At the heart of this argument is the assertion that children do not simply grow with the passage of time into adults. Development is not endogenous, spontaneous and inevitable. Children need to be cared for and supported in their maturation. More particularly their choices must be constrained; children need to be controlled and disciplined. Thus Purdy explicitly criticises a 'growth model' of human nature which would view children as 'essentially complete, needing only time and nourishment to develop'. Such a false view would support a regime of laissez-faire permissiveness, whereas in fact the natural impulses of children must be carefully controlled and appropriate dispositions must be deliberately taught.[14]

Of course, providing supportive boundaries within which development is encouraged need not amount to the denial of all rights of choice. Moreover, as Locke recognised, children 'grow up to the use of reason' and 'the rigour of government' may in consequence be 'gently relaxed' as they progress. What is appropriate constraint and discipline for one stage of childhood need not be so for a later stage. A still further point is that competence in the exercise of a right may only be acquired in the practice of the exercise. Giving children the freedom to make some choices is essential if they are to learn what it is to make choices and why it matters to be able to do so.

How plausible overall is the 'caretaker thesis'? An initial problem concerns denying rights of self-determination to children as a group. Surely each case deserves to be considered individually. Anyone who fails to display the requisite rational autonomy may be treated paternalistically. But this should apply equally to adults. It is unfair to categorise every child as an incompetent. Moreover, the liberal is happy for adults to make mistakes, arguing both that we learn from our errors and that a freedom only to do the right thing would be a hopelessly constricted and impoverished one. Even if children do not always choose the best for themselves, why should they not merit the same valued freedom as adults to commit errors?

Some of the reasons for treating children as a group and insisting upon age as a valid criterion for the attribution of rights will be discussed in the next chapter. It is worth noting here the claim that children are likely to make different kinds of mistakes from adults. In particular, a child unchecked by his caretaker can do things which seriously and irreversibly damage his future adult self. The point is a valid one, but two comments are in order. First, there is no reason to think adults could not and do not similarly make gravely and irremediably harmful mistakes. They too should be paternalistically protected from their errors. Second, the point justifies only a paternalism which is limited to the prevention of those childhood mistakes which seriously jeopardise future well-being. It does not supply a blanket justification of paternalistic adult caretaking as such.

The second set of problems about the 'caretaker thesis' concerns its answer to the question of how the caretaking should be conducted. The standard of safeguarding the future adult's interests is not a clear and unequivocal one, and I will review a number of ways in which it can be understood. Some writers who consider what justifies particular paternalistic behaviours appeal to the notion of *consent*. Treating people paternalistically may be permissible if they consent. In the absence of actual consent, hypothetical consent serves the same justificatory purpose. One is permitted to do that to which the other would consent if not in that state which makes the paternalism necessary. In this spirit some see parental paternalism as justified if it secures the subsequent consent of its object or may reasonably be thought of as likely to secure that consent. The child may not now assent to the manner in which she is being brought up. But it is the subsequent consent the child will give as an adult which retrospectively legitimates that upbringing.

The difficulty with this is that it conforms to what we might call 'self-justifying paternalism'. This is paternalism which changes others so that they approve it. It thus brings about its own subsequent vindicatory consent. We could brainwash someone to think that the brainwashing was a good thing. It is obvious that a child's upbringing could produce an adult who approved of how it had been brought up, and that this need not involve anything like the objectionable means of brainwashing. Nevertheless, why should we approve of an upbringing just because it can produce retrospective approval of itself? Surely we are interested in what kinds of adults are produced, and it is not enough simply that they approve their own upbringing. The point can be put another way. It is conceivable that one and the same child should have a number of interestingly different adult versions of himself, each of whom approved of the upbringing by which he came to be the particular adult he did. The standard of subsequent consent would not allow us to say that any one upbringing or adult thereby produced was preferable to any other. Yet it is surely probable that we would have well-grounded reasons for preferring some over the rest.

It seems appropriate then directly to ask what are the valued adult traits in the name of which a child's self-determination may rightfully be denied. We should distinguish first between a minimum and a maximum goal. We can seek to bring up the child either to be at least that which we think any adult should be, or to realise to the highest possible degree that which we believe to be valuable in an adult. In the former case an upbringing should only protect the child's basic needs or essential interests in so far as she will become an adult. In the latter an upbringing is judged against the standard of the very best that could have been achieved.

As for what is valued in adult human beings, the most obvious answer is self-determination. The 'caretaker thesis' then has a pleasing, concordant completeness. A child is denied the right of self-determination in order that he should be able to exercise this very right in adulthood. Indeed the argument can be expressed more strongly. Children will *only* acquire the rights of self-determination if they are denied them now. A good example is education. A child – so the reasoning might run – would choose not to go to school, preferring more immediate childish pleasures. But adult powers of reflective thought and adult knowledge about the world can only be acquired through education. Going to school is necessary for maturation into a rational autonomous being. Present compulsion is a precondition of subsequent choice. For this reason, compulsory universal education is insisted upon by liberals and is notable for being enforced against parents. Nevertheless, a liberal like

J. S. Mill is careful to distinguish between state enforcement of education and state direction of its content.

Rearing and educating a child to be a self-determining adult requires at least two kinds of thing. First, the child must have developed certain basic cognitive skills such as the capacity to reflect, deliberate and argue as well as the ability to acquire knowledge about herself and her world. Second, people's autonomy is greater the larger the number of options open to them. The child should be given knowledge of the choices he may make in his later life, and provided with the means to realise them. In this spirit Joel Feinberg speaks of a child's right to an 'open future'.[15]

We can also recognise here the classic liberal upbringing – tolerant of diverse life styles, flexible and wide-ranging in outlook, humanistic and tending to secular agnosticism in ideology. In contrast, the classic illiberal upbringing would be narrow, dogmatic, inflexible and perhaps best exemplified by that of religious zealots. The goal of nurturing a self-determining adult is plausible but there are difficulties. These can perhaps be best explored by looking at the tensions between bringing a person to full autonomy and bringing up someone to have character, that is a set of beliefs, desires and abilities.

In the first place, an autonomous adult does not and cannot choose in a vacuum. No chooser can be self-less. Choices are made by someone who has a character, dispositions, an outlook on life, commitments and loyalties. These may change. Indeed, the mark of self-determining persons is that they should be able to reflect upon and evaluate their own person, resolving where appropriate to change. But self-determination starts from a self. I choose the kind of life I want to lead on the basis of the kind of person I am, and I am the kind of person I am because of how I have been brought up. Parents cannot avoid forming their children's characters. It would be a caricature of ideal liberal parents to imagine them zealously striving to avoid the creation of any particular personality in their children. But a person's adult character moulded through inheritance, socialisation and parental upbringing has some considerable weight. It is absurd to believe that anyone could slough off their character through a simple act of will. Thus the question presses of what kind of person one should be brought up to be. Each and every upbringing has an obvious 'opportunity cost', namely the absence of some other upbringing. Upbringings can only be evaluated by recognising other desired adult traits apart from the single one of self-determination.

First, we should want someone to be able to make and act upon choices of the morally good. This will not be secured merely by developing a child's faculty of choosing. It also requires the inculcation of a sense of what is good and bad, and consistent exposure to good rather than bad ways of living.

Equally some sensibilities are preferable to others. We would surely wish a child to gain, for instance, an appreciation of culture, a respect for the environment and a love of humanity.

Second, the autonomous person should surely possess a certain kind of character. She should be someone for whom a commitment to values matters, who is resolute and strong in any commitment she does make, and able to stand by the values she endorses. Some liberal understandings of the virtue of autonomy place too much emphasis upon an ability to review and revise one's conception of the good life – and not enough upon an ability to adhere to what one believes in. Moreover, the inculcation of these desired character traits may be best secured within non-liberal cultures, those that do teach children a commitment to a set of fundamental values.[16]

However, third, it would be a mistake to offer an oversimplified contrast between a 'liberal' and a 'traditionalist' upbringing, the first preparing the child for an 'open future', the latter teaching withdrawal from choice into a single ideal. As examples of the supposed 'traditionalist' education many religious traditions in fact encourage criticism, deliberation, a preparedness to challenge orthodoxy, and to think anew about what has been received wisdom. They may do so within the terms of the inherited tradition but they instil critical dispositions nonetheless.[17]

Fourth, culture and tradition matter to people. Humans have a need to belong, to have a sense of themselves as members of particular communities with shared values and history. Some liberals even argue that a community's culture provides the individual with an indispensable context of personal choice. It is, in this sense, a necessary condition of self-determination.[18] Here too it is important to recognise that the child's caretakers may have a right to live their lives in the light of customs and values they esteem. It is most unlikely that the child will not thereby inherit a respect for his parents' way of life.

Fifth, there is the question of talents and the fulfilment of a child's natural abilities. An upbringing should realise the child's innate potentialities, whether in sport or music or intellectual scholarship or whatever. Yet, once again, each upbringing has an opportunity cost. This is not simply in terms of the skills that cannot be developed but, also and crucially, there may be a loss of self-determination. A precocious musical talent may be carefully nurtured to produce a concert soloist. But, as many personal careers can testify, this will have been achieved at the expense of other skills which could not be cultivated. Moreover, the soloist is limited as a result in the choice of life they can make. Even so, it is arguable that not to have been so intensively and exclusively trained in musicianship would have amounted to a culpable squandering of the child's native ability.

The good caretaker must strive both to realise the child's particular nature *and* to safeguard her 'open future'. The tensions between these two goals are significantly increased when they are defined in maximising terms. The 'caretaker thesis' rules out oppressive, stultifying, constricting upbringings, which would produce adults incapable of making real choices or bereft of valuable abilities they might otherwise have acquired. But the thesis is not so clear in its prescription of the ideal upbringing. It insists that it is in a child's own interests not to be self-determining. From the standpoint of the adult to come, these interests are various and not obviously consonant. This is important when it is remembered that the 'caretaker thesis' may legitimate only a limited denial of self-determination, for instance just to provide a basic education or merely to prevent the performance of seriously and permanently harmful actions. In sum, the thesis argues against the liberationist for a denial of self-determination but, in the last analysis, is unclear how much should be denied and what precise ends are served by the denial.

6

ARBITRARINESS AND
INCOMPETENCE

The dispute between the child liberationist and the defender of the 'caretaker thesis' turns on the question of whether it is right to distinguish between children and adults in respects that are relevant to the according or withholding of rights. This question divides into two further ones: whether making any distinction is not arbitrary, and whether the distinction made in terms of children's relative incompetence is accurate. I will deal with each issue in turn.

ARBITRARINESS

If nothing else, children are younger than adults. The child liberationist is correct to argue that a distribution of rights on the basis of age *alone* would be unfair. It would be morally arbitrary and unjust to deny children rights merely because they were younger than adults. It would be as arbitrary and wrong as denying rights to humans who were shorter than average, had fewer hairs or a lower pitch of voice than others. Clearly, some of the rhetoric of children's rights appeals to the general arbitrariness of age in this sense.

However, the denial of rights to children is not based solely on age. It is done on the basis of an alleged correlation between age and some relevant competence. The young are denied rights because, being young, they are presumed to lack some capacities necessary for the possession of rights. The argument from arbitrariness charges that it is unfair to correlate incompetence with some particular age.

Let me spell this out. Either one has a right or one does not. If age is to be the criterion then some particular age must be fixed as the point at which the right is first held. If it is, for instance, 18, then this means 17-year-olds on the eve of their eighteenth birthday lack the right but acquire it the next day. This prompts the charge of arbitrariness. How can a matter of hours, minutes, seconds even, make all the difference between being someone who can legitimately and someone who cannot legitimately hold a right? What possible capacity or competence of sufficient importance to warrant holding a right can be acquired within minutes? I shall term this criticism 'the arbitrariness of any particular age'.

It should be kept distinct from another criticism with which it is sometimes conflated. This is what might be termed the 'unreliability of correlation by age' and runs as follows. Some 17½-year-olds, indeed some 16- and 15-year-olds have those competences judged necessary for the holding of the right in question, whereas some 18½-year-olds, indeed 19- and 20-year-olds lack them. The use of 18 as a single point of transition is thus unfair.

Finally there is a view, which could be called the 'preferability of a competence test', and which is usually run in tandem with either or both of these two criticisms. It may be summarised as follows. It is one's competence or incompetence which is relevant to the possession or non-possession of the right rather than one's age as such. Thus it would obviously be fairer to accord rights if this competence is displayed by an individual than to do so simply when some designated age has been reached. The relevant competence could be gauged by some appropriate test. I now want to assess in turn each of these three criticisms – the arbitrariness of any particular age, the unreliability of correlation by age and the preferability of a competence test. It should be noted that none of them directly challenges the twin presumptions that competence should be the criterion of rights-possession and that age may supply *some* guide to one's relative competence. Together they amount only to the charge that passing a straightforward test of competence would be fairer than and preferable to the reaching of a certain age as the qualification for being a rights-holder.

The criticism that any particular age is arbitrary is an example of a more general charge which may be made against fixing cut-off points. We recognise that high speeds on the roads are dangerous and so set a legal maximum of, say, 70mph. But why should 70mph be dangerous, in the eyes of the law, where 69mph is not? Again, institutions bestowing qualifications must determine cut-off points. But, why should 40 per cent be a pass mark if 39 per cent is a fail? The examples can easily be multiplied. The problem is that the division of entities, actions or whatever into classes requires dividing lines. These need not necessarily correspond to any natural invariant intervals between the things in question. Indeed, such dividing lines are likely to be set by conventions, albeit with *some* eye on actual discontinuities. Crucially, the difference in import of belonging to one class rather than another does not seem appropriately related to the differences between the entities at the margins of the dividing lines. If 40 per cent is a pass and 39 per cent is a fail, a script receiving the first mark cannot nevertheless be that much better than one getting the second. If 70mph is dangerous, 69mph cannot be markedly less so.

However, this just is the inevitable and besetting sin of *any* dividing line. And if we are to have divisions then we must have dividing lines. No one who worries about the arbitrariness of dividing lines seems prepared to suggest that there should be no divisions. Should *any* driving speed be permissible? Should *all* students be awarded the same degree? Anyone who uses the language of rights – as do child liberationists – must be prepared to exclude *some* things from the class of rights-holders. Child liberationists are not necessarily animal liberationists, and the latter are not necessarily flora liberationists. Indeed, the very rhetoric of a liberationist argument would be devalued if *everything* had rights. Having rights bestows a moral status, and it is unjust to deny this status to those who are entitled to enjoy it. But there would be no distinguishing status at all if nothing lacked rights.

Still, it may be argued that these examples miss an important point. Students do not have a right to pass their examinations whatever mark they receive, and drivers do not have a right to drive at whatever speed they choose, whereas the distinction made between a child and an adult is for the purpose of denying rights to the one which are accorded to the other. *Prima facie* there is an injustice in the treatment of children which there is not in the case of low-scoring students and speeding drivers. Similarly, there is no reason to think that all examination marks or all speeds merit the same treatment. But it is surely sound to presume that, in the first instance at least, all human beings should be subject to the same moral regard.

Each of these examples raises the question of whether a certain kind of arbitrariness is unfair as such. It is not unfair to deny a right whose possession requires a certain competence to someone who is incompetent. It is not unfair to refuse someone a qualification if qualifying requires that a certain standard of work has been produced. It is not unfair to deny a car driver the freedom to drive at speeds which jeopardise other road users. The difficult question is whether the use of a particular age, a particular mark and a particular speed is not arbitrary and thus unfair. The argument so far is that it is not.

The presumption that all human beings are equal – and there are those who would dispute its soundness – does not establish that children are entitled to the possession of the same rights as adults. It shows only that in justifying any distinction between children and adults in respect of the possession of rights, no other considerations are relevant than those having to do with the criteria for possession of rights and their satisfaction by children or adults. It simply begs the important question to assume that the only relevant criterion is humanity. If someone must be x before they can have a right to y then it is the presence or absence of x which alone matters. It does not matter that one is or is not a human being. A non-human animal which is x should have a right to y and it would be 'speciesist' to think otherwise. The importance of being human can be overemphasised.

If society does need to separate and categorise persons, then lines of separation will have to be drawn, divisions between the categories agreed. This is especially likely when the society in question has a developed legal system. Law demands unequivocality, that it be possible to allocate cases unambiguously to appropriate categories. This requires clear boundaries between the categories. The alleged arbitrariness of any particular, conventionally established point is an acceptable price to pay for the benefits of clear categorial division. Perhaps the price can be reduced by adopting, where appropriate, a practice of discretion at the margins. For example, examiners may decide that marks of 37 per cent to 39.9 per cent merit consideration for a pass instead of automatic failure. Needless to say, the criticism of the arbitrariness of any particular point can now be directed at the new lower limit.

It is worth adding one further important point. The charge of arbitrariness directed at chronological points seems especially germane given that human maturation is construed in terms of a continuous development. If an individual develops from that state in which he lacks the property of x to that state in which he possesses x and if that development is a continuous one, then it seems impossible to fix a precise temporal point when the individual may be said to have x. He achieves x *over* time rather than at *a* moment *in* time. Yet developmental psychology does use the notion of 'stages'. Not only is childhood itself a stage in any human life, but there are stages within childhood. Developmental theory imposes upon the continuous development of the human a grid of successive stages such that, whilst it is not committed to the view that there are radical breaks in human maturation, it does see distinct cumulative and qualitative changes. In this way the idea of a division of human growth into notional periods, each with its own attributes, is easier to understand, and the charge of arbitrariness given continuous development correspondingly loses some of its bite.

The price of arbitrariness is acceptable only if the dividing point, even when conventionally established, bears *some* relationship to the terms under which and purposes for which the division is being made. If reaching a particular age is not to any significant degree an appropriate index of the achievement of some competence then it is simply unfair to use it as such. We come then to the claim that age cannot reliably be correlated with competence. Once again it is important carefully to separate points. There can surely be no disputing the thesis that, compared to normal adults, the very young display serious incompetence. Farson saw nothing wrong or inconsistent about conceding the 'obvious incapacity' of a 2-month-old baby to administer its inherited property, nor the 'obvious inability' of a very young child to vote.[1] Nor can it be disputed that the acquisition by human beings of various skills and abilities proceeds according to a fairly standard and universal chronology. Indeed, the pattern of human sensory, motor, cognitive and linguistic development displays a significant degree of cultural invariance. Children walk, recognise and manipulate objects, talk, etc. at roughly the same ages whatever the society in which they are brought up. There are some differences between societies and, within the same society, some individual children may, for instance, walk later or earlier than most do. But the degree of significant correlation between age and acquisition of competence is such that exceptions to the general rule are rarer the further they depart from the mean.

The fact that some individuals develop the competences required for possession of a right earlier than others is not surprising. Nor does it seriously impugn the value of using that particular age. What matters is the overall balance of probabilities. We need only to be confident that the competence is most probably not possessed by those in one age group and most probably possessed by those in the other. Here is an analogy. Drunk driving is illegal on the grounds of being an increased danger to other road users, and the law stipulates a measurable degree of intoxication beyond which driving is illegal. It is of course probable, indeed most likely, that some drivers below that point will be as dangerous as most of those above it, and that others above that point will drive as safely as most below it. But what is crucial is that it remains true that any driver over the legally stipulated maximum will most probably be incapable of driving safely, and correlatively any driver within the limit will most probably be able to drive safely.

Of course the wrong age for the competence in question may have been agreed. But that is a different matter. If ability to speak is thought the appropriate competence then, clearly, setting the age at 18 is ludicrously misjudged. Less dramatically, evidence that a substantial majority of 17-year-olds displayed the competence required for a right currently accorded at 18 would be a reason to consider lowering the age of qualification. Indeed, much debate over children's or rather teenagers' rights concerns the question of which age is the right one for the attribution of a particular right. But then this is all about finding the competence to fit the right and the age to fit the competence. It does not amount to a case against the view that reaching a given age may be a reliable enough indication that a person has achieved the requisite competence. No one who holds this view is committed to the absurd idea that every single individual on the stroke of midnight acquires, all at once and totally, the abilities associated, conventionally, with a particular age. The fact that precocious individuals are unfairly penalised and immature individuals are unfairly rewarded does not then constitute an overwhelming reason to abandon the use of a fixed age. It would only be a reason if the numbers of anomalous individuals suggested that the particular age used had in fact been poorly chosen.

It is also important to specify the competence required for a particular right. John Kleinig is right to point out that a 'child is likely to be able to decide with the requisite rationality whether and what games it will play before it will be able to decide whether and who to marry'.[2] This shows that someone should be free to enter into a marriage not merely as soon as they are capable of taking any sort of decision but only when they can understand what is involved in the specific decision to marry.

A final point remains to be considered. What ultimately counts, as far as the award of a right is concerned, is the possession of an appropriate competence. Age is at best a rough and fallible index of possession. So should not the right be awarded straightforwardly upon proof of possession of the competence, that is by means of a test? In this spirit, child liberationists argue that if children are denied the vote because presumed incapable of, for instance, making informed reflective electoral decisions then all adults should be compelled to pass a test establishing their electoral competence before *they* get the vote. It should be pointed out that age and proof of competence are not necessarily mutually exclusive alternatives. Merely reaching a certain age is not always enough to bestow a right. They may also have to show possession of some competence. To drive a car, someone must be of a certain age *and* have passed a test. And whilst there is normally no competence test for voting, insanity and incarceration do *dis*qualify even an adult.

However, the main relevant point is that a competence test must be shown not to have more significant disadvantages than those associated with the use of a criterion of age. Here the competence test fails, for it is vulnerable to a number of standard criticisms. First, it would probably prove impossibly expensive and cumbersome to administer in all the important areas. Imagine a 'suffrage test'. Not only would every individual have to sit it but each would have to *re*-sit it periodically. For it cannot be assumed that a competence, once acquired, is possessed for ever. Second, where tests are administered, and especially where the rewards of passing are so high, there will be risks of corruption, exploitation and the abuse of power. Think of the stakes of enfranchisement and consider how much it would be worth to get a vote not merited or deny others a vote they did deserve. It is always possible to cheat at examinations; it is not so easy to manipulate one's age.

Third, age is something over which there can be objective agreement, whereas both the initial terms of a competence test and the grading of responses to it could be endlessly controversial. They are also subject to cultural bias, as in the case of the alleged correlation between ethnicity and IQ score. It is one thing for some group to lack the suffrage simply and solely because of incompetence to vote. It is quite another for the group's alleged inability to have been established by false and discriminatory means. Fourth, and finally, the use of age as a criterion induces stable expectations on the part of a society's citizens. They know exactly when they qualify for a particular right. It is disturbing not to know when and even if one will ever have a right.

These are reasons to conclude that the use of a competence test would not be a preferable or fairer alternative to the use of age. Since the use of age has not been shown to be evidently arbitrary and unfair, I conclude that it remains, in principle, an acceptable basis on which to distribute rights. It must next be seen whether the possession of rights does require certain competences and, if so, whether children lack them.

INCOMPETENCE

In the last analysis, the dispute between child liberationists and defenders of the 'caretaker thesis' comes down to the following. For the former, children are unjustly deprived of rights because they are falsely believed to be incompetent. For the latter, children *are* incompetent and will only eventually become competent if rights are denied to them now. What does competence in this context amount to and why should it be required of a rights-holder?

We need to distinguish between the grounds for the possession of rights as such and those for the possession of certain kinds of rights or indeed for particular rights. In chapter 4 we saw that will theorists and interest theorists differ in respect of the first matter. A will theorist believes that rights are protected exercises of choice and thus that only those who can make choices can have, or at least exercise, rights. An interest theorist, by contrast, believes that rights protect significant interests – those of sufficient importance to merit the imposition of a duty on others – and thus that only those who have such interests can have rights. If a child cannot make choices then she cannot, according to the will theorist at least, have rights. Or at least she cannot exercise these rights; a representative of the child could.

Let us grant then that a child does have rights even if these are exercised by a proxy or representative. The next question is, which rights does a child have? Does the child have all the rights that an adult has or only some of these? In chapter 4 this was expressed, following Feinberg, in terms of which rights are C–A rights possessed by both adults and children. I said that very many who write on children's rights think that the C–A rights include welfare but exclude liberty rights. The CRC, by contrast, does give every child both liberty and welfare rights. Indeed, the distinction between 'participation' and 'protection' rights described in chapter 4 corresponds, broadly, to that between liberty and welfare rights.

Liberty rights are rights that essentially involve the exercise of free choices – voting, religious worship, speech, thought and association. Welfare rights, by contrast, are rights that essentially involve the protection and promotion of fundamental elements of our well-being – health, education, housing and work. Liberty rights are sometimes unhelpfully called 'negative' and welfare rights 'positive'. The background thought is that the duty that correlates with the right to make a choice is *not* to interfere with the exercise of that choice, whereas the duty that correlates with a welfare right is to provide goods and services. Yet this is too simple. The right to vote, for instance, imposes a duty on the state to provide, service and staff polling booths in reasonable numbers and at appropriate locations.

The distinction between liberty and welfare rights is a distinction between the kinds of things to which we may have rights. Now the ground for saying that we ought to have a right to x is that x is something of sufficient, perhaps even overriding, importance or value to us. If children cannot in fact make choices then, obviously, making choices is not something that can have value for them. Thus they should not have liberty rights. For instance, a child cannot be said to have an interest in voting if he is simply incapable of making a choice between candidates or policies, that is of recognising what there is that distinguishes them and the point of doing so. But children do have welfare rights, if they have any rights, because such things as their health are very important to them. This is essentially the thought behind the view that the C–A rights include welfare rights but exclude liberty rights.

Clearly we can have interests even if we do not recognise them. A child has an interest in staying healthy and in being educated even if she does not think so. Moreover, if a child cannot make choices then she cannot make a decision in respect of the exercise of a right she may possess. Article 24 of the CRC gives every child a right to 'the enjoyment of the highest attainable standard of health and to facilities for the treatment of illness and rehabilitation of health'. The child has this right, if he does, even though he may be incapable either of recognising that his health matters to him or of exercising the right to secure appropriate health care. Thus parents and the state may act on the behalf of children to exercise their welfare rights. However, in the case of liberty rights it does not seem that they can be exercised by anybody other than those who possess them. In talking of rights of self-determination I mean to cover both the possession of liberty rights and the independent exercise of welfare rights.

The child liberationist will not be satisfied with the view that a child has rights of self-determination but that these are 'entrusted' to a caretaker who exercises them on the child's behalf. The argument over whether children should have *and* exercise these rights turns on whether children are thought capable of exercising them. Children should only be permitted to exercise rights to self-determination if they themselves are self-determining agents. The child liberationist asserts that they are; the liberal defender of the 'caretaker thesis' denies it. Moreover, the defender of the caretaker thesis adds this: adults are only able to exercise *their* rights because they were as children not entitled to make choices. In other words, we deny children self-determination rights both because they cannot make choices and in order that their future adult selves will be able to make them.

I want to assess this debate, but my general strategy will not be to reach any firm conclusions, not least because the debate is bedevilled by a large number of complications, confusions and imponderables. I would like rather to marshal a number of considerations that favour a compromise position. This is that not *all* children should be denied rights, but not all children should be given them. Instead there should be a presumption that younger children cannot whereas older children, that is teenagers, can exercise rights of self-determination.

Liberals presume that normal, sane adult human beings are capable of making sensible choices about how to lead their lives. The capacity in question is most frequently described as that of rational autonomy. On the standard liberal account children lack rational autonomy. For our purposes rational autonomy may be thought of as comprising at least three elements – rationality, maturity and independence. I will consider them in turn.

The rationality in question is instrumental in character and may be defined, minimally, as the forming of generally reliable beliefs about one's surroundings, having a relatively coherent set of desires and consequently being able, in the light of these desires and beliefs, to order one's preferences consistently between alternative possible courses of action. This requires a certain cognitive competence, namely the ability to form generally reliable beliefs about the world. Piaget suggested that all children acquire cognitive competences according to a universal sequence. Nevertheless, he has been criticised on two grounds which are relevant to this discussion.

First, his ideal of adult cognitive competence is a peculiarly Western philosophical one. The goal of cognitive development is an ability to think about the world with the concepts and principles of Western logic. In particular,

Piaget was concerned to understand how the adult human comes to acquire the Kantian categories of time, space and causality. If adult cognitive competence is conceived in this way then there is no reason to think it conforms to the everyday abilities of even Western adults. Second, children arguably possess some crucial competences long before Piaget says they do. Pre-school children can take account of the point of view of other children, solve problems involving relative sizes, work with categories, appreciate possible causal action, construe objects symbolically and recognise discrete objects as persisting over time.[3] It is all too easy to cast children as cognitively incompetent when the standard of competence by which they are measured is both culturally specific and unrealised by many adults, but, even so, children may be cognitively more competent than we assume.

Our tendency to ignore this may be compounded by conflating cognitive competence with things like knowledge, experience and intelligence. The latter term in particular complicates matters, since it purports to offer an all-embracing measure of cognitive functioning, yet has proved notoriously difficult to define. It *is* clear that both experience and knowledge must be acquired and thus, on the whole, increase with age. A child may simply not know as much or have experienced as much as an adult. That is not to say that, relative to what they have experienced and do know, each may not have the same ability to make rational decisions. From birth humans fundamentally desire to make sense of the world and bring it under their deliberate control. They are also equipped from birth with the ability to use inner mental models of the world. In *that* sense children are as rational as adults. In the stronger sense of 'rational', which stipulates the acquisition of knowledge and experience, it is reasonable to think of children as incapacitated compared to adults. But it is not fair to presume that older children are obviously incompetent compared with adults.

J. S. Mill speaks of persons 'in the maturity of their faculties'. Maturity here can mean a number of things. It can obviously imply 'rational' in the strong sense already indicated. But Mill probably intends 'maturity' to mean fully-developed, where this implies settled and unlikely significantly to change. Mill has a view of adults as emotionally balanced, with stable and relatively invariant desires and clear plans for their lives. By contrast, the child is thought of as temperamentally unstable, prone to sudden and dramatic changes of emotion, flitting from one desire to another. There is a measure of truth in this. There is also a danger of overstating the temperate nature of an adult temperament. H. L. A. Hart famously criticised Mill's ideal of the rational autonomous adult as rather too much the staid middle-aged individual of modest, moderate and settled needs. However, there are reasons to think young children more likely than adults to make decisions whilst in the grip of strong emotions, which can change from one moment to the next. Again this is much likelier to be true of younger than of older children. Teenagers are more mature than young children and closer than them in this respect to adults.

The third element of rational autonomy is independence. Immanuel Kant maintained in *The Philosophy of Law* that children reached majority 'by their actually attaining to the capability of self-maintenance'.[4] The strongest sense of independence or 'self-maintenance' is self-sufficiency, that is, an ability to sustain oneself physically by providing for one's own food, clothing and shelter. Robinson Crusoe apart, this is inapplicable to most societies, which are defined by the economic interdependence of their members. Even if we speak only of paying one's own way, that is, making a contribution to the social product at least equal to the cost of one's own continued existence, things are complicated. Societies differ in their levels of both economic organisation and technological sophistication such that the terms of productive participation are different. This will affect the extent to which young persons can work for their keep. Societies also differ in their legal or customary expectations. Many non-Western cultures countenance children working alongside adults, whereas our society tends to think of work as inappropriate for children.

A broader interpretation of 'self-maintenance' is that people are self-maintaining when they can actually act out their choices. I mean not that they are permitted to do so but that they have the personal resources. It is sensible to think that an autonomous person not only chooses but, if allowed, can put these choices into effect. A child may be incapable of acting upon and in the world as an adult can. Even if he can understand the import of some options and is mature enough to settle upon a decision, he may be unable to make his choice effective. This is obviously the case where a choice requires physical abilities that are straightforwardly beyond a child. Kant certainly seemed to think that 'self-maintenance' was something attained 'with the advance of years in the general course of Nature'.

Yet there are adults who are as physically incapacitated as children in this respect. Moreover, a person's 'resources' are dependent on economic circumstances, and the level and amount of technological assistance available to them. Clearly, however, infants and the very young are dependent upon adults to act for them. The child liberationists overstate their case when they represent all childhood incapacity as mere conventional, enforced dependency. Some of it is natural. Being very young does mean being small and weak, even if the contrast between dependent child and independent adult can be exaggerated.

A final distinct sense of 'independent' relevant to the attribution of autonomy is that of having a mind of one's own. Independent people in this respect have a clear and distinct idea of what they think and want. When they make choices these are their own and do not simply follow the example of others. There is no doubt that children can be independent in this sense. What parents call childish stubbornness might be thought admirable resolution in an adult. On the other hand, children can defer to the authority of adults. Whether they do so from a natural respect for their elders, or only because they are given no other choice is debatable. Whether children are more *vulnerable* to the influence of other people is similarly unclear.

It is pertinent that how we think of children will affect how we act towards them and that how we act will tend to confirm our thinking. Two arguments of the child liberationists are particularly relevant and forceful here. The first is that an ideological presumption of 'childishness' on the part of children is a characteristic feature of the modern conception of childhood. We think of children as incapable by their very nature, and are disinclined to countenance the idea that they might be more competent than we presume. Moreover, the presumption retains its plausibility only by generalising across all childhood and ignoring the real differences between children of various ages. Thinking of all children as incapable is credible when the contrast is between a helpless infant and an able-bodied adult. It is less so when it is a teenager who stands next to the adult. A 16-year-old is just not an 'innocent incompetent' in the way that a 16-month-old is.

The second good argument of the child liberationist is that the modern presumption of children's incompetence is self-confirming. Presumed unable to do something, children may simply not be allowed to show that in fact they can. More subtly, it may be the case that a competence can only be acquired in the exercise of the appropriate activity. A child may display incompetence just because she has been prevented from doing what would give her the ability. This is a very valuable general liberationist argument. Groups are often disqualified from possession of some right or good on grounds such as that they have no relevant skill for it, express no interest in it or are unsuited to it. The liberationist may legitimately respond that the skill, interest and suitability come only with possession. If the group were entitled to the good and encouraged to exercise its entitlement then they would come eventually to display the skill, interest or whatever.

I have tried to suggest rather than conclusively prove that it would be a mistake to deny, on the grounds of incompetence, the rights of self-determination to all children. Teenagers should not be presumed incapable of exercising these. It would be a mistake to accord such rights to all children on the grounds that no child is significantly less able to be rationally autonomous than any adult. This cannot sensibly be said of infants and the very young. The argument has presumed that rights of self-determination require that particular competence described as rational autonomy. It is proper to sound a final note of caution against an over-'intellectualist' construal of adult ability and its alleged link to the possession of rights. Under the influence of contemporary Western liberal philosophy we have come to think of adult agency as characterised by a certain kind of continent, self-aware, prudent and rational pursuit of one's ends. Great emphasis is laid upon deliberation, reflection and consciousness of one's aims. We should be allowed to make free choices of what to do in our lives because and in so far as we know what we are doing with our lives, why we are doing it and how to carry on doing so.

This model of individual free agency is subject to familiar criticisms. Human beings are social, biological and historical creatures determined in their forms of life by circumstances outside their control and their reflective grasp. The model also seems to stipulate implausibly tough criteria of competence for the exercise of particular rights of self-determination. Should I be free to vote only if I understand the full significance both of voting in general and my own vote in particular? Should I be free to exercise sexual choice only if I completely understand my own sexuality, that of others and the full implications of any particular sexual encounter? I turn to these questions in the next chapter.

7

CHILDREN'S RIGHTS TO VOTE AND SEXUAL CHOICE

What competence exactly is required in order to possess and exercise a right of self-determination? I shall approach this question by looking at two key rights. One, the right to vote, is central to the public, political status of an individual as a citizen; the other, the right to sexual choice, helps to define private individuals as fundamentally in control of their own bodies. Why should adults be allowed to vote and express their sexuality as they choose, whilst children cannot? I shall have a lot more to say about a child's rights in respect of sex than about her rights in respect of political activity. This is because there is a lot more to say on what is a highly complex and deeply contested issue.

THE RIGHT TO VOTE

In a democracy, suffrage is the mark of citizenship. A citizen is someone who participates in the government of their society and, where that government is democratic, does so by casting votes in elections. Of course that is not all that is involved in being a citizen. Indeed, it is arguable that citizenship is constituted by a cluster of rights and duties that can be acquired progressively rather than all at once. In this sense a young person could play some of the roles of a citizen before she has the vote. Moreover, many political scientists and theorists have pointed to the limited utility of the vote in many democratic contexts. Thus where a clear majority exists – in some constituency or on some issue – there is little if any incentive for those in the minority to cast their individual votes. Correlatively, the extra vote of any one person in an overwhelming majority carries little, if any, extra weight.

Nevertheless, the possession of a right to vote is central to citizenship, and it is a symbolic affirmation of one's political status even when it seems to have little instrumental value for an individual. Thus, the defenders of democracy have always insisted that it remains incomplete and unjust as long as those who should be enfranchised are denied the status of citizenship. In the past, women and those without property were excluded; there are still states which refuse the vote to certain categories of people. It is a moot point whether the continued disenfranchisement of children constitutes an injustice and a violation of a fundamental democratic principle. Child liberationists of course say that it is both.

The key question here is whether the grounds on which adult citizens are accorded the vote are such that children can rightfully be denied it. Defenders of the status quo appeal to a competence required of the voter and allegedly possessed by adults but not children. The competence in question is normally defined as a capacity to make rational decisions about alternative parties or policies in the light of available information about them. Some critics of the status quo attempt to outflank this argument from competence immediately by appealing directly to what is alleged to be a fundamental principle of democracy. This is that all those whose interests are affected by the laws of a country are entitled to participate in the election of that country's government. Since children are affected in some way by a country's laws, it would follow that children should be given the vote.

I do not think this is a useful move to make. First, the category of being affected by the laws is hopelessly broad in its scope. There are many groups of people who may be described as having their interests affected by the decisions of a particular government and whom it would not be appropriate to enfranchise: temporarily resident foreigners, citizens of other states affected by the foreign policy of this government and the unborn, that is, both foetuses and future generations of citizens. Animals too may be thought of as having interests liable to be affected by government policy. Children are not a uniquely disadvantaged group in lacking a vote to help determine policies affecting them.

Second, the principle that nobody's interests should be affected without their being represented does not so much circumvent the competence criterion as underline its necessity. Someone is thought entitled to the vote because their interests are affected by policies which result, directly or indirectly, from an exercise in voting. It is thereby assumed that in voting someone would and could act to protect and advance these interests. And that presupposes a capacity to recognise both what one's interests are and which policies, parties and persons would best promote them. So even if children are affected by the laws passed and decisions made by a government, they would deserve the vote only if they are also competent to exercise it.

There is still a problem of consistency. It is not obviously inconsistent to deny those affected by a state's laws a say in their formulation and approval.

But there are other possible kinds of relationship between an individual and the law. There is a distinction between being affected by laws and being subject to them. The second means being thought of as legally accountable for one's actions, liable to punishment for offences. The first simply means that one can be better or worse off as a result of their being in existence. Children below the age of legal responsibility are affected by laws but not subject to them; children above the age of responsibility are affected by laws and subject to them, albeit normally in a special and restricted sense. Actually, as we shall see in chapter 9, there is another way to interpret the notion of an age of legal or criminal responsibility, but the argument from consistency is not thereby undermined.

It seems less obviously wrong to deny the vote to those who are not subject to the law than to those who are. But it does seem inconsistent for a jurisdiction to hold a given age group responsible at law for their actions, but not mature enough to play any part in the process whereby that law is shaped and validated. In general it makes little sense for a society to deny the vote to those who are thought old enough to be allowed to do those sorts of things which are equivalent to voting. By equivalent I mean that they require the same sort of competence or make the same presupposition of civic status. For instance, it is absurd that a country should continue to disenfranchise those who can, as enlisted soldiers, die in its service. Those in the UK who defend the lowering of the voting age from 18 to 16 rightly list the many things a 16-year-old can do, such as work full time and have sex, even whilst still deemed incapable of casting a vote.

So what competence is required of the voter? It is a silly fallacy of some child suffragists to appeal to the 'childlike simplicity' of voting, pressing a button or putting a cross against a name, as proof of the minimal demands upon reason and intelligence made by the vote. This is simply to confuse the technical means by which a vote is cast with the processes by which an electoral preference is formed and expressed. Wishing to see Smith elected is one thing: casting that vote by marking a ballot sheet in a certain way is another. A monkey might be trained to put an X against the name of 'Smith' whenever it appeared on a ballot paper. It would be acting intelligently but it would not be voting, since it would not be expressing a preference for Smith over other candidates.

Nevertheless, there is a difference in the competence required for different kinds of voting. Voting for Smith over Jones and Brown is considerably easier than, for example, ranking a long list of alternative public spending programmes. It is fair to point out that, standardly, voting in a Western democracy requires, at most, the ordering of preferences from a fairly limited list of candidates whose party affiliations will normally be identified. This is not the 'child's play' of putting an X on a piece of paper, but it remains to be seen whether it is a game which only adults can play.

The competence required of a voter is a minimal rationality, an ability to distinguish between parties, candidates and policies in terms of interests, aims and goals which can be identified as worth promoting. In short, the ability is that of making a choice between alternatives on relevant grounds. It cannot be required (though it can be desired) of voters that they make wise choices. Here we need to distinguish between what qualifies someone to vote and what would make them an ideal democratic citizen. To be the latter it is surely necessary that an individual have an interest in the character of the laws and government of their country. Residence qualifications reflect the requirement that this interest be a relatively serious and permanent one. It is doubtful whether the further linking of citizenship to national identity is warranted, especially where so-called 'aliens' play a significant role in the life of their adopted country.[1] 'Having an interest in' should not be confused with 'being interested in'. The actual indifference of voters does not disqualify them, and there may be many good reasons why someone with the vote is disinclined to use it.

It is, however, worth pointing out that research shows many young people to be interested in politics and to be keen to express their views on those matters affecting them. Small-scale experiments in involving children in political decision-making – for instance, at a local level – have proved enormously successful. Both parties – young people and the relevant authorities – report the experience to have been rewarding and positive, empowering for the youngsters and enlightening for those in government. Many young people below the voting age also already engage in a range of political activities, such as taking part in demonstrations, writing and signing petitions, staging mock elections at school, participating in schools councils, and campaigning for a lower voting age. If young people do view politics and politicians with indifference or cynicism, this can just as easily be attributed to the failure of those in power to talk to or about children as it can be to any basic lack of interest on the part of the children themselves.[2]

An ideal voter, by contrast with a merely competent one, would successfully identify the relevant issues in certain ways. Citizens who seek the good of the whole community are to be preferred to ones who pursue their own personal ends. The better voters correctly identify the probable outcomes of various policies and successfully relate them to their goals. Here what is required is intelligence and knowledge rather than minimal rationality. Adopting *these* qualities as criteria of competence to vote would entail something like an educational qualification for the vote or, on J. S. Mill's infamous suggestion, an entitlement to additional votes.

There are other qualities we might desire of the good democratic voter which could be summarised, somewhat vaguely, as responsibility and maturity. Good voters should not be subject to the undue influence of others. They should be able to make their own minds up as to the best way to vote. They should not be fickle or capricious in voting. Their support for certain fundamental ideals should be relatively fixed and reflected in a stable and identifiable pattern of voting. They should vote always on strictly pertinent grounds, discounting irrelevant factors such as the appearance of a candidate.

It seems clear that adulthood, marked by some such age as 18, is implicitly seen both as the threshold of minimum voting rationality and as presaging the desired maturity, responsibility, knowledgeability and experience. Defenders of child enfranchisement can quickly point to evidence of adult irresponsibility and immaturity in voting. There is considerable evidence of such irresponsibility: candidates being approved for their personal appearance rather than their policies or their integrity, candidates whose names appear at the top of the ballot sheet being more likely to be chosen than those lower down, voters not exercising their right to vote when it rains on polling day, and so on. But all of this is beside the point if there is a probable and general association of the desired qualities with the age difference. It is more appropriate, first, to repeat the important distinction between the qualification for voting as such and the esteemed qualities of the good voter and, second, to repeat the liberationist argument that some abilities and qualities are acquired only in the exercise of the appropriate activity.

In the foregoing I have assumed that a basic ability to identify one's interests and to express a clear political preference in the light of them suffices for an entitlement to vote. I have distinguished such a competence from a set of ideal civic qualities which we can allow are not possessed by adults to the same degree. However, at least since Plato, there has been a view of the different forms of political rule, democracy included, that measures their ability to secure desirable ends, such as the common good or justice for all. Judged in this manner, democracy may be thought a poor way of politically arranging matters. Giving the vote to everyone when all are not equally qualified to contribute to a determination of what is for the best or what is just is a recipe for disaster. What in principle would be best, as Plato and Aristotle thought, would be giving power to those who are best equipped to rule. Even a modified democracy – plural votes for the more capable adults and a denial of the vote to the poorly qualified adults – would be preferable to democracy proper on this argument.

However, the argument is an 'in principle' one. There may well be practical reasons for regarding full democracy as better than any of the alternatives –

the difficulties, for instance, of determining who in fact are the best to rule, or the risks of an elite, corrupted by power, ruling in their own and not in the public interest. Hence democracy may, as Winston Churchill famously remarked, be 'the worst form of Government except all those other forms that have been tried from time to time'.[3] Nevertheless, the rehearsal of these important anti-democratic arguments serves to illustrate the thought that if children are debarred from the vote on the grounds of their incompetence it need not, and should not, be assumed that all adults should have the vote on the grounds of their evident competence to share in self-rule.

What of the alleged incompetence of children? Are children as competent, in respect of a minimum voting rationality, as adults? One can do no better than quote the view of Olive Stevens whose *Children Talking Politics* (1982) is an empirical study of schoolchildren's ability to understand political matters:

> By the age of nine, much of the political language of adult life has been acquired. By eleven, many children have as good a working vocabulary for politics as many adults could claim, and a framework of ideas which, even if developed no further, will enable them to grasp the facts of current affairs, understand something of relation-ships between principles and issues in politics and make their choices at general elections.[4]

This finding does not conclusively show that 11-year-olds have the basic competence of adult voters. But it does suggest that, to adopt a ready and convenient age, teenagers could be thought capable of voting. As a matter of fact the voting age is 16 in a number of countries, including Brazil, Croatia and Cuba, and is 15 in Iran.

Second, the presumption that teenagers can and should be allowed to vote would lead to a change in current practices beyond the polling stations. Basic education in the theory and practice of democratic government would become a priority which would start even, as it does now in the UK, at the primary level. Fears that such an education could be political indoc-trination derive much of their force from the familiar presumption that children are 'innocents' in danger of corruption. Stevens's study clearly shows how capable young children, that is those between the ages of 7 and 11, are of acquiring information critically and making intelligent, independent use of it. To repeat the liberationist point, children will only become adept democrats, capable of exercising thoughtful choice in political matters, if they are presumed capable from the earliest feasible moment of acting as independent citizens.

At the very least, a civic education should prepare children for the eventual exercise of any democratic rights they are subsequently given. Article 29 of the CRC requires that the child develop a respect for human rights and fundamental freedoms, as well as being prepared for a responsible life in a free society. Article 42 dictates that adults and children alike be made familiar with the rights detailed in the Convention. A civic education should then comprise the following elements: citizens should command a basic understanding of key political concepts such as democracy, authority and the rule of law. Citizens should know about the particular features of their own society together with contemporary issues and events. Young people should be helped to identify and endorse core values, such as equality and mutual tolerance of difference. Finally, they should acquire certain dispositions, attitudes and skills, such as that of being able to think critically, independently develop their own ideas, defend their views, and respond intelligently to those of others.[5]

Children should not only be educated for their eventual citizenship, but actively be educated in citizenship at every available opportunity. This is especially so if we recognise, as noted earlier, that citizenship extends beyond the right to vote. Just because children do not have the vote does not mean that they are excluded from a range of participatory activities. In the first place, democratic practice can also apply in those institutions with which children are most intimately involved. Children can be encouraged to play their part in the running of schools, helping to determine such things as the organisation of the curriculum and discipline. There is no reason why the family should not also seek to be a democratic institution with each member having a say in how its life is arranged. Democratic participation should extend to all significant areas of one's life, and begin as soon as feasible.

Another initiative worth extending is that of Children's Parliaments. These have taken place in many countries supported both by national governments and by international organisations such as UNICEF. They give real expression to the CRC requirement that a child's voice is heard and also to the right to free association. Such parliaments can be, and have been, convened on an ad hoc or a regular basis, be devoted to a single issue or to many, and be regional, national or international. Such parliaments are not law-making bodies but rather fora for the expression of children's views. Nevertheless, their value is considerable. They do give a voice to children – to their views, concerns, and interests – which demands to be heard. They function both to instantiate and to proselytise for the CRC rights. Even if they do not allow children to participate directly in the determination of law and policy, they can help to make adult legislators aware of what children think and want. Equally, they serve to make politicians aware of the CRC. They help thus to strengthen the bonds of political understanding and possible cooperation between children and adults. Lastly, they provide an active education in citizenship, enhancing the abilities of children to participate. Indeed, they may help to create a group of children who can act as advocates for the needs and rights of children, not only now as children but also in the future as adult citizens.

THE RIGHT TO SEXUAL CHOICE

In the case of sex the relevant right of self-determination is that of being able to express oneself sexually. It is the right to choose whether or not to have sex, when to have sex, with whom and in what manner. The sexual abstainer as much as the profligate exercises a fundamental liberty right, one that is at the heart of our integrity, happiness and self-fulfilment as human beings, and whose denial is the source of a special, damaging kind of misery. It is thus critical to know if and when children can exercise this right. It certainly does not follow from the fact that children are sexual beings beyond a certain age that they should then have a right of sexual self-determination. Moreover, the detection and prevention of the sexual abuse of children must be a real and pressing concern. In whatever manner child abuse is defined – and chapter 14 addresses this matter – it should be recognised that its sexual form is especially vile and destructive. Nevertheless, our justified abhorrence of sexual abuse should not blind us either to the possibility that children can engage in sexually non-abusive activities, or to the realities of any child's actual sexuality. Indeed, talk of the child's essential innocence is in danger both of being mythic and, ironically, of being sexualised. The child, like a virginal woman, can be the object of a male sexual desire to corrupt what is as yet uncorrupted.[6]

The key to the possession of a right of sexual self-determination is the ability to give and to withhold consent to sex. One thing that certainly disqualifies a person from giving or withholding consent is ignorance. Hence if a child is to be competent to exercise a right of sexual self-determination then she must know about sex. Such knowledge does not come naturally but must be taught. Before speaking directly about a child's right to sexual choice, I need to consider a child's right to be sexually educated. Articles 28 and 29 of the CRC give the child a right to be educated and to be prepared for life in her society, but there is no mention of sex education in the CRC. Moreover, given that people disagree strongly in their views about sexual morality, it is not surprising that they also disagree about how and what should be taught to children about sex.

Some of this disagreement can be attributed to the existence of deeply held religious views. Yet providing children with a sex education does play an important role in promoting their sexual health – it reduces unwanted pregnancies and the incidence of sexually transmitted diseases. Lessons in simple abstention ('just say no!') do not appear to work, and expose those children who are sexually active to serious but avoidable risks. Moreover, there is no evidence to show that teaching children about sex somehow encourages them to engage in it. A frequently expressed worry about an early and explicit sex education is that it will result in premature or precocious sexual activity. Yet consider Sweden, where sex education is compulsory for all children from the age of 8 and which generally has more tolerant attitudes to sexual behaviour. Compared to their peers, Swedish children are significantly better informed about sexual matters at an early age. They also possess a larger and more explicit sexual vocabulary. Interestingly, they are less prone to see procreation as the main purpose of marriage or sexual intercourse, and more inclined to emphasise emotional reasons. They are also less inhibited about nakedness.

Moreover, it is a mistake for adults to maintain that sex education should only be given when children are judged by them to be ready for sex.[7] First, the ability to assimilate and understand sexual information appears related to general *cognitive* development and not, as is popularly assumed, to some degree of *sexual* preparedness. Here again the myth of childlike innocence obscures the truth by stipulating that purity requires ignorance. This is contradicted by children's actual capacity to comprehend themselves and their world. The difficulty children have with sexual information has to do not with its sexual explicitness, but its intellectual complexity. Children below a certain age may have difficulty, for instance, in understanding the role of genetic facts in the determination of the sexual identity of a foetus. Yet children given an early sex education seem capable of clearly comprehending the essential facts of procreation.

Second, children actually express a wish to be sexually informed at an earlier age than it is currently customary for them to be so informed. They are actively seeking answers to sexual questions from an early age and are not, as the theory of the latency period holds, uninterested in these questions during middle childhood. In the absence of proffered explanations children are quick to construct their own, often of the familiar mythological variety. Children, finally, see adults as withholding sexual knowledge. They are not only misled by the euphemisms and doubtful analogies on offer, but will come to think that information about sex is concealed for a reason. Thence comes children's feeling that sex is something about which one is expected, as adults clearly are, to feel guilty.

A clear and explicit sex education can also play a role in the prevention of child sexual abuse. The traditional injunction given to children to avoid strangers has proved of limited value, not least in virtue of the sad fact that children are most at risk from those with whom they are acquainted. A UK initiative some years ago, the Child Assault Prevention Programme, focused on teaching children that they have rights (to safety, privacy and their own bodies) and that they should exercise them to reject unacceptable adult behaviour.[8] A key premise of this approach was that children can and should be encouraged to say 'no' to what they do not like. To this end they are said to need only to know what they do not like, 'bad touches' for instance. But too much information is held to 'frighten' children.

However, the ability to say 'no' must presuppose an ability to say 'yes', and it is accepted by those who defend this approach that children can experience sexual pleasure when subject to sexual assault. This is, of course, not to condone the adult sexual exploitation of children, nor to deny that sexual abuse of children is a great evil. It is merely to point to the difficulty of an attitude which solicits the child's refusal of what it does not like, but seems reluctant to recognise the possibility of their accepting what they do like.

Of course sex must be taught within the context both of relationships and of basic core values. It does not suffice to teach the mere biological mechanics of sex and reproduction. This is because it is at least as important to understand that sex can be an expression of love, to learn to treat others with respect and to be tolerant of difference as it is to know what goes where and with what results. However, in the face of moral disagreement neither an appeal to agreed basic values nor to the provision of morally neutral information will be regarded as good enough. Basic principles can be differently interpreted. Can those who regard homosexuality as a repugnant perversion treat the homosexual with respect? Moral neutrality, on the other hand, will not satisfy those parents who do hold clear and strong views about sex.

A liberal state has no choice but to insist upon a common curriculum that does include an element of sex education. Such an education must insist upon respect for the choices of individuals and thus upon the central value of consensuality. Consistent with consent are a number of sexual activities that ought to be tolerated. Such a curriculum can be taught in a manner that is sensitive to the views of parents. Yet no parent has a right to demand how his child shall be educated and he is free anyway within the family home to teach those values he himself believes in. Moreover, any liberal education should teach every child the ability and willingness to examine, challenge and review the values it acquires from both home and school.

Should children be allowed to engage in sex when they can and when they know what they are doing? Puberty naturally marks the point at which humans are physically capable of sexual reproduction. Importantly, girls and boys are now maturing earlier than previously: the average age of a girl's first period, for instance, went from 16–17 in 1860 to 12–13 a hundred years later. But it would be wrong to make physical maturity the principal consideration in fixing the age of consent. An ability to hold, aim and fire a gun should not fix the age at which a gun licence may be issued. Moreover, it would be inappropriate to take the attainment of a reproductive capacity as critical. Sexual activity is not necessarily or essentially linked to reproduction, and there is good reason to regret its being represented as such, especially in the sexual education of children.

More importantly, pre-pubescent children are sexual creatures. This, at least since Freud, is a familiar, oft-repeated but important truth. It needs to be qualified with two cautions. First, the sexuality of young children should not be understood in the terms associated with adult behaviour. If young children are capable of experiencing something that may be called sexual pleasure, it does not nevertheless have the significance or meaning it would have for an adult. This applies equally to their commission of 'sexual' acts. Second, there is the ambiguous influence of Freud's notion of the 'latency period', extending from the age of five to puberty. Freud viewed this as a time of decreased sexual activity and the diversion of sexual energy into affection. This view, coming ironically from someone associated with the discovery of childhood sexuality, may have helped to confirm the current view that children are, for a significant period, non-sexual beings.

What is crucial is less the facts of biological development, important as they are, than how children understand their bodies, feelings and the behaviour of others. What matters is not just that one can have sex or even that, in addition, one knows what one is doing, but that one also has some appreciation of what it means to have sex. Hence – in addition to knowledge of what sex involves and the physical ability to have sex – a further precondition of the person's ability to consent, or not, to sex is her being in what John Stuart Mill called the 'maturity of their faculties'.[9] This comprises a certain level of cognitive development, a command of the facts, and, crucially, having a character that can properly appreciate the facts and make appropriate, considered choices in their light. English law has made use of this idea of a 'maturity of faculties' in the form of 'Gillick competence' which is further discussed in chapter 9.

Does thinking of the competence needed for a right of sexual self-determination in terms of a physical ability to have sex, knowledge of what sex is, and a maturity of character, give us enough to fix the age of sexual majority? There are further considerations. One is consistency. The reasons underlying the fixing of this age should cohere with the explanation of other ages of majority. Thus, for example, someone who is old enough to have sex is old enough to marry but someone who is old enough to have sex may not be old enough to consume alcohol or to serve in the armed forces.

A further question concerns what kinds of sex one may have a right to choose at particular ages. We can acknowledge that there are forms of sexual activity that fall short of full penetrative sex, and allow that young persons can engage in these whilst denying them the freedom to engage in full sex. The law has also distinguished between heterosexual and homosexual sexual activity.

For instance, the British Policy Advisory Committee on Sexual Offences, reporting in 1981, recommended that the age of consent in relation to sexual offences should remain at 16, but that the minimum age for homosexual relations should only be reduced from 21 to 18. The major reason given for preserving this anomaly was that originally given by the 1957 Wolfenden Committee, namely that 'a boy is incapable, at the age of 16, of forming a mature judgement about actions of a kind which might have the effect of setting him apart from the rest of society'.[10]

The reasoning here is curious. It may well make sense for the law to measure the competence required for a decision in terms of the nature of the act contemplated. Crudely, the bigger the decision the older one must be to be allowed to make it by oneself. Clearly a decision is bigger the more adverse its likely consequences, and being set apart from the rest of society can be seen as a large consequence of homosexuality. But the Committee appeared to ignore the possibility that a 16-year-old girl could set herself apart by becoming a single parent, and concerned itself solely with the 'apartness' of homosexuality.

Yet the law itself can play a role in the social meaning given to homosexuality, not least by continuing to make a distinction between it and heterosexuality in respects like the age of consent. The law characterises homosexuality as different and then cites that difference as a reason for continuing to treat it differently. More judiciously, the Committee made an attempt to relate any suggested age of consent to actual established patterns of behaviour, rather than to some ideal of maturity. Thus they took seriously the possibility, contradicted by nearly all the available evidence, that a child's sexual orientation might not be settled by the age of 16, and that, as a result, permitting consensual homosexual acts at that age would risk artificially 'converting' a heterosexual child to homosexuality. The facts are clear. Persons of 14 generally testify to a clear sense of their sexual orientation. For a variety of reasons, none sinister, the incidence of earlier sexual activity is increasing with a progressively lower mean age for first reported sexual intercourse. Thus the facts do not support a differential age of consent for heterosexual and homosexual sex.

Does it make a difference who the sex is with? The principal worry here is the sexual use of a young person by an older adult. In fact the vast majority of young people have sex with other youngsters their own age: the average gap at first sexual experience is one year. Thus most will find the idea of a 40-year-old having sex with a 14-year-old morally much more troubling than the idea of two 14-year-olds having sex. This is so even if the sex in both cases is consensual. The worry is that the age difference – and the corresponding disparity in experience, power, influence, money and social status – allows the adult to exploit and take advantage of the younger person.

Intellectual defences of paedophilia as permissible 'intergenerational' sex have been given on the grounds that children are sexual beings who can participate willingly in sex with adults.[11] However, at best such attempted justifications are self-serving rationalisations. Moreover, they appeal to the highly dubious idea of an adult sexual 'mentor' who can help to initiate the younger person into sex. A child is old enough to have sex with an adult but still young enough to need an adult's guidance on sexual matters. Of course sex can be pleasurable but it cannot, and should not, be insulated from the social relations which configure its character. Adult–child sex is never innocent.

A further worry arises when the adult stands to the child in a relationship of authority such as that of his teacher, doctor or guardian. An adult who has sex with the child is exploiting that relationship to a point where it is probably inappropriate to still talk of consensual sex, even if the child is willing and knows what she is doing. The law could recognise this by making provision to outlaw a misuse of a position of authority or superiority. The law might fix an age of sexual consent, let us say 14, but forbid sexual relations between someone over that age yet below a higher age, let us say 16, if there was a significant age disparity or a relation of authority between the parties. Thus it would be permissible for two 15-year-olds to have sex but impermissible for a 25-year-old or his teacher to have sex with a 15-year-old. Given these kinds of provisions we might feel confident in lowering the age of sexual consent to 14, an age fixed on in many European jurisdictions. Some have it even lower at 12. But in Holland, for example, where this is the case, sex between children aged 12 to 16 would be prosecuted if either party, a parent, or a child welfare organisation complained.

Yet in saying all of this the following should be borne in mind. It need not be denied that many children do and will continue to have sex below the age of sexual majority. The law does not deny that the sex in question may be consensual, that is, unforced and knowing. The law merely states that for its purposes such 'consent' does not count. In somewhat similar fashion the law does not regard the willing agreement to sex of those whom it deems incapable – the mentally disabled, those temporarily but severely intoxicated – as consent. The law has a duty to protect the young but is not naive in its expectations of them. Moreover, forbidding the young to have sex should not mean denying them a sex education and sexual health services, providing, for instance, information about contraception and access to appropriate resources. Such provision is not a case of condoning what the law forbids. It is protecting children from the consequences of what society would rather they not do but is realistic enough to acknowledge they might still do.

Finally, the law is a blunt and crude instrument for the regulation of human behaviour. Punishing those who break the law by having underage sex may not be the best means of dealing with them. Indeed it is likely, and desirable, that police forces should handle such cases by issuing no more than a formal warning and referring the young persons to child welfare agencies. Preventing the sexual abuse of minors is a legitimate aim of the law and social policy. But those below the age of sexual consent, yet capable of having knowing and voluntary sex, are badly represented if viewed simply as 'innocent incompetents'.

8

THE WRONGS OF
CHILDREN'S RIGHTS

The arguments considered so far have been concerned with what rights children should have. Child liberationists insist that the emancipation of children requires granting them rights of self-determination. Defenders of the 'caretaker thesis' urge that a child's interests are served by a denial of these rights of self-determination and their exercise on the child's behalf by a caretaker. None of these arguments challenges the presumption that the language of rights is the only or the best one in which to analyse and evaluate the situation of children.

This presumption derives from the general dominance of rights talk in current moral and political discussion. Major contemporary problems, such as abortion, justice, our treatment of animals and judicial punishment, are discussed in terms of rights. Indeed, they are often discussed *only* in terms of rights, with the implication that no other approach is possible. However, the hegemony of rights discourse has been subjected to criticism from a variety of angles and sources. A familiar criticism of rights is that they are individualistic in character and political import. This will not concern me here.

Three further strands of criticism are, however, especially relevant to the case of children. The first is that rights talk has a certain all-or-nothing character which may exacerbate the modern tendency to keep the worlds of adulthood and childhood separate. The second is that rights talk is morally impoverished and neglects an alternative ethical view of the world, in which the affectionate, caring interdependence which ideally characterises the parent–child relationship assumes an exemplary significance. The third is that ascribing rights to children rests on a misunderstanding both of rights and of the nature of childhood.

RIGHTS ARE ALL-OR-NOTHING

The claim that rights are all-or-nothing is in fact a convenient way of expressing a number of distinct worries about the implications of using a language of rights. These number at least half a dozen.

1. 'If someone lacks a right, then someone else has this right instead.' So, for instance, if a child does not have the right to decide whether to go to school then some adult, normally his parent, has it.

2. 'Where rights clash, the attribution of a right to one person means the complete denial of a right to someone else.' If my right conflicts with another's right then one of us can exercise our right and the other cannot. No other solution is possible. So only at the point where a parent's right over her child ceases does the child have any right at all.

3. 'A person either possesses all the rights normally possessed by an adult or none at all.' So if children are right-holders, they have all the rights an adult has; if not, they have no rights whatsoever.

4. 'A right is possessed either totally or not at all.' Someone cannot have some fraction of a right, since this is not how rights work. So if children lack a right, they lack all of what possession of that right would entail.

5. 'Either a moral concern is expressed in terms of rights or it is not recognised as a moral concern.' Moral claims to be treated in certain ways or to be allowed to do certain things are without any weight if they do not amount to the possession of a right. So a child who lacks rights has no moral claim.

6. 'People either have rights of self-determination or they do not.' Even if they possess welfare rights, this means only that they are entitled to certain forms of treatment, not that they are entitled to make important choices about how to lead their lives. So children, lacking rights of self-determination, have no freedom to choose, and their own choices count for nothing.

Taken together, these worries would suggest that the child without the rights an adult has suffers a radically diminished moral status. Correlatively, if children are to have any kind of moral status at all they should be accorded adult rights. When rights have an 'all-or-nothing' character and one thinks about adults and children in terms of rights, the resultant view of childhood is similarly infected with a certain 'either/or-ism'. Children are either essentially no different from adults, or essentially distinct from them.

I think all six claims are false. (1) is clearly mistaken. Unpossessed rights are not like items of unclaimed lost property which can be redistributed to new owners. If a child lacks the right to vote, there is not a vote left over to be cast by someone else; there is simply one less individual vote. A child may lack any rights of her own if, as the doctrine of *patria potestas* holds, she is owned by her parent. But on this view the parent does not have double the number of rights a non-parent has, his own plus the child's. Rather, he simply has rights of ownership over something, the child, which the non-parent lacks. But, then again, the latter may have rights of ownership of other objects which the parent does not.

However, it might appear that, following the 'caretaker thesis', some children's rights do transfer to adults. Parents are apparently entitled to decide whether a child should undergo medical treatment, whereas they, as adults, can choose their own treatment for themselves. But even this is not a simple case of a hand-over of rights from child to adult. The adult chooses for the child but is not unconstrained in her choices. She must choose with some regard for the child's interests. The preferred version of this constraint varies. On one account, the adult must choose for the child as the child would choose if capable of doing so and seeking to further his own best interests. On a less stringent account, the adult must choose for the child but so as not seriously to harm the child's interests. On either account, the adult is not entitled to choose just as she sees fit, as would be the case if the right in question were truly her own.

The law tends to protect the child when it deems that an adult's choices fail to satisfy a child's essential needs, or threaten to harm the child seriously. Medical treatment is a case in point. A parent may refuse a certain treatment on religious grounds, but is not normally entitled to jeopardise a child's life by refusing that treatment on her behalf. In short, children lacking rights do not thereby pass them over to an adult. At most, an adult exercises the right as the child would wish it to be exercised if she were an adult and protecting her own interests.

(2) expresses the claim that rights talk dictates a zero-sum solution to moral problems, and is a misleading oversimplification. It is of course absurd to speak of *the* parental right versus *the* right of the child; it is going to be a question of a cluster of rights. Some of a parent's claimed rights may come into conflict with some of a child's rights. However, it is not going to be the case that either the parents have rights or the child does, but not both. Naturally, some rights may cancel one another out in the way (2) suggests. Thus, the right of parents to bring up his child as he sees fit would straight-forwardly clash with the child's right, if she had it, to lead her life as she sees fit.

Nevertheless, the more interesting conflicts help to determine the scope rather than the actual existence of respective rights. The parent's right to rear her child as she chooses is not abrogated but limited by the child's right to certain forms of treatment, not to be beaten for example. Equally, the child's rights to self-determination might be limited, if he remained in the family home, by parental rights to the use of their own property. Few writers treat rights as 'unconditional' in the way (2) suggests, and the more interesting questions concern how the rights possessed by different parties constrain each other. This is especially true in the case of the relationship between parents and children.

(3) is also false. Both the child liberationist and the defender of the 'caretaker thesis' agree that the child should have welfare rights, that is, entitlements from birth to be treated in certain ways and to receive certain benefits. The former but not the latter think that these are not the only rights that a child should have. Becoming an adult does not guarantee possession of all the rights any other adult might possess. There are some rights that arise from the special roles individuals can fulfil and relationships they stand in to others. It is not possible for everyone to have *these* rights.

If we are speaking of the rights normally possessed by adults, there is nothing wrong in thinking that these are not acquired all at once, in a single dose. Indeed, it is common for 'adult' legal rights to be progressively acquired at various stages. Under British law an individual comes fully of age at 18, in that they can then, *inter alia*, vote, marry, make a will, apply for a passport and buy a house. However, they can buy a pet at 12, be gainfully employed under certain conditions at 13, consent to sexual intercourse and choose their own doctor at 16, and drive a car at 17.[1] This does not show that the law is inconsistent, though it may be. It may reflect a plausible belief that different rights require different competences, and that the acquisition of the latter is not an all-or-nothing affair.

(4) is true only in a relatively uninteresting sense. It is true that a right, fully specified in terms of its content and enabling conditions, is either possessed or not. But the same is not true of a right expressed in general terms. Take the right to vote. Strictly speaking, no one could possess half a right to vote. They might be described as having a right to half a vote – if, for instance, they were entitled only to vote in alternate elections, or if, on account of the size of their constituency, their vote effectively had half the electoral weight of other votes. This is a different matter. However, individuals do have different rights to vote in various contexts of greater or lesser importance. Only members of a party may be entitled to elect its leadership; only members of a legislature elect the executive. And there would be nothing absurd about according the right to vote in parliamentary elections to those over 18, but giving 16-year-olds the right to vote in an election for a school council.

115

Again, a right unconditionally held by an adult may be possessed by a child subject to certain conditions, and these conditions might be made the more stringent the lower the age. Sixteen-year-olds may marry subject to the consent of their parents or a magistrate. They lack the right to marry without consent, which is possessed by an 18-year-old, but they have more of a right to marry than a 15-year-old. Similarly, a 14-year-old may be gainfully employed, but only for certain hours and if the work is not of a kind likely to occasion injury. In this sense rights to generally described objects, such as marriage and work, are better described as all-or-less-than-everything than all-or-nothing.

(5) is a piece of exaggerated rhetoric which may describe the uses to which the language of rights is sometimes put, but does not identify a necessary feature of that language. Admittedly, some write as if rights were the only way in which moral concerns or claims can be expressed, exclusive of any other kind of claim. There has, perhaps, been a move from an insistence that rights must figure in the moral scheme of things to a claim that rights exhaustively define the moral, from a moral theory which includes rights to a rights-based moral theory.

The worry about too exclusive a reliance on rights in moral evaluations is that one may mistakenly think one has said everything of moral relevance when one has specified the relevant rights. If someone has a right to x then their doing x is permissible. But perhaps there are better or worse ways of doing x which are not indicated in terms of the right, nor prescribed by the existence of any other person's rights. Let us say a parent has a right to discipline its child and the child has a right not to be brutally or harshly punished. There is a range of disciplinary practices permitted by both the parental right and the child's right of which some are surely preferable to others. Again, a person's right to have y may be satisfied in different ways. All are consonant with the satisfaction of the right but some are better than others. Let us say a child has a right to education and healthcare. It is nevertheless desirable that they should receive better rather than worse education and healthcare.

If children do have rights then we can still do more for children than we are required to. This is morally commendable but not something to which the child is entitled. Rights essentially prescribe minimum standards. If, on the other hand, children do not have rights then it does not follow that we are not morally required to treat them well. We can be under obligations that do not correlate with rights possessed by others.

The last worry, (6), maintains that the denial to children of the particular rights of self-determination operates in an unacceptably all-or-nothing way. (6) again illustrates the danger of oversimplified dichotomies. The distinction between welfare and freedom rights is important but can be overstated. This is particularly so in the case of children. Farson assimilates the distinction to one between protecting *children* and protecting children's *rights*. Rogers and Wrightsman have similarly distinguished between 'nurturance' and 'self-determination' approaches to children's rights.[2] A clear implication is that children are either regarded as independent, active and strong persons equal in all significant respects to adults, or treated as dependent, passive, vulnerable individuals who do not merit the same moral status as their older and superior caretakers.

One reason for thinking this way is that if one has rights of self-determination then one's choices as to what one does should determine what actually happens. If, on the other hand, one lacks these rights then any such choices are beside the point. Either humans have the relevant competence, and can rightly make their own choices of life, or they do not and should not be allowed to have their choices count.

But this is mistaken. For the choices expressed by those who lack rights of self-determination need not be without weight. One famous reason given, as we saw, by J. S. Mill for according adults the right of self-determination is that their own expressed choices may be viewed as, in the main, reliable guides to what is in fact in their own best interests. They should be presumed the best judges of what is good for them. In the case of those who lack the competence required to possess rights of self-determination, their expressed wishes cannot be taken as completely trustworthy indications of their own welfare. But this does not mean they can be entirely discounted. They do give *some* evidence of what might be best.

Moreover, the weight accorded to expressed choices can be varied in accordance with an estimation of the individual's competence rationally to choose for their own good. This is an important point. Those deemed competent to choose for themselves are given a right of self-determination. It does not follow that those seen as unable to exercise such a right are regarded as entirely unable to judge their best interests. Possession of the right may be all-or-nothing, but estimation of the appropriate competence, and the amount of weight to give to their expressed choices, need not be. A child's desire to do *x* constitutes some kind of claim upon those in a position to allow it to do *x*, even if it does not amount to a right of self-determination on the child's part. Indeed, we saw in chapter 4 that a key principle of the CRC and of the English Children's Act is that a child's views on matters affecting her interests should be listened to and given a weight proportionate to her age and maturity. Thus, even if a child lacks a right of self-determination, she still has a right to *some* say in what shall happen to her.

In sum, rights are not all-or-nothing in any of the senses claimed. That some children do not have some adult rights does not mean that they have nothing. There are moral claims to be made on their behalf which are less than rights, but which still are not negligible. The acquisition of rights is a sort of moral watershed. But it does not follow that those on one side have everything morally flowing their way and those on the other have nothing.

THE IMPOVERISHED WORLD OF RIGHTS

Defenders of the inclusion of rights within moral theory maintain that a rights language enriches our moral vocabulary. They claim that allowing human beings to express their moral aspirations in terms of rights makes for a morally better world. They suggest a contrast between two worlds. In one, its inhabitants receive and even come to expect certain forms of reciprocal beneficent treatment as a result of the way they are naturally disposed to act. In the second, that same treatment is due to the possession by all of rights which are recognised and may be enforced. The defenders of rights argue that the latter world is to be preferred. This is because to be in possession of a right is to be in a position where one can think of oneself, in oneself and in relation to others, in a positive light. It is to stand with dignity, to make claims, to assert what is one's due, to be independent. By contrast, to be without rights is to be dependent on others, to have to plead, request or beg from others that one be treated in certain ways.[3]

In complete contrast, critics of the use of a rights language represent this world of rights in negative terms. This is done by suggesting a contrast different to and cutting across the one above. In fact, there are several contrasts deriving from different sources but which overlap to a significant degree. The language of rights is represented as part of a more general moral and political discourse which sees society principally as a contractual association of independent, autonomous, self-interested individuals governed by certain rules or principles. The contrary understanding of society emphasises community, interdependence, mutuality and affective bonds.

One famous expression of this contrast is Ferdinand Tönnies's distinction between 'association' (*Gesellschaft*) and 'community' (*Gemeinschaft*).[4] More recently, various critics of modern philosophical liberalism have been united under the description 'communitarian'. The term suggests their shared preference for an ideal of political community over contemporary liberal accounts of the good society.[5] Again, some feminists have defended what is alleged to be a distinctively female moral 'voice' in ethics.[6] Others have suggested that there is a special 'maternal thinking'.[7] Masculine morality is abstract, general, distant, formal and rational, emphasising the separateness and independence of persons who merit our respect. Feminine morality is

118

concrete, particularistic, intimate, contextual and emotional, speaking of people bound together in relationships and for whom we should care. Masculine morality sees individuals as having rights; feminine morality talks of our responsibilities.

Finally, there are critics of the language of rights who do not necessarily belong to any of the above camps, but who pejoratively characterise the world of rights. A world in which rights are the principal means by which its inhabitants assure themselves of reciprocal benign conduct is a cold, hollow one, drained of the sentiments of mutual care and love; a world in which humans are not bound to one another by affective ties; a world in which individuals assert themselves *against* one another, and in which they act beneficently from the recognition of a duty to be discharged and not as an expression of their love or care for others. Rights-holders are self-centred, pushy, assertive individuals, indifferent to others; those who discharge their duties do so bloodlessly, at most respecting those who possess rights but not feeling bound to them by any ties of sentiment or intimacy.

The general contrast then is between a society characterised by union, intimacy, affection, interdependence and sharing, and one marked by isolation, separateness, independence, distance and self-interest. The family is frequently cited as a paradigm of a community displaying the desired characteristics of affective union. Now there are in fact two distinguishable claims which could be made. The first is that society should be one big happy family; the second is that the family should not become a small-scale liberal association of independent rights-holders. Only the second is strictly relevant to the charge that talk of children as having rights is inappropriate and would lead to a morally impoverished world.

However, the idea that society could be organised on familial lines should be criticised for at least one obvious shortcoming. It is the small size of the family and the very special relationships defining its membership which permit the characteristically intense and particularistic sentimental bonds of familial attachment. We can feel as we do for our family precisely because of who they are, because they are not strangers to us and do not number the whole of society. This is not to say that society cannot be criticised for the anomic isolation of its members; nor that it should not strive to give these members a warmer sense of 'belongingness'.[8] But a large-scale modern society cannot simply be a family writ large.

The family is often defended as a haven of affectionate, close and intimate relationships to which the individual can retreat from the cold, impersonal anonymity of public life. Would it not then be dreadful if parent–child relations were constituted through the mutual recognition of appropriate rights and duties? Is it not obvious that the relationship would as a result be an attenuated, impoverished one, deprived of everything which makes it especially human?

The critic of rights for children argues then that family relationships can either be based on mutual affection or on the existence of rights and duties, but not both. The two forms are mutually exclusive alternatives and, for the critic, the preferability of affective union is a reason for children not to have rights. Some critics are content to say that a relationship based upon rights and duties follows the breakdown of love and affection. Others argue, more strongly, that the use of rights *brings about* such a breakdown. I will show that the first claim does not damage a thesis about the value of rights, and that the second claim is not obviously true. I will also give some reasons for doubting the alleged preferability of affective union over a rights-based relationship.

What is done from love and what is done in recognition of a duty need not coincide. I may very well be unable to discharge the duty 'to love *x*' (and this may be a reason to be suspicious of any supposed 'right to be loved'), even if I may be able to do as a duty most of what would be done to *x* out of love. Love, it may be thought, normally delivers something more and other than would be secured by an enforced right on the part of the loved one. However, some might say that love and duty do not coincide in a much more radical way. Duties and rights specify what is morally appropriate behaviour. Love is not something which has its own rights and duties. It is simply beside the point to stipulate what is and is not expected of the lover. Lovers who behave towards one another in certain hurtful ways need not be doing anything wrong *as lovers*. Love just does not have a code of conduct.

Love and duty certainly do not seem to coincide in terms of motivation. I can give to *x* what *x* is owed as of right because I love *x* or because I recognise and fulfil my duty to *x*. But I cannot act from both motives simultaneously. It has to be one or the other. I can do my duty but not from duty – when, for instance, I love my country and fight in its defence. I can also do my duty from a sense of duty – when, for instance, I fight on my country's behalf in recognition of what I owe to its defence. I may thus do from duty what I must do but what I am not otherwise naturally moved to do. Moreover, rights are exercised when the behaviour which is required by the correlative duty is not forthcoming. In that sense, the exercise of rights may be regarded as an indication that certain kinds of relationship, those of natural love and care, have broken down. Rights compel the performance of actions which do not come naturally to those under the correlative duties. The assertion and exercise of rights thus marks the absence or breakdown of relations characterised by mutual dispositions of benevolence.

120

That love has broken down is a matter for regret, and recourse to rights may well be what is second-best. But this is not by itself a reason not to have rights. It is always dangerous to reason that, in the absence of the best, nothing else will do, especially when the second-best at least secures something valuable. Moreover, the onus is on those who would rely on affection alone to indicate what happens when love fails. Someone who believes that it would never do so is simply credulous. To argue that there would be enough with neither love nor rights to protect individuals is culpably naive.

There is a still stronger claim, namely that the use of rights does itself bring about the fall from interpersonal grace. If I give to others from duty and claim from them as of right what had previously been secured through relationships of mutual trust and affection, I will change for the worse the terms of the relationship. I will introduce into it a suspicion, mistrust and distance, which are precisely the conditions under which rights are demanded. Michael Sandel makes this point when he argues that acting by principles of justice helps to create one circumstance of justice, namely limited mutual benevolence. Since the principles of justice are said to be needed only in circumstances of justice, their exercise can be described as self-confirming.[9]

To reply to this, we need first to distinguish between the exercise or assertion of rights and their possession. To possess a right is to be in a position to exercise or assert a right, and, normally, to be disposed to assert that right when appropriate. Now it is not obvious that the possession of rights in this sense is incompatible with relationships of love. The possession of rights is akin to having an insurance policy or a safety net. To be insured against theft is not to indicate your willingness to be burgled or your expectation that you will be burgled. Similarly, to walk a tightrope with a safety net below is not to say that you think you will fall off. In both cases, the taking out of insurance is not a prediction nor an expectation of, nor resignation to, the fact that you will fall or be burgled. It is an assurance that if these things do occur then you will be guaranteed a certain outcome. Similarly for a child to have rights against its parents is not evidence that parental love is not forthcoming. It merely offers the surety of the minimum which love would provide when that emotion is lacking.

Those who sign prenuptial contracts are often suspected of insufficient love or trust. But to countenance the possibility that a marriage *may* fail, and that it would be better to make sensible provision for that possibility, is not the same as entertaining doubts about its success. It is of course in the nature of present love to represent its future course as assured for ever; and to require pledges of sempiternal fidelity as evidence of current devotion. But, as Sartre famously observed, it is a paradox of love, and *mauvaise foi* on the part of the lover, to seek a future certainty which requires the negation of freedom for that which can only be an expression of freedom. The lover mistakenly 'wants to be loved by a freedom but demands that this freedom as freedom should no longer be free'.[10]

But does not even the possession of rights tend irreversibly to sour a relationship of intimate union? Will not lovers begin to suspect one another of insufficient love and trust when contracts are insisted upon? It is interesting to turn the terms of the argument around. The lover, disappointed at the suggestion of a contract, may be understood as asking, 'How can the other think of me as one who would not give from love alone?' But equally, the other could be construed as asking, 'What must the other think of me if I am not being guaranteed at least what would be mine as of right?' To see others as having rights is to view them in a certain positive light. It is to see them as worthy of, deserving and entitled to be treated in certain ways. A love which denies the independence and distinct worth of the other may be thought stronger in terms of some ideal, but it enervates its partners.

Throughout this discussion it has been assumed that where affection or love does characterise a relationship this is good enough. Indeed, it would be the ideal form of that relationship. There are reasons to doubt this assumption. In the first place, there are many perverted forms of affection even if the affection is sincerely felt. Affection can be informed by a false conception of the other person and their needs. Many a child's path to hell has been paved with the best of parental intentions. The sexual abuse of children has been perpetrated in the name of a kind of love. Love between adults may be able to tolerate what is deleterious to either or both parties. It is less obviously defensible in the case of a child.

Second, loving relationships need not be reciprocal. The lover need not be loved, the carer cared for. A parent can care for a child, whereas it is not obvious that a child can care for its parents. Even where there is reciprocity there need not be symmetry. A parent may love its child as one who is vulnerable and dependent upon it; a child may love its parents as those upon whom it depends and to whom it looks for care and protection. The very form of the affective union consigns one party, the child, to a position of subordination, weakness and dependence. It may well be that mutual caring can take place between equals. But it seems evident that in most relationships between parent and child, caring presupposes and reinforces a certain incongruence of roles.

Third, individuals can easily be trapped inside affective unions. Feminists fear that talk of maternalism and woman's commitment to the maintenance of loving relationships means only that she remains imprisoned within her traditional role as carer and nurturer. There is a danger that the desired attachments, even if intimate, caring and mutual, can exhaustively define the realm of possible relations to people. In this vein, Jeremy Waldron argues that the existence of rights furnishes a basis on which individuals can initiate new relations and break free from what may be a suffocating communality.[11] It may be important for a child to know that it does rightfully belong to a public realm with its rules, rights and duties and is not just a member of a private, if loving, community.

Parents cannot choose to love their child; they can choose to respect its rights. And that a child should have its rights respected when love fails is surely no bad thing; not least when it assures the child of beneficent treatment which might not be forthcoming on a basis of love alone. There is no reason of course to think that the child with rights will thereby cease to love and be loved by her caretakers. But relying on love alone to secure the well-being of children shows a misguided and perilous optimism. It surrenders the child to the embrace of an 'intimate union' without any assurance of minimum protection should the union fall short of its ideal.

RIGHTS TALK IS NOT THE WAY TO SPEAK OF CHILDREN

An argument that what we must do for children is not best expressed in terms of their having rights is due to Onora O'Neill.[12] It is undoubtedly true that we as adults owe something to children. When both what we owe and which children are owed it can be fully specified, we can speak of *perfect* obligations. So, for instance, each of us is under a perfect obligation not to ill-treat or abuse any child, and parents have a perfect obligation to provide a certain level of care for their own child. Contrasted with perfect obligations are *imperfect* ones whose scope and content are indeterminate. We are under these obligations but they cannot be owed to all children, for how could each of us possibly look after every single child? Nor is it specified under these imperfect obligations what we do owe to any particular child. This will depend on the context. For example, we are all of us, in addition to a perfect obligation not to ill-treat any child, under an imperfect duty to stop children from being abused. However, when a child is being abused and there is something I can do about it, what I ought to do will depend on the circumstances. These will include the laws and policies in place to deal with such cases. It might be that I ought to report my suspicions to the police or to a social worker, or it might be that I ought to intervene directly.

Corresponding to perfect obligations are rights, namely those of the specific persons to whom those under the obligations owe the specific duty. But this is argued not to be the case with imperfect obligations. Yet the discharging of our imperfect obligations is the principal manner in which we adults, in general, show care and concern for children. Hence it is a mistake to think about children in terms of their rights, and it gets it wrong about what makes their lives worthwhile and valuable.

But why should rights not correspond to imperfect as well as perfect obligations? If each of us ought to show consideration for the interests of all children, why should it not be said that they have the right that we show them this consideration? It could be true of each and every child that she is entitled to demand of all adults that she is treated properly by any one of them. Moreover, imperfect obligations can find institutional expression in a set of formally approved practices and roles. Our general duty as citizens to prevent the abuse of children gives rise to child protection laws, policies and agencies. It is then the case that a social worker is under a role-specific positive obligation to do certain things on behalf of the children she is entrusted with protecting. These children have corresponding rights to her protection. Of course the social worker ought morally to do more than simply discharge her positive, legally recognised and sanctioned, duties. However, this is true of all legal duties which specify minimal requirements. The law requires a parent to do certain things for his child and not to do other things. He must send him to school and not abuse him. Yet everything a parent ought morally to do for her child is not a legal requirement.

We do have imperfect obligations towards children, but it does not follow that they, in consequence, do not have rights against us. Indeed our imperfect obligations may by institutional means generate legal duties and corresponding legal rights for children. Our moral obligations to children extend beyond these legal rights, but children are not a special case in this regard. What morally we owe one another as adults is more than the law requires.

In denying that children do have rights, O'Neill is anxious to show that we do not thereby do them a great wrong. In the first place, we must still discharge our obligations to them. Second, the case of children is not analogous to that of other groups such as blacks and women. The denial of rights to the members of these groups did and does amount to a very serious injustice. However, children are not, as blacks and women are, human beings with a rightful claim to emancipation. The difference lies in the fact that childhood is not an enduring status sustained by systematic oppression and discrimination. Rather, it is a stage of being that all of us go through. Moreover, most of those who deny rights to children also believe that their adult caretakers have the duty of ensuring that children grow into adults who can and do possess rights.

9

CHILDREN UNDER THE LAW

CHILDREN AT LAW

Legal rights afford children a status under the law. So if children do have legal rights then they have a recognised legal status. But children do not only figure in law as rights-holders. There are a number of other contexts in which children have legal standing. First, the laws of any particular jurisdiction may provide measures of child protection, that is, provide for dealing with those children who are the victims of various forms of abuse and neglect and for the possible prosecution of those who are guilty of perpetrating the abuse. I shall discuss the principles underlying child protection laws in chapter 14. Second, children may feature in civil proceedings, for instance by suing for or being sued for a breach of contract. Third, children may serve as witnesses in court proceedings. Of course they may be, though they need not be, offering testimony in a case in which they are themselves also plaintiffs or alleged victims of a crime. A child, most obviously, can testify in court about her own abuse. Fourth, children may be defendants charged with the commission of a criminal offence.

There are still other ways in which, in principle, children could play a legal role, for instance as legal personnel – judges, barristers, jury members. However, the age – and associated immaturity – of children makes this highly unlikely. In the rest of this chapter I shall say something about the age of criminal responsibility since this – child protection issues aside – raises the most central and interesting issues concerning the legal status of children. First, however, I shall say something briefly about a principle of consistency. The following constraint seems plausible. The ages set, and the reasons underlying the setting of the ages, in one legal context should be consistent with the ages set in any other. Thus – to employ a simple-minded example – if a 13-year-old is deemed incapable of entering into an enforceable commercial contract, it seems wrong to hold her criminally responsible, and punishable, for her own actions; or to do so if she merits official measures of child protection because she is thought to be fundamentally incapable of looking after herself; or to do so if she is regarded as unable, by dint of her immaturity, to provide reliable testimony in a court of law.

The principle of consistency applies here within the law. But arguably it applies also between the law and non-legal domains. It is, for instance, inconsistent to think legally of a child at a certain age as possessed of a certain level of competence but, within the same society, to design his education on the assumption that he is at a very different level of ability. Consistency can also apply across jurisdictions. Indeed, one function of an international covenant of children's rights is to provide signatory states with guidance as to the normal expectations of competency at various stages of development. The CRC does not do this. However, the United Nations Standard Minimum Rules for the Administration of Justice ('Beijing Rules') does do so in a fashion. Article 4.1 demands that the age of criminal responsibility for juveniles shall not be set at too low an age level. The Commentary on this article asks that 'efforts should . . . be made to agree on a reasonable lowest age limit that is applicable internationally'.

The principle of consistency holds not simply that ages should be consistent across domains. For what would that mean? Rather, it holds that the reasons underlying the fixing of an age in one domain should be consistent with those underlying the fixing of an age (perhaps the same one) in another domain. Now it might seem that the reasons in question simply have to do with capacity: the ability to commit crimes, to bear witness in a court, to take care of oneself, and so on. But in the first place it is not clear to what extent, if any, these abilities are commensurate. Is the ability to give reliable independent testimony in a courtroom of the same kind as, or measurable against, the ability to understand the nature of one's actions and the distinction between right and wrong?

Second, the reasons for fixing an age are not exhausted by considerations of capacity alone. One very important factor in the determination of an age is the point or end of doing so. Thus, as we shall see, the purpose of fixing an age of criminal responsibility may not simply be to track a person's ability to comprehend the wrongness of their deeds but rather to determine if, and when, somebody should be subject to judicial processes. There are also the interests of the various other parties involved to be taken into account. Thus, for example, the question of whether or not a child of 10 is competent to give reliable evidence in a court of law cannot be taken as exclusively determinative of the issue of whether she should do so. We need also to weigh in the balance the harm to the child of requiring her to do so, as well as the interests of the defendant against whom she is testifying.

In short, it would be a mistake, appealing to an unadorned principle of consistency, to insist that the ages settled upon in various legal domains should have to reflect a uniform childhood capacity. What then of the age of criminal responsibility? Discussion of this important matter is deeply coloured, in the United Kingdom at least, by the Bulger case. The facts of this case were as follows: in 1993 two 10-year-olds, truanting from school, abducted 2-year-old Jamie Bulger from a shopping precinct. They took him on an extended two-and-a-half-mile walk through the streets before battering him to death and leaving his body on a railway line to be run over. The two defendants were tried against a blaze of publicity – much of it in the popular press depicting them as evil and sadistic little devils – and in an adult courtroom only slightly modified to take account of their ages. Every day of the trial a baying mob tried to attack their transport as it arrived at court. Convicted of murder and abduction, their sentence was raised from the judge's initial recommendation of eight years to fifteen years by the then Home Secretary.

The defendants took a case to the European Court of Human Rights. This rejected some of the boys' complaints, but it did find that the Home Secretary had acted unlawfully in changing their sentence, and that their right to a fair trial had been breached. Their eventual release provoked orchestrated howls of public protest and an unsuccessful attempt by the popular press to publicise their whereabouts after prison. The particulars of the case are less important here than its symbolic significance. The case was perceived as betokening a general crisis of childhood in modern society. After all, the horror of the crime lay *both* in its being the wanton murder of an infant and in its being perpetrated by those presumed incapable of such an act. How could two children – and this is what the defendants were – not see how terribly and utterly wrong it was to kill another child? Acres of newsprint and hours of television were devoted to this and associated questions. If 10-year-olds in our society could do such terrible things, what did this say about our society's children and our society? How responsible are those who stand by and do nothing when children are ill-treated? A significant number of passers-by saw the defendants hurrying along a clearly distressed child and failed to act. Were the defendants genuinely evil children or merely the unfortunate products of a poor social and familial upbringing? What punishment, whatever the age of those who commit it, is appropriate for so awful a crime?

The extended, and frequently overheated, discussion of the Bulger case cannot be allowed to distract us from one self-evident truth. Whether or not the defendants were morally culpable, knowing all too well what a terrible thing they were doing and yet doing it all the same, they should not have been subjected, as 11-year-olds and as they were, to the rigours of the court trial. They were tried in a court crowded with legal personnel and the public, to whose continuous scrutiny they were exposed by being in a specially raised dock. Throughout their trial they were suffering from untreated post-traumatic stress disorder. In their disturbed state, scrutinised by everyone, they could not have fully or adequately understood the proceedings which determined their fate.

These facts help to illustrate an important distinction in how we can understand the age of criminal responsibility. In one sense, the age marks the time at which children may be presumed to have the capacity to understand the difference between right and wrong and to act accordingly. According to the other sense, the age marks the time at which it is judged proper for children to be subject to certain kinds of juridical processes, in particular a court determining guilt or innocence and apportioning the appropriate penalties. It is easy to see why the distinction might be thought beside the point. It will be said that the same age applies whatever sense is intended. For it is only when individuals are judged responsible for their actions that it is appropriate to subject them to a procedure that may result in their suffering a penalty for these actions. Criminal liability should track responsibility for one's deeds.

Yet though this may be true, the converse does not hold. Even when we can reasonably hold a child to be responsible for her actions it does not follow that it is proper to try her in a court. To see why this is the case we must acknowledge both the point and the effect on those subject to them of juridical processes such as a court trial. Such processes can be in themselves very distressing to a child. It is daunting to be exposed in a court to the scrutiny of legal personnel and of the general public, to be cross-examined, to be asked to remember and to account for what one did in the past. The procedures of a court, the words and actions of judges and barristers, are arcane, complex and difficult to follow. It is thus fundamentally unfair to a child that her future welfare should turn on the outcome of a procedure she may not be able to understand adequately and, consequently, participate in properly.

A court of law does two things. It adjudicates on the truth of the matter. Did the child commit this act? Second, it apportions an appropriate penalty in the light of a determination of the facts. Given the child did commit the offence, how should he be punished? Thus the court serves the ends of truth and those of the good of the offender and of others (the victim, society as a whole). In the first place, it is not clear that a child's participation in a court of law does always serve the ends of truth. Consider the case where the child is not a putative offender but rather is a witness in a case. Remind yourself how distressing and intimidating it may be for a child to stand before adults and to testify to actions performed in the past. This is especially difficult if the child is giving testimony about his own abuse and the alleged abuser is also in court; or if the child is being required to testify publicly against members of his own family. Consider how alien the manner of eliciting information by means of agonistic cross-examination is to a child; or how difficult it may be for a child to recall past events in a consistent and convincing manner.

Of course, measures can be and have been taken to accommodate these difficulties. These include an elimination of court formalities such as the wearing of wigs, the installation of screens shielding the child witness from court scrutiny, the use of intermediaries to interpret both questions and answers, and the pre-recording and video transmission in court of evidence. Valuable as these innovations are as acknowledgements of the child's vulnerability in the witness box, it needs to be remembered that testimony serves the end of truth. Will a witness afforded these protections be as credible in her testimony as one subject to the standard rigours of open cross-examination? Is the solemnity of court procedure, including the formal swearing in of any witnesses, necessary to ensure that those who testify recognise the significance of what they are doing and cleave, in consequence, to the truth? Moreover, the interests and rights of others must also be recognised. Can a defendant denied the opportunity to confront his accuser be assured a fair hearing?

Returning to the issue of criminal responsibility, even if the child's appearance in court, appropriately modified in its proceedings, did serve the end of determining the truth, there would still be the further question of whether it was appropriate, having made an adjudication of the facts, to punish the child for what it was found she had done. Let us take the case of the child who is legally responsible for her actions in the sense of possessing, and displaying, an appropriate capacity. We need first to be clear about what this capacity amounts to. Central to Western jurisprudence is the idea that criminal responsibility, that is, liability to suffer penalties for an offence, requires the demonstration of two facts in respect of the offence: the *actus reus* and *mens rea*. The first is the performance of the act defined in law as constituting the offence. The individual pulled the trigger of the gun whose fired bullet pierced the heart and occasioned the death of the victim. The second fact is often badly translated as a 'guilty mind'. It describes not the act but the agent, her intentions, motivations, attitude. Thus an individual who did not and could not reasonably have been expected to know that the gun, whose trigger she pulled, was loaded might be held not to display the *mens rea* needed for her to be guilty of a crime.

Very young children are as a rule presumed in Western law to be *doli incapax*, incapable of committing a crime. The presumption is also normally qualified in the following manner. Below a certain age, let us say 7, a child is *conclusively* presumed incapable of committing a crime. A 6-year-old who manifestly does know what he is doing and that it is wrong is nevertheless

129

assumed at law not to be capable. This is just to say that below a certain age the presumption of *doli incapax* is irrebuttable or indefeasible. In respect of a child above that age but still below a still higher one, let us say 12, the presumption of *doli incapax* may be defeasible. It is rebutted if it can be shown, to an agreed standard of certainty, that the child committed an act he knew to be wrong.

It is obviously important to be clear what it is for a child to know that an act is, as has been said, 'seriously wrong'. Even a very young child may think of her actions as naughty or mischievous. What the law requires is an appreciation by the child of the serious wrongfulness of her acts. Moreover, it is not enough that the child understood that her act was seriously wrong. She must also be able to act on her understanding of the distinction between right and wrong. She needs to be independent and capable of assuming responsibility for her actions.

So let us imagine that an 11-year-old has committed a serious crime and could be shown to have fully understood that what he did was very wrong. Should he be subject to the same court procedures and to the same kinds of sanctioned penalties that an adult would be if she had committed the very same act? An 11-year-old who is capable of understanding the nature of her acts and their moral import might nevertheless be incapable of understanding and hence contributing appropriately to a court trial. Again, it need not be fair to punish even a knowing child in the same way and to the same extent as an adult who was guilty of the same offence. We ought to acknowledge, by way of an obvious example, what 15 years' incarceration would mean to an 11-year-old boy as opposed to a 35-year-old man. Locking up young persons for that period of time – even if in a special juvenile prison – deprives them of their liberty during the most important and formative years of their prospective lives. Such treatment is clearly more onerous than the life imprisonment of an adult.

We ought not to take any of the foregoing to show that a child guilty of an offence should not be subject to *some* process and to *some* penalty. However, society can appropriately determine that there are better ways of proceeding in respect of a child who has committed an alleged offence than requiring her to appear before a court of law and punishing her as they would an adult. The Scottish Hearings System, for instance, is a unique and extraordinary quasi-judicial mechanism for dealing both with children who have committed offences and with those who are the victims of offences. Both sets of children, argued the Kilbrandon Report that recommended the institution of a Hearings System, may be properly viewed as 'children in trouble'.[1] As such, child offenders should be disposed of in ways other than by the infliction of a penalty – through the requirement that they be subject to supervision by a social work agency, for instance. The Hearings System thus separates the issue of the determination of truth (did the child commit the offence?) from that of the disposal of the case. The Hearings System does not, as does the adult court, tie a determination of guilt to the apportioning of a penalty. In general terms it may be appropriate to put in place diversionary procedures whereby children guilty of crimes go not to courts – juvenile or other – but are dealt with by other non-judicial agencies.

If a child *is* to be dealt with by a court of some kind then it is proper that the court's business be conducted in a manner that respects the child's immaturity. It is fundamentally unfair that a defendant's judicial fate – the reaching of a verdict and the subsequent apportioning of a penalty – should be determined by procedures which preclude his full and knowing participation. A child cannot contribute to a trial whose conduct he is incapable of grasping, and it is wrong to punish him – even for deeds he did commit – if he cannot. If juveniles are to be tried in courts they should be juvenile courts.

Nevertheless, there are arguments from the other side that ought to be considered. In the first place, even if the general presumption is that children below a certain age are not subject to court proceedings there may, in some instances, be a public interest in so treating them. Regarding the defendants in the Bulger case, someone might say the following: there was a proven public interest in prosecuting these minors in a court and subjecting them to the full rigours of the criminal law. This is because the crime they committed was so awful that the public had a legitimate concern that they should, notwithstanding their young age, be severely punished and be publicly seen to be subject to punishment. In general, we might argue that the more serious the crime the greater the public interest in treating the children who commited the crime as if they were adults, or very close to adulthood.

Of course the fact that there is a general expressed, and widely shared, sentiment that a child guilty of some terrible crimes should be treated in certain ways does not show that there is a legitimate public interest in doing so. The sentiment in question may be no more than a reactive desire for vengeance. In the Bulger case there was reason to so view the prevalent feeling. But children – even the authors of dreadful acts – are not to be treated as scapegoats. The following considerations are also relevant. Very few very serious crimes are committed by children. Moreover, the great majority of the children who do commit such crimes are, the evidence shows, the products of seriously disturbed backgrounds, often the victims of abuse or suffering from the loss of a significant figure to whom they were deeply attached.[2] It seems a double penalty to punish those who have done wrong in large part because they themselves have been wronged.

131

There is a further argument for treating irresponsible young offenders as if they were adults. This is the thought that it is precisely in virtue of their *not* being responsible that adult punishment is appropriate. Those who cannot see the difference between right and wrong, and act accordingly, should be taught the difference and how to behave. Is there any better form of education in good behaviour than exposure to the rigours of a trial and subsequent punishment? The question is posed rhetorically but can be answered in the negative. For it is not clear that children can be, or can best be, taught the lessons of responsibility for one's actions by judicially sanctioned punishment. Remember John Locke's reasonable fear that corporal punishment would lead a child to associate the forbidden action with the pain suffered rather than bring him to recognise the reasons for its being forbidden. His concerns about corporal punishment extend to punishment in general.

WELFARE VERSUS JUSTICE

In all of the foregoing discussion a distinction has been alluded to but not named. This is one between 'welfare' and 'justice' models of dealing with young offenders. The distinction can be broadly drawn as follows: a welfare model addresses the needs of the child, viewing these as the source of her misdeeds. It seeks to rehabilitate or treat the child, not to punish her for her errors. By contrast, the justice model focuses on the deeds of the child, viewing those which are misdeeds as meriting appropriate penalties. The child is to be punished, not reformed. The Scottish Children's Hearing System, briefly discussed earlier, is often cited as providing a classic welfare model that speaks to the 'needs not deeds' of the child.

It would be an oversimplification – though it is easy to see how the distortion is attractive – to think that the welfare model represents the child as not responsible for his actions, whereas the justice model presupposes a capacity for wrongdoing on the part of the punished person. Certainly, to repeat what was stated earlier, it is unfair to punish someone whom we hold to be not responsible for their actions. Yet the converse does not hold. Even when we can reasonably hold a child to be responsible for his actions, it does not follow that the justice model is appropriate. It may be better, on balance and all things considered, to deal with the child as somebody whose needs should be addressed. Nevertheless, the fact that these needs provide some explanation of why he acted as he did may not acquit him of responsibility for these actions.

The welfare model has in recent years within Western jurisdictions been displaced by the justice model, and one plausible explanation of this change is the increasing tendency to view children, or young persons, as responsible for their actions. Certainly this is where something like the principle of consistency may exercise considerable influence. Judgments such as *In re Gault* accord children the same juridical rights as adults. If children are entitled to the same legal protections as adults, then perhaps they should be subject to the same legal liability for their actions. It is hard to see a child as a possessor of adult rights because she is thought of as being as competent as an adult to exercise them and yet also as incapable of answering in law for her actions.

However, it is imperative to keep two matters distinct. There is, on the one hand, the question of when children may be held to be responsible for their misdeeds, in the sense of being properly described as knowingly and avoidably doing wrong. On the other hand, there is the question of when it is proper to require that children be liable to judicial trial and punishment. A child may be responsible, in the first sense, and yet ought not to be liable in the second. It is not contradictory to think this way, and indeed there are many good reasons to do so.

Nevertheless, the contrast between the welfare and the justice model can be overstated. Obviously, in the first instance, any institutional arrangement for addressing the needs of young offenders must be regulated by just rules. More importantly, any such arrangement cannot turn a blind eye to the fact of wrongdoing. A child who has done wrong must be given the opportunity to acknowledge as much. A young offender who is made the subject of a compulsory order – such as one requiring him to cooperate with a social work plan of action – is not punished. But he is compelled to do that which he would not otherwise do, and the terms of the compulsory cooperation may be burdensome. Lastly, it would be wrong to think that welfare and justice are mutually exclusive. A juvenile court can, for instance, both impose a penalty on a child *and* make provision for the child's needs to be addressed. Both punishment of the offence and amelioration of the conditions of the offender can be within the remit of a judicial body.

Part III

CHILDREN, PARENTS, FAMILY AND STATE

What the best and wisest parent wants for his own child, that must the community want for all of its children.
John Dewey, *The School and Society* (1900)

10

BEARING AND REARING

Thus far the talk has been of children's rights. But what about their caretakers? Do not adults have rights over children, especially if they are natural parents and the children are *their own*? But if parents do have rights, what kind are they and how are they to be balanced against those of children? Finally, what role should the state play in enforcing these respective rights? In this chapter I will consider the two most obvious putative rights of adults, namely to bear and rear children. In particular, I want to consider the relationship between these rights. Does the fact of giving birth to children in some way ground the right to bring them up as one chooses?

A RIGHT TO REAR

Charters of human rights have recognised a right of adults 'to found a family'. For instance, Article 12 of the European Convention on Human Rights, incorporated into UK domestic law by the Human Rights Act of 1998, accords 'men and women of marriageable age' 'the right to marry and found a family, according to the national laws governing the exercise of this right'.[1] This right may be interpreted as comprising a right both to form a legally recognised cohabiting relationship and to have children. 'Having children' may be taken here to mean not simply bearing them but subsequently bringing them up. I will say something in turn about bearing and rearing.

The right to bear must be qualified in two respects – first, the entitlements of the infertile and, second, the constraints upon its exercise. There is no general right to have children. If there were, an infertile couple would be entitled to take possession of at least one of another, fertile, couple's children. We do not think that it is a requirement of justice that children be distributed across couples such that every couple desiring to have a child has at least one. Of course, those who wish to adopt a child freed for adoption by her

137

parents should be permitted to make an appropriate application. Nevertheless, it is entirely proper for the state to vet prospective adoptive parents strictly. Sadly, adoptive practices in the West display a mismatch between the kinds of child adoptive parents desire and the children actually freed for adoption. Moreover, the official control of adoption can all too easily be subverted by those wealthy enough to buy children from poorer countries.

The right to bear children is not the simple corollary of the right not to bear children. This latter is a right of control over what shall happen to one's own body. It gives women the right to contraception and, more controversially, to abortion. The right to bear, by contrast, is a right to bring into existence another human being. It is in the first instance a negative liberty right not to be stopped from doing what one could and would otherwise choose to do. Thus it is a right not to be compulsorily sterilised or to be forced to undergo an abortion. It is not a right to be assisted in the performance of something one would wish to do but could not otherwise do. So, for example, my right of emigration is a right not to be legally prevented from leaving the country. I do not have a right to official financial support of my travel to another country. Hence, in similar terms, the negative liberty right of reproduction need not entail any right on the part of the infertile to assisted reproduction.

Nevertheless, having one's own child is something most people regard as of enormous value, as giving their life a tremendous purpose and significance. It engages some of the deepest, most enduring, and significant interests of adult human beings. Those who want but cannot have children experience an overwhelming sense of loss. Should we not then make provision for the infertile to be helped to have children? One argument in favour would be that infertility does occasion very serious mental distress that can be more effectively treated, and at less cost, by providing such assistance than by psychiatric therapy.[2] Another argument claims that infertility is properly thought of as a handicap and that liberal egalitarian principles provide that individuals be compensated for any handicaps they suffer which cannot be viewed as their fault.[3] Someone born infertile can thus claim treatment, whereas someone seeking the reversal of earlier voluntary sterilisation cannot.

Both arguments rely on the thought that the desire to have children is both very strong and somehow also unavoidable. Thus the desire if checked causes serious mental distress, and the inability to have children is experienced as a significant handicap rather than as an inability to which one is indifferent. Yet very many individuals have no desire for children, and many of these have a strong aversion to the very idea of having children. Moreover, there are dangers, which feminists will be quick to identify, in seeing women as innately disposed by their biology to want to reproduce, such that the lack of any desire on their part to have children is viewed as unnatural. Indeed, there is considerable evidence that the desire to parent is socialised. Our culture tends to sanctify natural parenthood and to stigmatise the childless. In these circumstances it greatly oversimplifies to say that the desire for children is one we cannot avoid feeling.

I said that having one's own child engages some of the deepest, most enduring, and significant interests of adult human beings. What are these? Adults can want to have, and do have, children for a variety of reasons, some of which are without doubt morally suspicious and some of which are downright morally repugnant: to prove it can be done, to spite or to blackmail another adult, to bring about a life that avoids the errors of its begetter, to try to save a disastrous relationship, to create a companion and an assistant for one's dotage, to add another soldier to the army of the motherland or another true believer to the ranks of the faithful, and so on. Yet there are good reasons to have children. One lies in the idea of creating another being. To procreate is to be responsible for the existence of a new and distinct human being, somebody who is one's original creation but who has his own value. Another is to make real or concrete the sexual love of a couple. In charmingly abstruse if suggestive language, Hegel believed that only with the birth of a child does conjugal love become a 'knowing that knows'.[4] Another good reason to have a child is to be motivated by a concern to dedicate oneself to the welfare of what is one's own and not another's offspring.

Yet if we grant that there is a right to bear children, it is surely not unconditional. The propriety of bringing a child into existence is governed by a number of considerations.[5] One set of these concerns the well-being of the child. Arguably, a new human should not be brought into being unless its own rights – to life and to the provision of an adequate level of welfare – can be secured. So any right to bear should be conditional upon acceptance of an obligation to provide properly for one's offspring. Rousseau happily admitted in his *Confessions* that he had abandoned to the care of foundling institutions five children by his mistress. In *Émile* he evinced a profound change of heart, stating that, 'He who cannot fulfil the duties of a father has no right to become one. No poverty, no career, no human considerations can dispense him from caring for his children and bringing them up himself.'[6] Rousseau is perhaps too strict. Parents may bear if they at least ensure that their child will be well cared for, even if this is not actually by themselves.

Yet interesting issues arise with the following kind of case. Imagine a prospective child whose life will fall below a certain threshold but will still on balance be worth living. We can obviously specify this threshold in various ways, but the essential idea is that someone below it lacks some significant part of what makes any life worth living. The child enjoys a very poor life but nevertheless it is one that is still worth living. Now imagine that the prospective parents cannot have any child but one whose life is below the threshold. So this is not a case where they could have a child whose prospects are significantly better. If this were the case we would rightly condemn them for deliberately having the child whose life prospects are so much worse. Of course there is still a puzzle as to why we would condemn the parents, since the better-off child they do not have is not the same child as the one – the worse-off – they do have. Given this non-identity, we cannot say that the parents harm the child they do have by condemning her to a worse existence than she might otherwise have – by being conceived later, for instance.[7] It would seem then that wrong is done by the parents who nevertheless do not harm anyone.

The case under consideration, by contrast, is one when any child born to the parents will only have a very poor existence, yet one that is still better than non-existence. The poor life is unavoidable in the sense that the parents can only avoid creating such a life by not having any children at all. A number of philosophers who discuss this kind of case think that no wrong is done to the child by bringing him into existence.[8] The child cannot be said to be harmed. Harming someone means making her worse off than she would otherwise be. But there are only two possibilities. Either her existence can be compared with her non-existence, in which case she is, according to the specification of her case, better off alive. Or no such comparison of existence and non-existence is possible, in which case the question of her being harmed, or not, does not arise, since harm is an essentially comparative notion.

The exercise of a liberty right is constrained, according to familiar liberal principles, only by a harm principle. An adult should be free to do whatever does not harm another. Hence the would-be parents are entitled to exercise their right to bear so long as they do not harm any future child. In this imagined case they do not, and thus should be perfectly free to have the child. Many will find this conclusion unappealing. Can it really be right for two adults to bring into existence knowingly and deliberately a child whose life will be very miserable, even if they could not have any child with happier prospects? One way to block the conclusion of the argument is by asserting that the right to bear is constrained by the requirement that parents bring into existence only those children that they can be reasonably sure will enjoy a minimally decent life, one that is above the threshold and thus more than merely better overall than non-existence. A powerful reason for thinking this way is that procreating is not just the exercise of one's freedom but the creation of another life.[9] Can it possibly be morally acceptable for adults to exercise *their* right in such a way that somebody who will enjoy very few rights is brought into being? Can it be acceptable to claim that it is very much in one's interests to create a human being whose own central interests cannot be enjoyed? The satisfaction of one person's rights and interests cannot be at the expense of another's. Hence it is wrong to bring about a life whose prospects you can be reasonably sure will fall below a minimal threshold of decency.

A second set of factors governing any right to bear has to do with the consequences for society of any birth. A new life might seriously threaten the continued existence of persons already alive. This would be the case with a woman suffering from a highly dangerous and contagious disease known to be automatically transmitted to the foetus. Or the existing members of a population subsisting on scare resources would be put at risk by any addition to their numbers. The general goal of maintaining population at a desired level may be argued to constrain the exercise of any right to bear. We might concede a right to have at least one child, as is the case in China, thus limiting the size of any family founded rather than abrogating the right to bear.

The right to bear is then not unconditional. What of the right to rear, and who might be said to have it? The right to rear is the right to determine the conditions and manner in which a child is brought up. It thus entitles a person to choose, amongst other things, what a child shall eat and drink, where he shall live, who he shall associate with, what he may read and view, what moral rules shall govern his behaviour and how he shall be punished for any transgressions of these rules. Of course, the child liberationist denies that there is any such right, incompatible as it is with the child's own rights of self-determination. Even the defender of the 'caretaker thesis' accepts that a parent's right to rear is limited and has conditions. For the moment I am interested in the question of how someone might acquire a right to rear. The most obvious answer is in virtue of being the child's parent. Parents have the right to rear and they do so *because* they are the parents.

I BEAR THEREFORE I REAR

There are four sorts of argument for the conclusion that natural parents should be entitled to bring up their own children. I shall call them the 'proprietarian', the 'blood ties', the 'interests' and the 'least detrimental alternative' arguments. The strongest conclusion that any argument could seek to establish is that a parent has an unconditional right to rear his own children, and the weakest is that a parent has only a defeasible claim to do so. In support of the arguments, considerations can be urged either on the part of the parent or on the part of the child. In other words, parents may lay claim to rear their children because they are their parents. Or this claim may derive from the child's own interests in being brought up by his parents. This latter support for a parent's claim is indirect, since it merely provides a warrant for bringing about a situation in which the parent does rear her own child. Support for each argument displays a certain balance between parent- and child-centred considerations, and some considerations are not exclusive to any one argument. For instance, showing that children are least badly off by remaining with their own parents requires evidence that there are some costs in separation. And demonstrating this forms part of the 'blood ties' case.

The 'proprietarian' argument reasons that a natural parent owns her children, and the right to rear would be included within a right to dispose of what is rightfully owned. The ownership of a child by his parents is in some way grounded in the child's production by them. The thesis first found expression in Aristotle, who spoke of children as belonging to their parents: 'for the product belongs to the producer (e.g. a tooth or hair or anything else to him whose it is)'.[10] In fact, Aristotle's examples suggest something more than the relation of producer to product, namely that of part to whole. A child is, in some sense, a part of the parent's body. This could only be taken as applying, if at all, during pregnancy, and even this claim is deeply controversial.

It is in Locke that there is a more credible version of the 'proprietarian' argument which derives from a general theory of property. For Locke, one owns the product of one's labour in virtue of owning one's body and thus one's labour. Self-ownership generates ownership of the fruits of one's labour. The felicitous association of 'labour' with childbirth helps support the idea that one's child is owned because she is one's product. Locke also thought that one 'owned the turfs my servant cut', that is that one acquired rights in the products of another's labour when that labour was itself owned or the other's services purchased. So, by analogy, a childless couple could 'own the baby their surrogate bore' through buying her 'labour'.

Yet, as we saw in chapter 1, Locke himself denied that parents own their offspring. But his reasons for thinking the labour of bearing children any different from forms of labour which *do* ground property entitlements are unconvincing. There are then two ways of responding to the 'proprietarian argument'. The first is to deny the general validity of the Lockean thesis about labour generating ownership; the second is to show that there are good reasons, other than Locke's own, to exempt children from the scope of that thesis.

Locke's argument that people own that with which they have 'mixed' their labour is subject to a number of familiar criticisms. The move from owning one's own 'self' to owning what that self works on is not obviously valid, and may depend upon conflating labour as activity with labour as product. If the move derives its plausibility from the idea that labour improves, then perhaps one has an entitlement only where there is improvement, and, even then, merely to the value added by one's labour. Why should the act of labouring be thought of as a process whereby entitlement passes from labourer to laboured upon, rather than a loss of that labour in its object? How is entitlement to be apportioned in the case of collective labour or where something results from a number of successive productive stages?

Procreation illustrates many of these difficulties only too well. Giving birth to a child might be viewed not as a property-generating labour but as a dissipation of one's genetic stock in a new existence. Can begetting be construed as improving something? If so, are there degrees of improvement such that parents might be entitled only to the equivalent of the amount by which their particular procreation is improving? For instance, should we reward parents only to the extent that their coupling can be justified eugenically? Is the relevant 'labour' the conception (which *sounds* odd), the gestation and birth, or both? Strictly speaking, only the mother 'labours' to produce the child, and the father's contribution may be seen as a freely given gift (this may be explicit in the case of semen donation and artificial insemination). In many circumstances, others besides the parents, most notably medical personnel, make a significant productive contribution. Do they have rights to the child proportionate to their contribution?

Such problems notwithstanding, if Locke's labour argument is valid, is there then a good reason to exempt children from its scope? As we saw in chapter 1, modern critics have suggested one. This is that the child has, as a new human being, a right to liberty. It is this right which, in the case of adults, underpins the right to dispose of one's body as one chooses and thus the right to own the product of that body's exertions. Since the right to own derives from a right of liberty, the former could not conceivably trump the latter. The child's liberty undercuts any presumptive rights of another to its ownership.

This reasoning is not ad hoc, since it derives from the general presumption of self-ownership. However, it can seem paradoxical, since it denies precisely what the labour thesis affirms, namely that you own what you produce. If labour always generates ownership, it is because one always owns oneself. But if parental labour creates ownership then children do not own themselves. If parental labour does not create ownership of children then labour in general does not always generate ownership. The paradox is not vicious. Rather, it seems to be a case of a principle or thesis limiting itself. Self-ownership is universal and universally generates ownership in things other than oneself, except where the products of labour happen to be human beings.

A defender of the 'proprietarian thesis' may simply insist that this is to beg the question. If children *are* owned then this is not a case of self-ownership failing to be universal. It is rather that children are not the sorts of things that can be self-owning, any more than domestic animals are. Children *become* self-owning when they reach adulthood. Thinking this way seems to fly in the face of deep moral convictions. But previous cultures have not felt as we do. A major principle of Roman law was that of *patria potestas*. The father as head of the family, *paterfamilias*, had the absolute power of life and death over his son; he completely controlled his person and his property. The son was released from this state only by his father's death or by manumission. In practice, the son exercised *de facto* administration of his own property, *peculium*, and instances of his father exercising his *potestas* to the limit seem to have been rare. Moreover, Romans were worried about the anomalies caused by the father's power – they were, for instance, concerned that a father should not make a slave of his free-born son by selling him – and *patria potestas* was progressively attenuated.

This shows that the idea of a child as something over which parents have total power has been seriously entertained. In the last analysis, consequently, rejection of the 'proprietarian' argument requires that one either be sceptical of Locke's general labour theory (and reasons have been given for being so), or insist that children are just like adults in being self-owning and thus exempt from that thesis's scope.

For all of that, the 'proprietarian' argument casts a long shadow over much thinking about parental rights, and it is easy to find modern examples of arguments or claims which appear to make proprietarian assumptions. The talk of 'ownership' may not be explicit but something very like it seems to be argued for. Thus some speak of children as 'extensions' of their parents. Charles Fried, for instance, writes that 'the right to form one's child's values, one's child's life plan and the right to lavish attention on the child are extensions of the basic right not to be interfered with in doing these things for oneself'.[11] Or, again, Robert Nozick writes that children are 'part of one's substance [. . .] Part of a wider identity you have'.[12] In other words, the rightful exercise of parental control over one's children is just a part of one's rightful self-disposition.

It should be noted that given that there are always at least two parents, the 'one' who chooses is not a single person. Indeed, each parent may choose very differently for his or her child. Although the idea that one's child is an extension of one's own self is lent support by the tremendous significance a child can and does assume in most parents' lives, it surely does not ground a parental right over the child. After all, many things are 'part of one's substance' or 'wider identity' – for example, friends, place of work and work colleagues, sports team, private club. My rights to choose for myself do not extend to these things, so why should they extend to my children? The thought that the case of children is different is probably then only a thinly veiled version of the basic proprietarian claim. In general, Mill's stern rejoinder to thinking we can choose for our children just as we may choose for ourselves is apt:

> It is in the case of children that misapplied notions of liberty are a real obstacle to the fulfilment by the State of its duties. One would almost think that a man's children were supposed to be literally, and not metaphorically, a part of himself, so jealous is opinion of the smallest interference of law with his absolute and exclusive control over them.[13]

The idea that parents own their child may seem to follow all too obviously from the biological fact of parentage. But it is important to make this reasoning explicit. For some write that parental rights to rear arise out of the natural facts without any indication as to why. For instance, H. L. A. Hart claims that there is 'a type of situation which may be thought of as creating rights and obligations: where the parties have a special natural relationship, as in the case of parent and child'.[14] Philosophers have always been suspicious of the idea that natural facts of themselves generate moral claims. In this particular case it is instructive to try to discern what is doing the moral work between the facts and the rights. For non-natural conventional relationships, such as that between adoptive parents and their child, might be thought to create similar rights and duties. Equally, there are non-special natural relationships, such as that between second cousins, which do not. This leaves us with the strange idea that the irreducible brute fact of procreation 'creates' moral rights and duties. Whilst it is not too odd to think of a created duty to care for what one has brought into being, it is mysterious how this same event generates a right to rear.

The only way to make sense of this idea is to argue that something follows from the fact of progeneration which *is* morally relevant to the existence of rights and duties. This is where the 'blood ties' argument comes into its own. This argument appeals to certain facts, chief of which is that of 'bonding'. By 'bonding' should be understood the way in which parents and children naturally feel bound up with each other, so that parents display a strong, self-sacrificial affection for their children, and children on their part would be lastingly damaged by separation from their parents. Bonding can reasonably be represented as a well-attested and prominent fact about human beings, indeed about very many species of animal in relation to their offspring. The 'blood ties' argument says that parents have an innate tendency to bond to their children, and therefore the parents have a claim on their children which amounts to a right to rear. This is a strong argument and, once clearly separated from the 'proprietarian' argument, a widely accepted basis for a parental right to rear.

There are in fact two arguments which need to be separated. The first is what could be called the 'best suited' argument in which the facts of bonding form one premise. The second amounts to a claim about the costs of separation. The 'best suited' argument is that a child's caretaker ought to be the person best suited to care for her and most likely to give her the best upbringing, that natural parents are the persons best suited and should thus be the child's caretakers. Bonding explains why the parents are best suited. The existence of bonding can be supported simply by an appeal to the facts, by a claim about the evolutionary success of natural parenting, or, as in John Locke, by talk of an inborn, God-given disposition.

The 'best suited' argument has a number of weaknesses. The first is that the crucial fact is only a *tendency* to bond. What the argument needs is a clear statement that every parent *does* bond to her child. The likelihood, even probability, that a parent will bond does not give a claim. Still less does it give the parent a weaker or paler probable claim. Either the parent bonds to his child and is best suited to rear, or he does not bond and is not best suited. The probability of a parent's bonding cannot somehow be related to her suitability to rear, any more than the likelihood of my passing my driving test would strengthen or weaken my claim to have a licence to drive. Clearly, some parents do not bond to their children in the appropriate way. After all, this is the sad lesson of child-abuse cases. A parent in such a case cannot be said to have had a measure of suitability to rear her children in virtue of its having been probable that she would bond.

The second thing to say about the 'best suited' argument is that it is child-centred. The claim of a natural parent to rear arises from the child's claim to have the best possible caretaker. If a natural parent does feel self-sacrificial affection for his child, then that qualifies and motivates him to fill the role of best possible caregiver for the child. But his being that caregiver is required by what the *child* needs, namely the best possible care. Put another way, it seems clear that one person's self-sacrificial affection for another cannot, of itself, give the first a claim in respect of the latter. My loving you does not give me rights over you. But if you have a right to certain kinds of treatment and my love for you guarantees that treatment, then it may follow that I am the person to love you. This, however, is your right not mine. Finally, we

146

should still remember that the existence of affection does not, as the last chapter argued, guarantee the right kind of treatment.

The existence of 'blood ties' also suggests that for children not to be brought up by their natural parents would be costly in psychological and emotional terms. These costs of separation may just be considered as reasons to think a child would fail to have the best possible upbringing if not reared by her natural parents. But they can also be considered independently of the 'best suited' argument. There are two different sorts of evidence which point to parent–child separation as having serious costs.

The first kind of evidence is of the actual alleged trauma of separation. It is claimed that both children and parents suffer great distress, possibly lasting, on being removed from one another. There is clearly some truth in this. The idea that separation is deeply and lastingly damaging derives from a certain account of infant attachments whose most celebrated and influential defender is John Bowlby. Bowlby's claims – that attachments are instinctive and enduring, and that their disruption does permanent psychological damage – are not without their critics. Modern 'revisionist' psychologists have suggested that children are more adaptable to changes in their environment than Bowlby believed. They have also argued against the enormous importance formerly ascribed to parent–child bonding.[15] It is worth adding that the significance given to attachment is both culturally specific and relatively modern. The idea that secure parent–child bonding is critical for the future healthy development of the child is not evident in the practices of non-Western culture and even European societies in the past. Feminists too may rightly be suspicious of talk about a natural and sacred bond between mother and child.

The second kind of evidence cites the extent to which even happily adopted or surrogate children may seek out their natural parents. It could well be that one's genetic nature is crucial to one's sense of identity. Or even, simply, that a sense of affinity, given by biological relations, exerts a very real influence on people's discovery of their 'self'. It does not follow that this is an irreducible biological fact about human beings. The way in which society defines the proper family as a biologically based unit may be critical. It is all too easy for a child brought up without natural parents to feel stigmatised as incomplete and lacking something when the familial norm is cast by society in biological terms.

A final point should be made about the attachments parents feel for their children. It is undoubtedly true that parents may suffer real agonies upon separation, and it would be improper to discount *their* needs and emotions. Such considerations may not establish a parental right to rear. But they may help to support a presumption in favour of natural parents bringing up their own children, and it would be wrong simply to discount the feelings and interests of parents.

The third argument from natural parentage to a parental right to rear is the 'interests' argument. In general, an individual's right to some thing is based upon the individual's having a strong interest in it. Recognition of a right requires both that the interest should be of value and that its protection should not interfere with the securing by other individuals of things in which they have a valuable and comparable interest. For instance, we are right to have an interest in being as free as possible, and it is evident that we may claim a right to the maximum liberty compatible with a like liberty for others. Now it can be argued that parents acquire an interest in what happens to their children by bearing them; indeed that the fact of bearing a child is itself a powerful statement of one's preparedness to be interested in that child. Further, the facts of attachment, if true, testify to the way in which a parent can feel her child's interests to be bound up with, perhaps indissoluble from her own. That interest is then best protected by giving the parent a right to rear.

It is unfortunately true that some natural parents do not feel an interest in their children's future. Indifference to one's offspring may be rare but it happens. It should not then be assumed that bearing automatically generates an interest in rearing. One should also be cautious about the idea that getting pregnant in some way displays an interest in rearing the eventual offspring. Pregnancy occurs against the parents' will, and can result from carelessness or unconsented sex. Moreover, a woman can clearly be casual about and even culpably negligent of the health of her foetus.

As we have seen, there are many possible bad reasons to have a child, those that serve morally suspicious and even repugnant interests of prospective parents. These cannot ground a right to rear. Moreover, at least one of the good reasons to have a child is child-centred. This is that a parent is strongly motivated to care for her own child. It is the child's interest in receiving a devoted and loving upbringing which here provides the warrant for a putative parental right to rear her own.

The final argument for the parents' claim to rear their children can be briefly stated. It is that parents' rearing their own represents the 'least detrimental alternative'. Various reasons have already been offered for thinking that children will benefit from staying with their natural parents and will suffer if separated from them. Natural parents tend on the whole to love their children and show a willingness to care for them disinterestedly. Children and parents will suffer significant distress if separated. They may even be caused lasting damage. Children need their blood ties for a sense of their own identity.

These reasons support a presumption in favour of allowing parents to rear their own children. Arguably, this presumption is defeated only if it can be shown that the only feasible alternatives have no greater benefits and worse harms. Defenders of the 'least detrimental alternative' argument argue just this. Proper assessment of their claim must await a review of the alternatives. However, at least two sorts of immediate response are in order. The first is that much depends on how the alternatives are specified. It is assumed that the only choice is between natural parenting within the family and the collective rearing of all society's children, or between the first and some centrally organised system whereby children are compulsorily allocated at birth to the 'best possible' caretakers. This ignores the extent to which there may be other alternatives less extreme than these collectivist options.

The second rejoinder follows on from the first. The costs of the alternatives will depend on how they are described. Much of the prejudice against child-rearing institutions, which complemented the emphasis upon the importance of parent–child attachments in the immediate post-war era, arose from studies of poor examples of institutionalised rearing. A good instance is Anna Freud's critical survey of nurseries operating during the Second World War in conditions of Dickensian austerity.[16]

PARENTAL DUTIES AND PARENTAL RIGHTS

We saw that the right to bear is constrained by a duty to ensure that any child born has the reasonable prospect of enjoying a minimally decent life. On Rousseau's behalf it was suggested that parents can discharge this duty by ensuring that someone else provides adequate care for their child. But parents who do undertake the task of rearing their own child should also honour the duty. Hence it is arguable that any right to rear, that is, to determine the conditions and manner in which a child is brought up, derives from and is constrained by this prior duty to make sure that a child is properly cared for. This is the 'priority thesis'. Kant, for instance, thought that procreators 'incur an obligation to make the child content with his condition as far as they can' and that 'from this duty there must necessarily also arise the right of parents to *manage* and develop the child'.[17]

Some will argue that these rights are not rights proper but only a degree of discretion in the discharge of the duty.[18] If I must repay my debt to you, I certainly can choose whether I pay you in cash, by cheque, or by bank transfer, and whether I do so directly or through an intermediary. But it would sound distinctly odd to say that I have a right to repay you. However, I can have a right to what I am also obliged to do. Those who are legally obliged to vote cannot choose whether or not to vote. But they do have a right, which non-voters lack, to choose who shall receive their vote. Moreover, parents have rights over their children when they are entitled to make those choices for their children that the children cannot.

How must the parent choose for his child? What is the scope and content of this perfect obligation a parent owes her child, and to which corresponds a child's right? I do not discount the question of what society and the state owes the child, something to which I will return in the next chapters. Under the CRC, states are enjoined to guarantee the child a range of fundamental rights. In addition to protection from abuse and exploitation under Article 24, the child must enjoy the 'highest attainable standard of health'. As for parents, Article 18 insists that they, or the legal guardians of the child, having primary responsibility for the upbringing and development of the child, shall have the 'best interests of the child' as 'their basic concern'. Article 27 adds that they also 'have the primary responsibility to secure, within their abilities and financial capacities, the conditions of living necessary' for the 'physical, mental, spiritual, moral and social development' of the child.

In chapter 4 I argued that it is implausibly demanding to regard the 'best interest principle' as prescribing that parents and the state shall do what in fact is the very best for each and every child. It is notable, therefore, that the Articles of the CRC just quoted make the best relative to what is 'attainable' and 'within [the parents'] abilities'. Moreover, the standard of living parents are responsible for securing is one 'adequate for', not one that maximises, the child's development. Children do not have a right to the best upbringing, nor even to the best possible upbringing. They do have a right that their parents shall do whatever they can to ensure the conditions of their development. To require that parents shall do everything they possibly can to promote their child's development and welfare treats them as no more than altruistic paternalists, devoted agents of the good of their offspring.

But might not other parents be able to do more for a child? Does a child not have a right to be allocated those parents who will do most for her? Even a right to an optimal upbringing would not entail wrenching children from their natural parents and allocating them to 'better' caretakers; nor would it mean moving children from caretaker to caretaker whenever another could be judged 'better' than the existing one. I have given reasons for thinking that the separation of a child from his parents may have serious costs. It is even more certain that a radically disrupted childhood, one without a relatively stable and permanent context of affectionate care, can be harmful. Considerations of self-identity are also important, and so too then is a child's relationship to her origins – national, ethnic and social. The extent to which a child's upbringing may in fact be improved by his being moved from one rearing context to another is significantly limited.

Even with the best possible upbringing, how well a child can do is significantly constrained by his genetic inheritance. Yet recent rapid developments mean that genetic engineering is possible, both with living humans and *in utero*. It is increasingly accepted that genetic therapy for the purposes of saving an existing or future child from suffering a serious disease is morally appropriate. Since we can or will soon be able to identify the genetic bases of all those positive factors, such as intelligence and certain physical traits, predisposing to human well-being, can the child claim that she ought to be born the best she can be? Can the child claim a right not only to be free of serious inherited diseases or disabilities but to have the most perfect nature it is scientifically possible to produce?

Engineering the best child is possible either by genetic manipulation or by selection of the genetically superior gamete, embryo or foetus. Those involved in *in vitro* fertilisation (IVF) can choose which embryo to implant on the basis of preimplantation genetic diagnosis (PGD). In this latter case, the child that results from whichever embryo is implanted cannot make a claim to be harmed by having been chosen, since she would not exist if not chosen. Consistent with what was said earlier, the child can only claim to be wronged if born without the reasonable prospect of a minimally decent life. This is true also of the child who is born when earlier genetic intervention would have removed the inherited obstacles to leading such a decent life. Whether parents ought, given such a choice, to produce the best possible child is moot. There are a variety of considerations – equality, freedom, and beneficence – that bear on a complex issue. It is important here only to acknowledge that no child has a right to be the best he can.

The very difficult question remains of how to distribute the responsibilities for the kind of upbringing a child receives between parents and society. A child's start in life is a function of her own genetic inheritance and the character of those guardians to whose care she is allocated. Should society act to ensure, by genetic engineering, that the genetic bases of inequality are eliminated or at least significantly reduced? Should, as an alternative, society accept initial inequalities due to different genetic inheritances but seek to compensate for them? For instance, we might re-allocate children from less favoured backgrounds to better-off households. As we saw, Article 27 of the CRC gave parents 'the primary responsibility to secure, within their abilities and financial capacities, the conditions of living necessary' to their children's development. Should society ensure that the economic abilities of parents to provide such conditions are equal? Whether or not children do have a right to an equal start in life, and if so how this is to be ensured, raises issues of social justice whose resolution lies beyond the terms of this present book. Nevertheless, it is proper to comment that no full account of what is owed to every child by parents and state can be given without resolving them. The implications of a principle of social justice for family privacy are briefly discussed in the next chapter.

The arguments of this chapter can now be summarised with the help of a distinction between biological and moral parenthood. Biological parenthood is the existence of a physical causal tie between begetter and offspring. This might arise through gestation or conception. Moral parenthood is the giving to a child of continuous care, concern and affection with the purpose of helping to secure for her the best possible upbringing. 'Parent' should only be understood as meaning one or several adult caregivers. Thus moral parenthood is not restricted to any particular familial form. It is consistent with natural, adoptive, foster or multiple parents, as well as a children's residential institution. A child must have some parenting, and whatever parents a child has are obligated to fulfil the terms of moral parenthood.

It is reasonable to argue that the discharge of these duties requires something like a right to rear. The moral parent can only properly care for his child if he is permitted to make important choices on the child's behalf. This at least is uncontroversially true in the case of young children. In other words, the parental right to rear derives from and is conditional upon the fulfilment of the duty of moral parenthood. It is not that a right to rear pre-exists but is limited by a duty to meet certain minimum conditions of upbringing; it is rather that those who undertake to discharge the duty to give children decent upbringings thereby acquire the right to rear.

Biological parenthood does not guarantee moral parenthood. But the facts considered earlier do suggest that natural parents will probably be moral parents, that bearing a child does dispose a human, on the whole and in the main, to be deeply concerned for and affectionate towards their child. Both natural parent and child normally have a strong interest in remaining together. Thus it may be reasonable to presume that biological parents should act as the child's caretakers, especially if the feasible alternatives can be shown to be unacceptably poorer. In short, there may be nothing wrong with a state permitting natural parents in the first instance to bring up their own children as they choose and within specified limits. What the state should not do is presume that natural parents have a right to rear which derives simply from biological parenthood.

11

FAMILY AND STATE

THE LIBERAL STANDARD

We are led by talk of rights and duties to the question of how the state should act to protect the interests of children whilst at the same time respecting the rights of those who may act as their caretakers. This question is immensely complicated for at least two important reasons. First, what is regarded as the proper role for the state in the protection of children's interests will be crucially influenced by how the state itself is viewed. In particular, socialists and feminists have long charged that, in a society marked by significant structured inequalities, it would be a mistake to see the state as the neutral enforcer of impartial law.

Second, it remains likely that in the first instance children will, where possible, be reared in families by their natural parents. Or, at least, this is a natural presumption to make. Moreover, the 'family' and 'state' have most commonly been represented as mutually excluding spheres of action; so much so that an endorsement of the family's social role in bringing up children may be taken as already setting certain limits to the proper role of the state. Consequently, it is important to be clear how the family is to be regarded. Here again, socialist and feminist critiques are especially relevant.

It is impossible to tackle the issue of who should care for society's children without first being clear about state and family. In this chapter I will offer some general remarks about the state and the family. I shall do so by simultaneously critically examining the presuppositions of what may be called the 'liberal standard' and reviewing the main criticisms made of family and state by socialists and feminists. These remarks will serve as a background to a more direct consideration, in the next chapter, of the role of the state in relation to children and families.

The 'liberal standard' prescribes the proper relations between state, family and children, and in some form is presently the most influential account of

153

how the law should govern families within liberal democratic societies. It comprises three elements. First, there is a commitment to the paramountcy of the best interests of the child. Second, parents, that is, those accorded responsibility in the first instance for the welfare of particular children, are entitled, subject to standard conditions, to autonomy and privacy. Autonomy here means the freedom to bring up children as they see fit; privacy means the absence of unconsented intrusion upon the family's domain. Third, there is a clear specification of the threshold of state intervention, that is, a statement of those conditions whose satisfaction would warrant the state in breaching parental rights to privacy and autonomy. Normally these conditions concern either the proven breakdown of the family or the occasioning of significant harm – actual or probable – to the child.

The three elements of the standard are mutually reinforcing in this way: it is in the immediate best interests of any child to be reared by her parents as they see fit and within a family context protected against intrusion upon its privacy. However, when a family fails or the child is exposed to serious harm, the parents forgo their rights of autonomy and privacy. The guardianship of a child then passes from his parents to the state which, guided by the best interests of the child, determines an appropriate course of action – eventual return to the parents or the reallocation of the child to new caretakers, such as a residential insitution or foster parents.

THE STATE

The 'liberal standard' presupposes a number of things about both the state and its nature and role, and the family. These need to be spelled out and then critically examined. The presumptions of the 'liberal standard' concerning the state are as follows: first, the state has a legitimate interest in the welfare of children but, second, it acts as their caretaker in the last, or at least not first, instance. Third, the state assumes a public role in protecting children which is initially circumscribed by the private space of the family. Fourth, the state does or can act neutrally and impartially to promote the interests of all children within its domain.

That a state should assume some responsibility for the well-being of its children seems obvious. That, historically, the state has seen fit to do so is also true but to widely differing degrees. A longstanding influential doctrine holds the state, in succession to the monarch, to be *parens patriae*, 'parent of the nation', and thus responsible for the upbringing of its youth. However, the first legislation in Britain and America specifically and deliberately directed at protecting children's welfare rights dates only from the end of the nineteenth century. A significant and often noted fact is that the first prosecution for child cruelty around this time had to be brought under laws protecting animals, since none existed specifically for the protection of children.

The state may claim a legitimate interest in the welfare of children both as *current* human beings to be cared for and as *future* citizens who must now be trained for their eventual roles in society. Of course, it may be hard to separate these concerns, since the standards of education and rearing observed now can crucially determine future levels of civic fitness, both physical and mental. Indeed, it has been argued that the assumption by the British Liberal government (1906–14) of collective responsibility for child welfare reflected a sudden, and militarily exigent, obsession with 'national efficiency'. Large numbers of army recruits for the Boer War had to be rejected on grounds of physical debility, and this, more than anything else, focused public attention on the poor social conditions in which children were being brought up.

The liberal doctrine presumes that the state is not its children's 'parent' in the first instance. It concedes parental responsibility in the first instance to the child's own parents. The question of whether it is right to do so lies at the heart of the debate about the proper role of the state, and will be considered in the next chapter.

As for the way in which a state actually operates, it is a common mistake to think that power is exercised only by the state, and that the influence of the latter is confined to its explicit political–juridical interventions into the lives of citizens. These errors are especially relevant to the case of the family. In the first instance they lend false support to the view that the family inhabits a politically neutral 'private' space into which the state intrudes only when it acts 'publicly'. Second, they help to reinforce the idea that the modern 'nuclear family' is more private, and secure in its privacy, than previous familial forms.

Each error needs correcting. Power may be exercised over individuals and families by agencies other than those of the state, and by means other than the legal-coercive ones associated with the state. Two writers in particular – Christopher Lasch and Jacques Donzelot[1] – have drawn attention in their different ways to what they view as the emergence of a peculiarly modern Western form of 'policing families'. This consists less in explicit state intervention into the life of the family than the subtle and pervasive intrusion of experts, involving, to use Donzelot's own phrase, government *through* families as opposed to the government of families. A therapeutic medical model stipulates a norm of familial 'health' which, by means of professionals, insinuates into the 'private' life of families. These professionals fill the quasi-official occupations of doctor, psychiatrist, lawyer and social worker. It is the

155

view of both writers that the modern 'private' family is more thoroughly governed, albeit in less public fashion, than any of its historical predecessors. Both write from left-wing positions and yet lament this most recent, and insidious, displacement of parental (patriarchal even) autonomy by socially dominant forces.

The policing of families may extend beyond the state. But it is also true that the state's role in respect of the family is broader and more significant than might be implied by attending only to its explicit interventions. There are a number of ways in which the state, through its laws as well as its social and economic policy, may crucially influence the way the family and its members' roles are defined. These suggest that the distinction made between 'private' family and 'public' state is fundamentally mistaken and dangerously misleading.[2]

In the first place, the significance of the distinction between 'public' and 'private', and the respective boundaries of each, are not things which were laid down once and have then remained constant ever since. Rather, the distinction itself owes much to the emergence, from the sixteenth century onward, of the modern, sovereign nation-state and a corresponding movement to define a countervailing sphere safe from its encroachments. The legitimating practices of the market, especially in the nineteenth century, were critical in sanctioning the separation of public law from the law of private transactions; and it is historical developments in the form of the family which have contributed to its acquiring the status of a paradigmatically 'private' institution.

But, second, the family is not 'private' in the sense of being a non-political institution, if 'political' refers to relationships and structures of power. Feminists have rightly exposed the extent to which men and women are expected to fulfil stereotypical roles within the family, roles which reproduce relationships between unequals of subordination and oppression. It is the further contention of child liberationists that children are also, and unjustly, the victims of domination by their adult caretakers. The representation of the family as 'private', and the consequent pressure to protect it from 'public' scrutiny and regulation, serve only to shield and reinforce these relationships. Indeed, there is a sense in which the 'private' domain ideologically reproduces itself. For what the state will not intrude upon is defined as 'private', and the 'privacy' of the private is what then serves as the principal ground for non-intervention.

Third, the state sanctions a social, economic and legal background which supports these particular familial roles. Indeed, it is a general failing of the notion of a neutral, non-interventionist liberal state that it cannot show how it upholds, by not changing, what is already 'given' by the economy and society. Thus, for instance, the liberal state tends to assume that the natural family is a unit in which the father is the earning head of the household, with wife and children as economic dependants. It confirms that standard when it fails to institute alternative sources of support which might make it possible for women and children to leave families. If this is now less true for women, it certainly remains the case for children.

Finally, the state may sanction certain intra-familial patterns of conduct by exempting them from the normal processes of law. For example, a parent may, short of serious abuse, corporally punish her child without being liable to charges of assault. In these various ways the state's non-intervention actually serves to bolster the structures and roles of a particular kind of 'private' family. These structures and roles clearly have public import.

The fourth presumption of the 'liberal standard' is that the state does or can act neutrally and impartially to promote the interests of all children within its domain. In modern Western societies, which are structured by serious class, gender and racial inequalities, the state cannot sensibly be viewed as such a neutral agent. If we restrict ourselves to consideration of the state's possible interventionist role in respect of children these inequalities will reveal themselves in the following ways.

First, the children whose treatment by their parents is monitored by the state will probably come from families which are *already* under surveillance for other reasons. Working-class households are more likely than middle-class families to come to the attention of social service and legal agencies on account of financial, housing and welfare difficulties. Middle-class children may thus be less well observed because their families do not have the same socially depreciated status.

It is, of course, important to recognise that there may well be some significant correlation between the incidence of child abuse and conditions of social and economic deprivation. Poorer parents may, for whatever reason, be more likely to mistreat their children. A self-conscious attempt to see all parents as equally possible abusers may fall victim to the 'myth' that child abuse is classless. On the other hand, a predisposition to view parental failure as strongly connected to a certain socio-economic status may amount to a class bias which is blind to the occurrence of poor parenting elsewhere. Moreover, the bias may become self-confirming in so far as only those parents from certain groups are reviewed and consistently found to be probable abusers.

Second, the agents of the state regulation of child welfare are disproportionately drawn from the white middle class. Notwithstanding an official professional ideology of non-judgmentalism, social welfare and legal workers are prone to proceed on the basis of particular values about the proper ways to rear and treat children. At best this may amount to an insensitivity about different possible standards of family behaviour, standards which may be entrenched within a particular well-established class or ethnic culture. At worst there is a disposition to impose one particular and socially dominant set of familial values on those who do not share them.

Third, the effects of state policy may be inegalitarian in that they actually reinforce existing inequalities. For instance, the placement of children who come to the attention of the state is presently much influenced by the priority of 'permanency', that is, returning the child to its original parents or, where that proves impossible or undesirable, settling it as quickly as feasible with another set of permanent parents. It has been argued that, given the social and ethnic status of, respectively, 'problem' and foster families, this amounts in practice to a transfer of children away from working-class and black to white middle-class households.

Fourth, any child policy may be inegalitarian in the simple and straight-forward sense that its opportunity cost is a failure to tackle directly the inequalities which give rise to the problems. If the neglect and abuse of child-ren *is* related to social deprivation, then it is the elimination of the latter rather than a welfarist or judicial response to the former which should assume priority in the allocation of a state's resources.

There are, of course, independent reasons for thinking that a state should act to promote social justice or to eliminate the grossest forms of social injustice. These reasons, in turn, provide the state with a warrant, other than that of child protection, for broaching family privacy and autonomy. It is worth briefly spelling out the respects in which the protected privacy of the family may serve the end of social injustice. In the first place, injustice *within* the family may vitiate the achievement of social justice. Women confined to the performance of unduly burdensome domestic tasks may be disabled from the full performance of their civic role. Again, families may function as 'schools of injustice' where children unfortunately learn to accept and to play their own future part in the reproduction of injustice by living under an unjust familial regime, one, for instance, where there is an unfair division of gender roles.[3]

Injustice *between* families may also serve to perpetuate social injustice. Parents can pass on their advantages (and disadvantages) to their children. They can do so directly through the transmission of their genes or through the inheritance of material goods; they may do so indirectly by being able to give their child a more favourable upbringing and education. The liberal who is committed to the ideals of family autonomy, appointment on merit, and an equalisation of life chances faces a serious problem.[4] How well a child can expect to do in life depends crucially on where she starts from, namely the family into which she was born and within which she was raised. This is a matter of her good or bad luck. If we appoint strictly on merit, then we cannot take an adult's unfortunate start in life as a relevant consideration when allocating jobs and offices. Yet the only remaining option is to interfere in families, something at odds with the liberal presumption in favour of leaving parents to bring up their own children as they see fit.

We can of course give up on the principle of family autonomy altogether in the name of social justice; or permit the state to seriously constrain the degree to which parents are able to pass on their advantages (and disadvantages) to their children. Yet surely the family will endure in some form, and the collectivist alternatives, as I shall show, are beset by their own difficulties. Moreover, the family serves other valued purposes, such as the moral education of children, and, perhaps most importantly, seems an essential element of leading a recognisably full and fulfilled human life. Simply abolishing the family in the name of justice does not seem an option.

I have given reasons for thinking that it would be naive and short-sighted to believe that the state is what the 'liberal standard' presumes it to be. The state does have a legitimate interest in its children, though it may display it for pragmatic rather than purely principled interests, and, for the liberal at least, it does not act as a caretaker in the first instance. It is too simple to see a 'public' state standing over and against a 'private' family; further, it is ingenuous to believe that the state acts neutrally and impartially to promote the interests of all children within its domain.

THE FAMILY

I now turn to the question of whether the 'family' is not a similarly controversial institution. The twin presumptions about the family at the heart of the 'liberal standard' are that it is probable and desirable that children will be brought up within families, most likely those constituted by their natural parents, and that familial rearing requires privacy and parental autonomy.

It is important, first, to stress that there is no such thing as *the* family, as a single, historically unchanging kind of social unit. There always has been a diversity of familial forms. It is clear, however, that most who presently speak of the family have in mind a particular and, so it is often argued, particularly modern variant. This has at least the following distinguishing features: a membership normally restricted to parent(s) and child(ren), and a clear distinction between its sphere of activity and the rest of society, especially as concerns work. There are familiar arguments to the effect that developments in the nature of production, leisure, education and even architecture have combined to make the modern nuclear family paramount and paradigmatic. And it can seem especially hard to separate this sort of family from the exemplary 'privacy' it allegedly enjoys and is entitled to.

This modern family has been the subject of well-known criticisms from the left which, to simplify greatly, have charged that the family is undesirable in itself or in so far as it is the instrument of an undesirable society. The family is undesirable in itself inasmuch as its relationships are oppressive, and the roles it allocates to its members stereotypical. The family is undesirable on instrumental grounds in so far as it is an agent for the transmission and reproduction of the oppressive social structures and roles, that is by, for instance, socialising daughters to become mothers or by securing the inheritance of property.

What remains unclear in this criticism is whether socialists and feminists favour the abolition of the family as such (or, less starkly, view its historical supersession with equanimity) or are committed only to the radical restructuring of the present familial form. One can imagine something that is clearly a *form* of family whose members enjoy equal status, share all significant familial tasks and which functions within an egalitarian society; a family, moreover, whose sphere of existence is not dramatically distinct and set apart from the 'public' domain.

There seem to be only two respects in which a socialist or feminist could object to the very principle of the family: that it requires an unacceptable monogamy or permanency of coupling between parents, and that the family represents the objectionable privatisation of reproduction and rearing. There need not of course be any reason to believe that the maintenance of a family requires its parents to be monogamous. Conservative prejudice rather than hard fact may be why one is tempted to think differently. Adultery is a cause of divorce and hence familial disruption. But it is the inability of one or both parents to tolerate infidelity rather than the infidelity itself which is the relevant factor here. Within some cultural contexts polygamy – albeit normally one male to many women – is accepted both as normal and consistent with familial stability.

But is monogamy in itself wrong? It would seem perverse to deny that a couple should express their mutual love in an abiding and exclusive fashion. The parties to an 'open' relationship, on the other hand, might view its primacy as consonant with both having other sexual partners. However, it would be as wrong to insist upon 'openness' as essential for all progressive couples as it would be to impose a requirement of monogamy on everyone. What surely matters is that unconstrained choices can be made in the light of what is felt to be best for each and every partnership. Suspicions about monogamy and fidelity derive from a concern that these ideals may be only ideological constructs which work to the detriment of women, not least by concealing a serious duplicity of standards. Men have historically bound women to them in a contract of sexual exclusivity whilst at the same time and for their own part breaching its terms. Women's fidelity is required by male jealousy and possessiveness, whilst man's promiscuous 'nature' is argued to make reciprocal faithfulness an impossible demand.

Is the family unacceptable because it represents the privatisation of reproduction and rearing? How private this needs to be depends very much on the form of the family and the role the state is permitted to play in regulating the family's activities. Nevertheless, the family does seem to require, to some degree and in some form, exclusive control by parents over the bearing and rearing of *their* children. Bearing and rearing raise different issues. As to the first, some radical feminists have argued that women's oppression is ultimately rooted in biological facts of parturition. Women not men reproduce. But scientific developments such as *in vitro* fertilisation and artificial insemination by donor have dramatically changed the force and character of these facts. There is now no reason to think that women need be forever condemned by their biological nature to reproduce.

The crucial and pertinent point is that there is no necessary relationship between the collectivisation of reproduction and the emancipation of women from their 'natural' reproductive role. It is possible to imagine the collectively administered propagation of the species, with fertilisation and embryogeny managed, respectively, without sexual intercourse and *ex utero*. In literature such social experiments have either been seen as seriously dystopic (as in Aldous Huxley's *Brave New World* (1959)) or as forming an essential part of a feminist utopia (as in Marge Piercy's *Woman on the Edge of Time* (1976)). On the other hand reproduction might be collectively run but by utilising some women solely and principally as brood-mares. Margaret Atwood's *The Handmaid's Tale* (1985) offers a vivid portrait of such a sexist dystopia.

At this point it is worth briefly remarking upon a possible inconsistency, or at least difficulty, for feminists.[5] Many feminists have said that they would favour a collectivisation or communalisation of social existence. They have certainly argued against the public–private divide, chiefly because women are condemned to live an unfree life on the 'private' side. They have recommended a society in which all important matters would fall under the public, collective democratic control of society as a whole, men and women equally. Now one such matter must surely be reproduction.

Yet feminists have also struggled to secure for individual women rights of choice over their own fertility. This has had especial relevance in the campaign for access to free, safe and legal abortion on demand. The asymmetry is obvious: the right *not* to have children is a private individual choice; the right to have children would be subject to collective control. It is not satisfactory to point to the difference between a campaign waged within existing structures which deny women any real choices, and decision-making within an envisaged future but as yet unrealised society. For the fact remains that, in the latter, if reproduction *is* subject to collective control then abortion could not be a private choice, at least not to the extent that is implicit in present demands for a 'right to choose'.

The choice between the 'private' and 'public' rearing of children will be discussed in chapter 13. However, one distinction is worth drawing in the present context. One of the seven demands of the early women's liberation movement was for free 24-hour childcare. The rationale for this demand was evident, namely the emancipation of women from their enforced role as sole familial childcarer with all its consequent isolation, drudgery and misery. Yet it has remained unclear in what form and by whom this care is to be provided. Are there to be state managed, staffed and funded nurseries or merely state financial support for whatever local initiative might be favoured by a particular group of mothers? We might in this spirit draw a somewhat crude distinction between two systems of care. 'Community' care is informal and devolves upon a network of relationships between people sharing a locale, strong personal ties or occupation. 'Collective' care is formal, structured and tends to be institutionalised. The relevant contrast would be between the local creche and the children's residential home.

Feminists have rightly been suspicious of a recent revival in the prominence accorded 'community care', fearing that in present society 'community' reduces in effect to 'family' and that this in turn reduces to women.[6] When politicians speak of the community's need to look after the weak and dependent they condemn women to their traditional role as carers. In general, 'communalism' as an alternative or supplement to the family may only represent a broader context in which gendered roles are still maintained. Housework and childcare may be spread across women but not across the gender divide. On the other hand, 'collectivism' is not congenial to the libertarian and anti-statist sentiments of the feminist left, and institutionalised forms of care have received a notoriously bad press from Anna Freud through to Irving Goffman. Feminists are wary of openly urging a system of state nurseries and residential children's homes.

In sum, the 'public' alternative to 'private' childrearing by the family has not, in feminist criticism at least, been well enough defined to conclude that the family is obviously unsatisfactory for being 'private'. We have also seen no reason to conclude from feminist criticism that the family as such, rather than particular familial forms, is obviously undesirable. Is the liberal then right to presume that the family is both desirable and inevitable?

As for its desirability, it would be a mistake to discount the very real benefits which families may achieve. The family is a set of unchosen but intense affective relationships. Within the family the individual can feel emotionally secure, loved and protected; one can be intimate with others and show oneself emotionally; one can be oneself safely and securely, where outside one would be vulnerable and exposed. There are important familial bonds of mutual dependence and belonging. Consanguinity may also bring with it a vital sense of similarity and familiarity; people may need to feel that these others are their kind.

Chapter 8 gave reasons for mistrusting reliance on affective bonds alone. But a stronger accusation – that the intensity and exclusivity of the family is positively dangerous – probably lacks justification. Such a claim is associated with radical psychoanalytic critics of the family, most notably R. D. Laing. For them it is the family's very closeness that forces some of its members, who cannot withstand the imposition of an identity upon them by others, into madness. The limitation of such criticism is that, whilst it may be able to argue from schizophrenia back to the family, it cannot with the same measure of plausibility argue from family in general to schizophrenia. Laing's cases are of families gone wrong, those where qualities – of closeness, intimacy and mutual dependence – which otherwise might be virtues are vicious in their effects. But this no more shows the family in itself to be injurious to one's mental health than all sexual love is condemned by the perpetration of occasional crimes of passion.

Many social and political theorists have been happy to appeal to the contrast between a public realm, where strangers without ties interrelate like the parties to a legal contract, and the private sphere of familial bonds, warm, loving and reciprocally caring. Indeed, the family can, in the phrase Christopher Lasch chose for the title of his book, be the 'haven in a heartless world'. The contrast can be overdrawn, not least if it reinforces both the public–private divide and the sense of the family as essentially private. Against that, arguments to the effect that the public can be familialised, that is that all our social relationships can be transformed to resemble a large family, are simply naive. The family's appeal is that for each person there is some discrete set of known individuals with whom they can enjoy a special and exclusive mutual regard.

The family is special and has definite merits which cannot be ignored, even if the contrast between it and the rest of society should not be exaggerated, and its occasional dangers should not be overlooked. Is it also inevitable? Social critics are chary of claims that anything is 'natural'. Yet it is particularly easy in view of the family's cultural prevalence and long historical survival to think of it as one institution with a right to such a title. Moreover, the family can be represented not just as 'natural' but as desirable because natural. The more closely a particular family approximates to the paradigmatic form of the family, the more ideal it is said to be.

Now it is important, if difficult, to separate what is due to facts of nature and what may be attributed to ideological and social practices. For instance, it has frequently been argued that children brought up by single parents suffer compared with those from 'normal' families. The relevant comparative indices are such things as educational achievement, eventual occupation, incidence of criminal behaviour and disposition to mental illness. It would be easy to conclude that the facts show children to benefit from being reared within a natural environment, that is, a stable family with a couple of parents.

However, in the first place, children may be the victims of imposed social expectations and values. If a child is brought up to believe that he is less well-off and abnormal for having only one parent, then that belief can only too easily be self-confirming. Second, facts other than those having strictly to do with familial form may be influential. Single parents will tend to be on a lower income, experience greater difficulties in finding suitable employment and housing, and so on. It is these facts rather than simply the singleness of parenthood which may adversely affect the children. Finally, public policy, whether in pursuance of an ideological agenda or not, may penalise the single parent relative to the couple by means of such things as discriminatory welfare payments. This too will contribute to the relatively poorer position of the lone parent.

Even accepting these points, it can still be tempting to view the paradigm family as the best system for bringing up children. Perhaps much of this feeling derives from a popularly assimilated Freudianism. We feel, somehow instinctively, that a child should have parents of both sexes in order to make those identifications and form those attachments which are a prerequisite for healthy development. Happy, self-sufficient children need a mother *and* a father. Again, much of this may be self-confirming ideological prejudice, especially when what is understood as 'mother' and 'father' are, in fact, specific and stereotypical gender roles.

It is important not to rule out the choices that may be made by individuals for atypical family forms, those headed by single parents, multiple parents or gay and lesbian couples. Of course, there is something weighty about the choice that has been made and continues to be made by millions of couples, across many cultures and throughout history. But these choices are not a vote for one familial form over all others. A tolerance of diversity is consistent with a recognition that large numbers of children will continue to be brought up within standard families. Even so, the cumulative effect of various social and demographic changes is that the 'standard' is by no means as obviously prevalent as previously. Increasingly, the modern nuclear family may be seen as one choice amongst several, even if it probably remains the most popular.

The extent of these changes, and their effect, can be exaggerated by talk of the 'end of the family'. Nevertheless they are significant. The changes are principally threefold. First, there has been and continues to be greater social and legal tolerance of single-sex couples, whose unions and rights over any children are given as much recognition as those of heterosexual couples. Second, marriage continues to decline, with a rise in the number of children reared by cohabiting couples, lone parents and step parents. Third, and most striking, is the rise of a reproductive technology which allows those who cannot, the infertile, and those who would rather not procreate, such as gays and lesbians, to have children.

The new reproductive technology is striking because it directly challenges the idea of 'natural' parenthood. In particular, it forces us to recognise both a distinction between causal and custodial, or what in the last chapter was termed 'biological' and 'moral', parenthood, and the contingency of the relation between them. The essential idea is that biological or causal parents play a causal role, through gestation or genetically, in the existence of the child, whereas the moral or custodial parent is the individual, or individuals, entrusted with the guardianship of the child and devoted to her continuous care during childhood. The idea that it is a brute natural fact that the causal parents of a child are also her custodial parents has been dramatically, and probably irreversibly, subverted by the new reproductive possibilities. Individuals can choose to be either causal or custodial parents, and they need not be both to one and the same child.

Natural facts are often taken, though they should not be, to support moral claims. Thus it was only too easy to assume that only those who can be his causal parents should also be the custodial parents of the child they bring into existence. Yet if custodial parenthood is cut loose from causal parenthood there is no longer the same reason to privilege the causal relation. Perhaps what matters most is not the blood tie as much as the commitment to care for the child. Re-thinking matters in this way thus not only changes our view of what the obvious or 'natural' family is; it also disposes us to judge claims to parent not by reference to natural facts but by intentions, skills and dispositions. 'Who ought to parent?' is more easily asked once the question 'who *is* the parent?' admits of no ready answer. These remarks reinforce the general scepticism about parental rights to rear that follow from alleged rights to bear which were rehearsed in the previous chapter.

The liberal standard presumes that the family is both desirable and, in some sense, 'natural'. I have given guarded and qualified reasons for thinking there is some merit in this presumption. The next issue is whether childrearing within the family requires what the liberal standard prescribes, namely privacy and autonomy.

12

PARENTAL RIGHTS TO PRIVACY AND AUTONOMY

INDIVIDUALISM VERSUS COLLECTIVISM

The 'liberal standard' is essentially a prescription that the state should not interfere in the rearing of children by their parents, unless it can be shown that the child is exposed to a serious risk of harm. In chapter 14 I shall consider the whole issue of harm and abuse. In this and the next chapter I want to review the liberal standard's presumption of non-interference, by contrast with alternatives. I shall think of this standard as essentially individualistic. By this I mean that childrearing is left to individual parents. Standing opposed to individualistic policies are collectivist ones where the state or society assumes a responsibility, to greater or lesser degree, for the upbringing of children. At one extreme this can mean that childrearing is collective or communal and under the direct control of the state or society – as in kibbutzim or Plato's *Republic*. Closer to the individualist model, we can envisage children being brought up in the first instance by families, but subject to a range of forms of legal supervision and control. The state might, for instance, initially allocate children upon birth to families; or closely monitor their development in their respective families, reserving powers to remove and redistribute children among other families or institutions.

There are a number of arguments for and against the individualist and collectivist positions. I want to review the most important of them, and will start by looking at the strongest case that can be made for the individualist liberal standard, namely that parents have a right to autonomy and privacy. The right to autonomy entitles the adults of a family to make important decisions in the rearing and educating of the children within that family; the right to privacy entitles the adults to refuse unconsented intrusions into the family's domain.

An admirably clear statement of these rights can be found in the United States's Supreme Court decision in the case of *Prince* v. *Massachusetts* (1944).

The case arose out of an attempt by Massachusetts to use its child labour legislation to prevent a family of Jehovah's Witnesses sending its child out upon the streets to sell religious literature. The judge commented,

> it is cardinal with us that the custody, care and nurture of the child reside first in the parents, whose primary function and freedom include preparation for obligations the state can neither supply nor hinder. And it is in recognition of this that [previous Court] decisions have respected the private realm of family life which the state cannot enter.[1]

This judicial thinking was echoed in the celebrated and influential defence of minimum state intervention on behalf of children by Goldstein, Freud and Solnit in *Before the Best Interests of the Child*:

> The child's need for safety within the confines of the family must be met by law through its recognition of family privacy as the barrier to state intrusion upon parental autonomy in childrearing. These rights – parental autonomy, a child's entitlement to autonomous parents, and privacy – are essential ingredients of 'family integrity'.[2]

A number of things should be noted about these rights. First, they appear to be a pair, perhaps so closely linked together that one cannot have one without the other. Second, although Goldstein, Freud and Solnit talk about '*family* integrity', the rights in question are held by the parents alone. Moreover, they imply a lack of rights on the part of the children – respectively to make important choices about their own rearing and education, and to invite monitoring of their treatment within the family by outsiders. Third, these rights are held by the adults against society as a whole, but obviously are most important in disallowing certain kinds of action by the state. Finally, they are not construed as absolute rights. Their exercise is subject to the satisfaction of what might be called the 'harm condition', that is that the children are not subject to any serious risk of harm. I will look at each right in turn.

PRIVACY

The right to privacy can either be defended independently of the right to autonomy, as derivative of it or as equivalent to it. To take the last possibility, some write as if the right to privacy is just the very same thing as the right to rear one's children as one sees fit. If one has this right, then it cannot be legitimate for others, without permission, to interfere in or obstruct the exercise of this entitlement. Although some construe things this way, it seems clear that privacy should be understood as something other than autonomy.

The only plausible way to defend the view that parental privacy is valuable in itself lies with a more general and influential defence of privacy in terms of intimacy.[3] It has been argued that some of the relationships we enjoy with other people are special because of their intimacy. Intimacy in turn is characterised by a mutual disclosure of information about one's self which would not normally and willingly be disclosed to others. The standard examples of such special relationships are those between husband and wife, lovers and friends. Privacy is seen as the necessary condition of such intimate relationships, for only if some things about us are kept private can they be exclusively revealed to our intimates.

Sometimes the family is offered as an example of an intimate relationship. But it seems clear that the family comprises at least two different kinds of relationship. There is not only that between the parents, but also that between them and their children; and *this* relationship is crucially different from the others given as examples. In the first place, intimate relations are between equals, or at least between two persons each possessing rights of choice. That between a parent and their child is one between an independent superior and a dependent subordinate.

Put another way, if the relationship between parent and child is an intimate relationship in exactly the same way as that between lovers or friends, then a child should have a right to co-determine the terms of that relationship, and to withdraw from it. Second, our relations with lovers and friends are chosen, whereas a child does not choose her parents. I do not mean that we can choose who to fall in love with or be drawn to as a friend, but we can choose whether to continue the affair or the friendship. A child cannot elect to have a different set of parents, or indeed to have none at all.

Third, what is at stake in protecting intimate relationships by means of privacy is the possibility of a selective disclosure of information. But the sharing of personal knowledge between parent and child is not what defines parenting – or at least this is not what gives purpose and meaning to a parental right of privacy. Of course it should not be thought that disclosure need be the explicit utterance of some truth about oneself. Lovers can reveal themselves through nakedness and physical contact. Even so, the behaviours of a parent which a parental right to privacy might reasonably be said to protect – including, for instance, caring for, disciplining, helping, educating and comforting a child – do not seem to be essentially about the uncovering of the parent's self.

Fourth, intimacy can only provide a compelling reason for its precondition, privacy, in the absence of any equally or more compelling countervailing reason. Intimates should have their privacy respected only so long as there is no good reason to intrude upon it. It is naturally very hard to see what, in general, such reasons could be in the case of lovers or friends. But in the case of the relationship between parent and child there is one. This is that some parents do abuse or seriously neglect their children. The harm done a child is undetected if perpetrated in 'private'. Moreover, it can continue unobserved. Whilst physical abuse may show itself in lesions, sexual abuse has no obvious public face. Abused children may also have no sense that what is happening to them 'privately' would not be publicly acceptable. Many victims have subsequently reported that they did not think of their abuse as anything other than normal. Finally, the abused child can be 'privately' pressured by his abuser not to make or to retract any accusation of abuse. These are all reasons for thinking that a 'right to privacy' on the part of parents can seriously collude with the perpetration of very significant harm to children.

Fifth, and finally, it is worth noting that the absence of a right to privacy does not mean that the family home is without walls or doors, subject to constant observation and invasion by outsiders. It means only that the parent cannot complain of every intrusion upon the family's domain simply because it is unconsented. Without parental rights to privacy, the state is permitted to intrude into the family's space. Whether it should actually do so, with what frequency and on what occasions, is a matter for debate.

A related point is this. A person may be judged not to have a right to something without its following that they have no kind of moral claim to it. Privacy may be valuable or important to parents, or indeed to the family as a whole. And this will be a relevant consideration when deciding whether to respect their privacy. What is critical is that such a consideration need not amount to the recognition of a right, that is, it need not require the imposition on all others of a duty not to invade that privacy.

Perhaps then it is worth considering what could be the reasons for valuing familial privacy if it is not required for intimacy or, as we will come to, required by parental autonomy. Some have suggested that we need to be able to do privately what can reasonably be called private kinds of thing.[4] These include, most obviously, sexual intercourse and defecation. However, it is very hard to see which kinds of familial activity can be private in this sense.

Again it may be said that what is special about an intimate relationship is not so much the reciprocal disclosure of personal information as its emotional closeness and mutual caring. Arguably, the kind of openness and spontaneity that characterises this kind of relationship is inhibited by the presence of observers. It may be hard to be loving under the watchful gaze of others. However, it is certainly not impossible or unknown. Public displays of familial affection are certainly not taboo or even rare. Moreover, it may well be a peculiarity of our culture, and not a particularly appealing one at that, to regard public expressions of intimacy as improper.

At this point it is worth emphasising that the kind of privacy to which the twentieth-century Western family feels entitled and which it has come to expect is historically and culturally very specific. The phenomenon of the private nuclear family, a self-contained household of kin only, living within its own well-defined space is a peculiarly twentieth-century and Western one, a compound of various changes – social, economic, demographic, cultural and even architectural. Families in previous times, and in other societies, have enjoyed a quite significantly smaller degree of privacy. Of course, it is possible to demonstrate that in all cultures something is done to allocate space, demarcate activities or specify roles so as to constitute a division between the public and the private. This may be managed by conventions, taboos, etiquette or the literal movement of individuals and groups. However, it remains true that in many non-Western cultures households can comprise several kin groups living and sleeping in one unpartitioned building. There is no obvious evidence that the children of such cultures develop into any less normal or sane adults as a result. There is no reason to think that the kind of familial privacy modern Western nuclear families believe it proper to enjoy derives from an invariant, irreducible and inevitable human need.[5]

We come then to the claim that the right to privacy is required if the right to autonomy is to be properly exercised. It is easy to appreciate the common-sense reasoning which probably lies behind such a claim: parents can only effectively exercise direction of their children's lives if they are able to do so unmolested. However, this reasoning needs to be clarified and a number of distinct points separated. Part of what is intended by talk of being unmolested is that parents should not be observed. It may be thought that the mere presence of others undercuts or in some way makes impossible the successful practice of parental autonomy. It is generally true that people can feel discomfited and thus less able to do things when observed. We have all complained of being unable to complete a task whilst someone is watching.

But there are differences between merely being observed, being observed and consequently judged, and being observed and judged with a view to possible intervention. As to the effects of observation alone, the evidence is anecdotal, but many of the subjects of 'fly-on-the-wall' documentaries have stated that, after a period of acclimatisation, the presence of a film crew has ceased even to be registered. Thus it is conceivable that a family could be filmed going about its 'private' business without in any way significantly altering its patterns of behaviour, or, crucially, feeling that its family 'integrity' had been violated.

On the other hand, it can be unsettling to think that an observer not only watches but evaluates. Nevertheless, this is a familiar feature of a great deal of human activity. Moreover, much parenting occurs in situations where outsiders may not only observe but also judge. Families cannot help but conduct business in public, and, even in private, there will be visits to the family home. Most people cannot help but pass judgment, albeit silently, on other people's parenting abilities. Once again, it is worth adding that in many non-Western cultures parenting is shared amongst a number of adults, all of whom may feel ready to offer advice on how best to look after a child.

It is of more significance that, even in our culture, parents countenance outside expert advice for at least the early stages of infancy. The health visitor and midwife are not obviously unwelcome when they offer assistance concerning the care of a young child. Indeed, it is understandable that parents should want to get the feeding, bathing and general minding of their infant right. In this context familial privacy is willingly sacrificed in the interests of the child. We should also remember the claim made by Lasch and Donzelot that the insinuation of rule by the expert into modern Western family life is so thorough that talk of parental privacy is largely mythical.

It would seem to be a very different matter when observation is linked to the possibility of explicit intervention. Doing something while knowing that failure to do it right will lead to restrictions on doing it in future, or even withdrawal of permission to do it, can be deeply disturbing. Yet much will depend on the standards of evaluation and consequences of failure. Normal car drivers are not disconcerted by knowing that a clearly observed and serious departure from standards of safe driving – such as dangerous or drunk driving – will lead to a suspension or withdrawal of their licence. But it would be otherwise if all drivers knew both that their every manoeuvre was being monitored and that the slightest error would jeopardise their future right to drive.

The terms of the observation are also a crucial factor. There is a great difference between continual observation and the possibility of being observed at any one moment, both where the moment in question is signalled in advance and when it is not. There is also a difference between knowing that one is being or might be observed, and the situation in which one is led to believe, falsely, that one will not be observed. Curiously, we would perhaps find it easier to cope with being continually observed than with being deceived. Even so, it may obviously be in the interests of the observer for the observed not to know that they are being observed.

How are all these considerations relevant to the case of parenting? No plausible standard of state intervention can commend none at all. Nor can it seriously be recommended that all parenting be a solely private business. The 'liberal standard' specifies a threshold for action by the state which has to do with the risk of serious harm to the child. The liberal seems to countenance breaching familial privacy only *after* there is a reason to believe the child is being exposed to serious harm, and not to establish that such harm is occurring. It is not that intruding into the private domain shows evidence of a need for statutory protection of the child. It is rather that once the mistreatment of the child has become public then her protection can include measures which override family privacy. For the liberal, it would often seem, harm to a child is serious enough to warrant intervention if it is also and at the same time public enough to come to the state's attention without any need to invade the family's privacy.

It is in this way that the liberal standard privileges familial privacy and links it closely to a preference for minimum state intervention. Without favouring a collectivist solution, it is possible to argue against the value accorded privacy by individualist policies. Continual observation of parenting is almost certainly not feasible in our society, so long as the family persists in something like its present form. But it is fair to insist, against the liberal, that some harms to children are both serious and private in the sense that neither their occasioning nor their effects need be evident publicly. Sexual abuse is of this kind. Yet parenting could be monitored more closely than a right to parental privacy would permit.

To make this point, imagine that there were a child welfare agency with statutory powers of entry into the family home, and rights of access to children. These powers would apply in the case of all children from birth to the mid-teens. Further imagine that the powers did not need to be 'triggered' by any specific evidence – such as a neighbour's complaint or school-teacher's expressed concern. As a matter of regular practice, these visits are not announced in advance, yet parents can reasonably expect to be visited a certain number of times each year.

Now there is no doubt that the parental right to privacy has been abrogated. Equally, it cannot be doubted that these visits would disclose evidence of serious harm to children, which would meet even the liberal standard's threshold requirement for intervention. It is also reasonable to speculate that the prospect of such regular visits would deter parental abuses. Both the disclosure and the possible deterrence would supply a very powerful reason for not respecting parental privacy, namely that the children's own right not to be harmed would thereby be adequately protected.

Would parental privacy still have some powerful countervailing weight in so far as it is needed for the proper exercise of parental autonomy? It is hard to see how the kind of intrusion upon familial privacy which the example envisages would make it impossible or even difficult for parents to go about the business of bringing up children. Certainly, parental autonomy would more likely be exercised in ways which respected the child's right not to be harmed. But even the liberal standard only envisages parental autonomy as legitimate if exercised subject to the child not being seriously harmed. The observation contemplated is not continuous and does not even in itself directly deny parental autonomy. Parental autonomy is only subverted if, as a result of visits by child workers, decisions are taken as to the subsequent upbringing of the child.

What *these* decisions are depends on what standards are adopted for evaluating parenting and what courses of action are deemed appropriate for failure. In other words, the monitoring of parenting is not in itself interventionist. We could imagine the same statutory powers of entry granted to child workers, but solely for the purposes of gathering evidence over a certain period as to the extent of parental abuse of their children.

Liberal writers on child-care policy have a tendency to conflate monitoring or observation as such with the actions that may be taken as a result. They do so by using the single rubric 'intervention'. Thus they tend to assume that more monitoring of parenting (and an abridged right to parental privacy) must be associated with a lowered threshold of harm and a greater willingness to remove children from their parents. In this way a single collectivist bogey is invoked as the only alternative to the liberal standard. Closer observation of children and reduced familial privacy is seen as all part of the state stealing responsibility from parents. But it is important to separate the issues of observation, judgment of parenting and intervention – just as it is important not to speak as if 'autonomy' and 'privacy' comprised a single, indivisible value of 'family integrity'.

AUTONOMY

In so far as parental privacy is clearly separated from parental autonomy, it does not have so obvious or high a value as the liberal standard presumes. The case of autonomy is more complex. The right to autonomy is the same thing as the right to rear, that is, a right possessed by caretakers and enabling them to make significant choices on behalf of the children under their care. It has already been considered in two previous contexts. The first of these was chapter 5. The child liberationist denies that any adult has a right to make choices for children. The defender of the 'caretaker thesis' argues that there is such a right, provided that it is exercised in the long-term interests of the child. I argued that the 'caretaker thesis' has merit in regard to young children, but that it needs to be clearer about what adult interests the caretaking serves to promote.

The second context was chapter 10. There it was denied that natural parents have a right to rear which derives from the fact of their having borne the children in question. If they do have a right to rear, it is plausible to think that it derives from and is consequently dependent upon a prior duty to give a child the best possible upbringing. Children should be reared by what were termed moral parents. Nevertheless, reasons were given for thinking that biological parents should, in the first instance, be presumed to be a child's moral parents. In what follows I want to consider two further considerations which are relevant to any presumptive claim to rear. One has to do with the value of stable parental care; the second concerns the putative value of diversity in adult lifestyles.

Arguably, a child benefits from stable, consistent and continuous parenting. The idea is familiar enough. In order to enjoy normal healthy development, a child needs to be able to form a strong and persisting bond with a parental figure, or pair of parents. This is impossible if, in the most obvious case, the child is moved from parent to parent. The import of this claim is twofold. First, where there is a presumption that a child should be brought up in the first instance by its natural parents, there is now a further presumption that he should stay with them. Second, even if it is shown that the child's interests are on balance best served by removing her from her parents, an alternative which can supply the prospect of a long-term and stable parenting should be found as quickly as possible.

The relevance of this to any right to rear is as follows. If someone does have a right, or even a strong claim to rear children, then they also have a good claim to exercise it uninterruptedly over the period of the child's minority. The latter claim is the stronger the greater the value and importance that is attached to the stability of caretaker–child relationships.

The second set of considerations relevant to the parental claim to rear has to do with the value of diverse adult lifestyles. Talk of the kind of upbringing to which each child has a right is arguably empty unless we have a clear and agreed ideal of the adult. The measure of any upbringing is its outcome. The better the eventual product, the better the process of rearing by which it was produced. We saw in chapter 5 that the 'caretaker thesis' remains equivocal as to the kind of adult an upbringing should aim to produce. In particular, there is a difficult tension between realising a child's particular nature and safeguarding his 'open future', between ensuring that his innate character is properly developed and giving him the self-determinative capacity to make a full choice between various adult options.

At this point it is relevant to introduce the liberal ideal of tolerating a diversity in adult ways of life. Each person subscribes to a way of life, informed by more or less explicit beliefs and ideals. One individual favours asceticism, another aestheticism, yet another athleticism and so on. The liberal believes that, subject to its not harming others or denying them a like freedom to lead *their* lives, each person's choice of lifestyle should be tolerated. If parents exercise a right to rear their children then this diversity is reproduced in so far as the young inherit the values, beliefs and general outlook of their adult caretakers. That they should do so is readily understandable.

First, parents *share* their life with their children, and in conditions of considerable intimacy and emotional closeness. Families live, eat, play, holiday, travel, entertain themselves and worship together. It is natural that the children should come to share the outlook which informs that life. Second, the young naturally *identify* with the significant adults in their lives. They seek to follow the example of those adults they see as models.

Third, parents want to see the values and beliefs that matter to them *survive*. They want an esteemed way of life to persist. Children are naturally seen as the means to do this. Parents cannot remain indifferent to the general outlook on life that their child acquires. In this sense Charles Fried, quoted in chapter 10, is correct when he says that a parent's right to rear her children in her own values is merely an extension of her own right to live by these same values. He was wrong to think or imply that this is so only because the child is merely an extension, a part or a product of the parent.

For the liberal, the transgenerational reproduction of outlook, culture, values and tradition is acceptable so long as it is not accomplished at the expense of the child's self-determination or particular nature. The child must still have an 'open future' when he reaches adulthood. He must be able to review and evaluate what he has inherited from his parents, choosing a different life for himself if he so decides. It is important to add that an adult can exercise her own autonomy only in relation to the character she already has. An autonomous person must have *some* values, beliefs and dispositions, and it is precisely this that someone acquires in their upbringing. Ironically, parents would fail to produce an autonomous adult if they gave their children *no* outlook on life.

A problem remains. Why is diversity a good thing? Is there not one good way to lead a human life, and is there not as a consequence only one kind of upbringing that can be described as the best possible – the one that leads a child to lead the best possible adult life? At this point the liberal can appeal to an idea which serves as a philosophical foundation of contemporary liberalism. This is that sincere, rational and autonomous individuals disagree in quite radical ways about what the good life is, and that, in consequence, the state should not, by its policies or laws, favour any particular conception of the good life. It should be officially neutral on the question of the good.[6] There are at least as many conceptions of the best upbringing as there are conceptions of the good life. As the state should be neutral on the latter, so it should not take a view of the best upbringing.

The liberal society seeks to be tolerant of diversity in lifestyles, and this will inevitably be reflected in various modes of parenting. The right to autonomy ensures and protects plural parenting. Each parenting may secure a good upbringing for the child so long as it safeguards the child's 'open future' and does not neglect her particular nature. Any further prescription of how any child must be reared would presuppose some ideal of the good life, and that is not the proper prerogative of the state.

Yet even these minimum requirements do set limits to permissible parenting. And the more a society is agreed on the value of certain lifestyles, outlooks, talents, sensibilities and dispositions, the more it will encourage the kinds of parenting that introduce children to them. The contrast between collectivist childrearing according to a single standard and the toleration of as many styles of parenting as there are parents is thus too stark. Much will depend on the extent of social agreement on the good life.

13

COLLECTIVISM

Thus far the 'liberal standard' and its presuppositions have been subjected to extended criticism. In this chapter I want to seriously examine collectivist alternatives.

PLATO'S PROPOSAL

The most notable philosophical defence of the view that the state should assume direct and unmediated control of its children's upbringing is Plato's. In the *Republic* he argues that the Rulers of his ideally just society should have no family and that the upbringing of their children should be collectively managed: 'in a State destined to reach the height of good government wives and children must be held in common; men and women must have the same education throughout and share all pursuits' (*Republic*, VIII.543a).[1]

Plato offers three broad reasons for his proposal. First, the regulation of marriage and childrearing is urged on eugenic grounds to ensure the perfectibility of the Rulers:

> if we are to keep our flock at the highest pitch of excellence, there should be as many unions of the best of both sexes, and as few of the inferior, as possible, and . . . only the offspring of the better unions should be kept.
>
> (*Republic*, V.459d)

Plato also insists upon a rigorously specified public education for leadership.

Plato's second reason for his collectivism is his belief that men and women may equally fulfil the offices of state. Certainly, he sees no reason why women as well as men should not be competent, and therefore trained, to rule. Thus childrearing will not be an exclusively female occupation: 'As soon as children are born, they will be taken in charge by officers appointed for the purpose, who may be women as well as men or both, since offices are to be shared by both sexes' (*Republic*, V.460b).

However, Plato's main explicit reason for his proposal is to ensure the unity of the state which is its highest value: 'nothing does it more good than whatever tends to bind it together and make it one' (*Republic*, V.462b). He takes communality in all things to be the guarantor of unity, just as, correspondingly, disunity and dissension are assured when claims can be made to something as 'mine' or 'not mine' (*Republic*, V.462). Rulers, having no family of their own to distract them, look instead to each other as their family: 'For all wives and children were to be in common, to the intent that no one should then know his own child, but they were to imagine that they were all one family' (*Timaeus*, 18c). The abolition of the family is the corollary of the abolition of private property. Both are institutions which, by disposing to self-interested individualism, subvert the ideal motive of collective loyalty.

Having given these reasons for his collectivism, Plato simply discounts any claims that might be made against it on the basis of a parent's rights over children. He defends compulsory education, for example, 'on the ground that the child is even more the property of the State than of his parents' (*Laws*, VII.804d). And in the *Republic* he argues that between certain prescribed ages, a woman should bear and a man beget children 'for the commonwealth' (*Republic*, V.460e).

Remembering all the criticisms to which Plato's proposal has been subsequently subjected, it is worth noting that he himself saw its desirability as indisputable. Only its feasibility was a matter of serious contention (*Republic*, V.457d). I will briefly review these criticisms having particular regard to the implication that Plato's 'collectivism' may somehow stand as a contemporary alternative to liberal individualism. In this fashion critics also speak easily of Plato's 'communism' and 'feminism' as if the *Republic* were a present-day tract which might unproblematically be cited alongside contemporary defences of these ideals.

It should first be remembered that Plato's 'communist' proposal applies only to the state's leadership; it does not include the largest class of producers. Moreover, it is a 'communism' which does not affect the class-based nature of production, or do away with rigid social hierarchy. As for Plato's defence of the proposal, eugenism is, perhaps rightly, regarded nowadays with deep suspicion. It is enough for our purposes to note that the proposal requires collective agreement both as to 'excellence' in the human species, and on the methods of education to ensure perfect nurture. Lacking such agreement, the proposal could only be imposed by the 'wise' Ruler. What might disturb the modern progressive outlook as much as eugenism is Plato's assumption

179

that sexual union exists solely or mainly for the purposes of procreation. Whereas the Christian Church sees marital intercourse to procreate as being a fulfilment of men's and women's 'natural' and God-given roles, Plato views procreation as exclusively serving the state.

However, it is not inconceivable that a society should wish to exercise some collective control over reproduction. This could, least controversially, be in the interests of population control. But there are feasible measures to this end which both fall short of the infanticidal brutality hinted at by Plato, and would be consistent with the preservation of the family. For instance, the government could penalise couples who exceeded the prescribed number of children by the withdrawal of important benefits or by the imposition of graduated fines. The Chinese government has since the 1950s sought to impose a 'one child' per couple policy in an effort to curb its rapidly burgeoning population. The problems this policy has encountered – traditional preferences for a son encouraging the infanticide of daughters, rich couples viewing financial penalties for breaching the policy as merely a price to be paid for extra children – are a good indication of the practical difficulties of enforcing population controls. It should be added that a state may seek to *increase* the population when a national birth rate slumps. Again, there are real practical difficulties in effectively controlling reproduction.

The frequently voiced view that Plato is a 'feminist' has drawn merited criticism.[2] His is certainly not a 'feminism' which urges the emancipation of women as of right. Rather, he wishes the state to be more efficiently served by having the use of women currently wasted in the maintenance of households. It is notable that, in general, Plato does not see the abolition of the family as a means to individual liberation but rather as facilitating the better functioning of the state.

Plato's main reason for collectivising the propagation and rearing of children is to secure unity. It is this idea which has provoked most criticism, ever since, in the *Politics*, Aristotle rightly challenges the twin assumptions that unity in Plato's sense is a desirable political end, and that his 'communism' would serve such an end.[3] It is Aristotle who insists that a political community is an association, an aggregation of different, mutually dependent individuals whose efforts can be complementary and reciprocally useful. Echoing this notion is the modern liberal view of society as necessarily comprising a diversity of individual lives.

When political theory commends the unity of the state, it normally means harmony between its disparate elements. However, when Plato talks of unity he seems to intend unicity, that all differences should be abolished and every distinguishing identity effaced in the name of one single entity, the state. The family is abolished not because it is somehow opposed to the state's purposes, but because it is a source of identification for the citizen other than the state. This emphasis upon oneness, together with Plato's insistence that everything be evaluated in terms of its functionality for the state as a whole, supports the familiar charge that the *Republic* is a manifesto for totalitarianism. One need not go that far. Aristotle's criticism is telling enough. To seek Platonic unity for the *polis* is self-defeatingly to seek its destruction. A functioning self-sufficient *polis* needs its internal elements to be differentiated and mutually supporting.

More relevant here is Aristotle's second criticism, namely that a community of wives and children cannot yield the unity Plato desires. Plato presumes that the intensity of attachment which defines familial membership can be redirected into feelings of loyalty towards the whole state. Aristotle claims that such communalistic feelings will not be familial emotions writ large but rather attenuated and diluted ones. He speaks of there being only 'a watery sort of fraternity'.[4] The ties of kinship cannot survive when they extend across a society. As Ernest Barker glosses, 'when 1,000 are father to the same child, each father is only 1/1,000 father'.[5]

This is an important general point. Many critics of the family take greatest exception to its parochiality and partiality. Yet they are unable to deny the very real strength and depth of the ties and loyalties which it engenders. In response they urge that these affections be generalised to society at large. The whole community should become one big happy family. But it may well be that its very particularity is the source of the family's intimacy. I can love my family with the emotional profundity I do only because it is my family, and is confined to a well-defined circle of persons. I could not love all my co-citizens as I do my parents, siblings and children.

Now it might be thought that this criticism is guilty of begging the question if it simply assumes that family feeling can only be felt for family. After all, evidence from communities like the kibbutzim suggests that an individual might successfully be brought up to think of the collective as its parents and its peers as its siblings.[6] But Aristotle does suggest two considerations which support his argument. The first is size. Plato prescribed 5,000 as the membership of his ideal *polis*; Aristotle recommended that each citizen should know all the others by sight and ruled out anything over 100,000. The kibbutz's membership would be measured in hundreds rather than in tens of thousands. Modern social solidarity cannot, however, be based on such familiarity. The difficulties Aristotle thought there would be in extending one's familial feelings to all of the *polis* are surely multiplied beyond resolution when it comes to a modern nation-state. That is not to say that co-nationals may not feel bound together by ties of loyalty towards and affection for their shared traditions, culture and identity. But the nation cannot be anything more than a metaphorical family, and the fellow feelings of national attachment cannot approach the devotions of shared kinship which Plato envisaged.

The second consideration concerns the source of one's feelings. Aristotle argues that you cannot care for what you do not like. There is in the fact of consanguinity, even in the simple fact of sharing together a life apart from the rest of society, a basis for affinity and affection. One's fellow citizens need not be strangers but one does not start off from anything other than shared membership of the state. And it can be hard to love those with whom one has so little of obvious significance in common.

Aristotle's objections are not decisive, but they are weighty. What does count against not only Plato's proposal but any collectivisation of childrearing is that it requires unanimity concerning the purposes and ends of parenting. A community must agree on how best to bring up its children; it must form a single wise parent. And the agreement must be not only that children are to be brought up collectively, but also on the precise form of this upbringing. Everyone must agree to see their parenting role transferred to the state and its officers. Failing that, the collective rearing must be imposed on all, including those who dissent.

It is surely significant then that the kibbutzim were voluntary associations. Not only were they formed in a self-consciously pioneering spirit by individuals keen to create a new kind of society, but the kibbutzniks' willingness to see their children brought up communally derived from an almost Platonic desire to instil a new sense of identity in the next generation, and to extirpate individualistic attachments and interests which might undermine communal loyalty and devotion. In a modern society it is unreasonable to demand of individuals that they should be forced to live as others may choose. This is not to deny people the right to experiment with communal forms of existence. Some may wish to forswear the family and rear their children within a group. They should surely be allowed to do so as long as their communal forms of childrearing are consistent with the protection of the child's interests. Any child who is communally reared must be assured at least the minimal level of welfare guaranteed to all children. The state's acknowledgement that children can be reared in communes as well as within families does not amount to an abandonment of its role as *parens patriae*, ultimate protector of all minors within its jurisdiction. As long as there are those who seek to found a family and bring up their children within it, the writ of a Platonic republic can only be extended by force. The coercive imposition of communal rearing practices would mean that parents faced the stark choice of living against their will under a communal regime or giving up their children. Either way, they would have to forsake their parental role.

In this way Plato's proposal offends against the liberal view that individual liberty entails a diversity of lifestyles, and thus of childrearing. Plato's monism is simply and straightforwardly incompatible with liberal pluralism. The right to autonomy is the right to bring up children within a family as one chooses. It is violated by Plato's scheme. However, there is an even more general right which cannot be countenanced by Plato's collectivism, and that is the right to bring up children within a family if one chooses. The right to have, or found a family – even if its children are subject to close supervision by the state – is one which seems so fundamental as to be undeniable, and yet it is plainly abrogated in the *Republic*. But, without going as far as Plato recommends, does even this right have to be accepted as basic?

THE LICENSING OF PARENTS

The right to have or to found a family, the right to be a parent, is an entitlement to some combination of bearing and rearing a child. One might bear and rear one's own child, or rear another's after some process of adoption. What sorts of reason might be given for thinking that an individual should not be free to have and bring up their child? In chapter 10 I gave some reasons for thinking that the right to bear is not absolute. There I mentioned two possible kinds of constraint on such a right. The first had to do with the effects upon others of the birth of a child; that it might, for instance, contribute to a problem of overpopulation or inherit a contagious, lethal disease. The second had to do with the well-being of the prospective child, that she was guaranteed at least a certain level of existence. We can note now a third constraint which concerns the well-being of the prospective parent.

It would be unacceptably paternalistic to deny someone the opportunity to bear a child solely on the grounds that to do so would be injurious to the bearer. This is because it is generally thought impermissible to prevent someone from doing something which has, or carries the risk of having, adverse personal consequences so long as they are aware of these consequences and are deciding in a tolerably rational state of mind. A woman may know that continuation of a pregnancy is dangerous but feel that she wants to take the risk. However, a judgment that someone is seriously incapable of appreciating the effects of pregnancy or childbirth may be viewed as warranting a refusal to permit the pregnancy to continue. It is at least partly for this reason that occasional, if controversial, decisions have been taken to sterilise compulsorily or perform an abortion on a severely mentally handicapped person.

Returning to the issue of the child's welfare, a child has, as we argued in chapter 10, a right to an upbringing that meets a specified threshold. Any upbringing should be an adequate one and every child is entitled to a minimum level of care. For any prospective child there are three possibilities: that his own parents are able to discharge their duty adequately, that there is some set of parents but not his own who can do this, and that there is no possibility of the child being properly looked after. In the last case there is good reason for concluding that the parent should not bear the child. In chapter 10 I argued that where any child born to some parents cannot be assured a life that is not just better than non-existence but one that is tolerably decent, then no child should be conceived by those parents. In the second case it would follow that the parent should be allowed to bear but not herself rear the child. The natural parents should make provision for their child to be adopted by those guardians who can afford the child a minimally decent life. Only in the first case does the natural parent appear to have a claim both to bear and rear his own child.

Chapter 10 argued that the mere fact of bearing a child did not ground any right to rear her, and that any parental right to rear was conditional upon the discharge of a duty to give the child a minimally decent upbringing. It also suggested some reasons for thinking that natural parents might be best placed to act, in the first instance, as the child's caretakers. Chapter 12 pointed to the value of stable parenting as a reason for children to stay with their caretakers. The import of such reasoning is, in effect, that decisions are made after the birth, and to that extent tend to favour the natural parents. The child, being born, is (normally) with his natural parent(s) and should stay with them unless good reasons can be given for moving him. The facts of attachment and parent–child bonding are such that any post-natal removal of the child to other parents is bound to be deeply traumatic to both parent and child. Making choices for a child after she is born has serious costs. But why should decisions not be taken in advance of any possible birth? Why shouldn't the state, or society as a whole, decide whether a child should be born and, if he is, to which parents he should be allocated?

One obvious means of doing this is the 'licensing' of parenthood. As this is sometimes discussed a licence to parent is a permission both to bear and to rear a child. A licence only to procreate – where this meant that someone could bear a child only for her to be reared by another – is imaginable. Indeed, this would apply to a commissioned surrogate mother. And such a type of licence, if required, might be refused on the grounds that a woman was judged incapable of ensuring the health of the foetus during pregnancy. Similarly, a mother might be refused a licence to have further children because her behaviour during a previous pregnancy was deemed to have harmed her child as a foetus. Recent American law cases, permitting children or their representatives to sue retrospectively for damages done to them before they were born, at least suggest that a mother can be held responsible for the level of care given *in utero* to her prospective child.

A licence only to rear is also imaginable, and this is what is normally meant by talk of licensing. Directed at natural parents, licensing presupposes that the mere fact of procreation is not enough to demonstrate fitness to parent. Individuals must show that they can rear their own children.

The proposal to license parents may seem so outrageous, so wrong-headed and unjust, as to merit immediate rejection. It is worth offering three reasons why it should be given serious consideration. First, society does presently license a range of activities which are potentially harmful to others and whose safe performance requires a proven competence. Driving and practising medicine are obvious examples. There are good reasons to think parenting is such an activity. It exposes children to harm which can be avoided through the exercise of demonstrable skills. Parenting is thus an activity which should be licensed as the others are.[7]

Second, society is prepared to license *some* parents. Child welfare agencies must be satisfied that prospective foster and adoptive parents are suitable, and this is normally done by observing stringent guidelines for their assessment. It is surely inconsistent and unfair to evaluate possible parents in these cases but not in others. *All* parents should be evaluated for their fitness.

Third, the apparently obvious wrongness of licensing parents may derive from a basic belief that humans should not need the state's permission to rear their own children. But this is to say that they have a right to rear, and that is what has been disputed. Moreover, what is denied is not a right to cohabit, or have sexual relations, or even to bear children. What is at issue is the right to bring up one's own children. Licensing parents cannot then be dismissed as manifestly wrong, and there are some grounds for thinking it might be justified.

Licensing parenthood is closely linked to the proposal to separate the institutions of marriage and family, so long as marriage is thereby regarded as an essentially private and voluntary matter between its partners. Nothing should prevent two people from choosing to cohabit. They can make a more or less formal agreement on the terms and length of their cohabitation, disposition of any jointly owned property and so on. Again there seems no reason why they should not be free to celebrate or sanctify their agreement to cohabit in a more or less public ceremony with a religious content appropriate to their convictions. However, should they wish to procreate then, so the proposal continues, their decision requires public sanction, since the bringing of children into the world and their adequate subsequent care

are legitimate concerns of the rest of society. Individuals do not need to demonstrate a competence to become cohabiting lovers; they do to be parents.

Arguably, it is very important to break the normative link between marriage and family. For it is too often assumed either that the purpose of marriage is to found a family, or that, conversely, a family requires a marriage at its heart. Severing the link permits individuals to form a couple without any expectation that they will, as a matter of course or what is 'natural', have children. Equally, the absence of the link means that families can be countenanced whose parents are neither a couple nor married.

There is, though, one difficult problem for the proposal. A major concern of those who suggest the separation of marriage and family is the instability of the former and the need for stability in the latter. A marriage, being between two freely consenting adults, cannot be guaranteed to last. It would be wrong to require that individuals stay with uncongenial partners just because they once contracted to cohabit. However, it does seem that the child benefits from continuous and stable parenting. If the family and marriage are linked, then this desideratum is likely to lead to pressures to keep a marriage together, even in the face of its partners' unwillingness to remain married. Certainly, conservative defenders of the family are consistent in wanting to make marital separation and divorce harder to secure.

If, on the other hand, the family and marriage are separated, then a way must be found to ensure stable parenthood in the face of a marriage's breakdown. This may be done by society's defining parenthood in such a fashion that its duties are dischargeable whether or not one parent remains married to the other. Many divorced parents manage this, whereas others find it very difficult. Or a solution may be to think of parenthood as devolving less exclusively on the child's parents. Stability is assured for the child by the community, or a network of adults, caring for her alongside her parents. The importance of a 'network' is something to which I shall return.

If a parental licence is to be granted, then it will be on the basis of an ascertainable fitness or competence to parent. Being part of a married heterosexual couple is certainly not a sufficient condition of such fitness, and probably not necessary. Fit parents may be married or unmarried, single or multiple, heterosexual, gay or lesbian. The liberal tolerance of diversity in childrearing practices should, if consistent, extend to at least the possibility of these alternatives. Yet it is noteworthy that most liberals who speak of permitting parental autonomy in a child's upbringing seem to mean only that a heterosexual couple should decide how to rear their child.

There are at least three kinds of reason why individuals should not be given a licence to parent. The first is the probability that the child would inherit a serious disease or disability. There are a number of difficult and interrelated issues here. There is the question of whether a very seriously handicapped child should even be brought into existence. As we saw in chapter 10, the terms of this question change according to whether the choice is between a handicapped child and no child at all, or between a handicapped child and a normal child. If – and this can be controversial – the key consideration is whether such a child would have the reasonable prospect of leading a life worth living, then it is relevant to know whether the parents can guarantee such a life. Being the parent of a seriously handicapped child involves significant extra burdens. A couple who showed no understanding of the difficulties in raising such a child, or no willingness to take on the responsibility, might be thought unfit to parent *this* child.

The second reason for denying a parental licence would be the social and economic situation of the prospective parents; that they were, for instance, financially incapable of offering an adequate home for the child. The third reason would be the psychological character of the parents; that they were, for instance, so immature as to have no idea how to raise a child properly, or disposed to cruelty and abuse. The defenders of the proposal to license parents presuppose that evident fitness to parent can be identified. The proposal apparently receives strong support from the fact that adoptive and foster parents are screened. This process presumes not only that unfit parents can be detected, but also that there is a real point in doing so, namely the protection of the child's interests. If this is the case with adoptive and foster parents, then why not also with natural ones? The only plausible difference rests on an assumption that biology alone equips an individual to be a good parent. This, it may be replied, is not only an implausible but a dangerous assumption.

What then are the objections to 'licensing parents'? The most fundamental theoretical one, that natural parents have a right to rear their own children, has been shown to lack foundation. That natural parents should not have to show their competence to parent because they do not need to, being 'naturally' good parents, is also a false generalisation. The important objections to licensing are practical and of four kinds: the first is that no acceptable standard of competence could be devised; the second is that the fair and efficient administration of licensing could not be managed; the third is that sanctions against licence violations would be impossibly difficult to organise and the fourth is that the purposes by which licensing is justified could better be secured by less objectionable means.

The first objection has less force if what is to be identified is palpable unfitness rather than fitness to parent. It is easier to know who is a bad parent than to agree on what counts as a good one. This is reflected in our current willingness to tolerate different styles of parenting, subject to no serious or obvious harm coming to the child. Yet even if a society can agree on what a bad parent is, it must, for the purposes of licensing, know this *ex ante*, that is, before the child is born. This requires a well-established predictive theory as to the relationship between present characteristics and future abuse. On the assumption that a person's socio-economic circumstances could change overnight but their character remain fairly constant, the need is for an exclusively psychopathological portrait of the abusing parent. The problems are whether there is one, and even if there were how reliable it could possibly be.

Research into child abuse has failed to yield a single, uniform cause, and has certainly not managed to produce a clear and distinct psychological picture of the abusing parent. There are factors, other than individual psychopathology, which are thought to play some role in the incidence of child abuse. Importantly these include circumstances, such as social and economic conditions, which cannot be guaranteed to remain as they were at the time of the licensing review. Someone who is not now a likely abuser may become one later in worsened conditions.

Clearly, social workers and policy-makers would like an account of child abuse that made possible rigorous prediction of its occurrence. They could identify abusers in advance or predict that abuse would occur from a recognition of certain predisposing parental traits. To the extent that theories of abuse have conformed to a medical model, those dealing with abuse have been misled into thinking that such prediction might be possible. The first attempts to characterise and understand abuse were made by medical professionals, and they have continued to represent it as a disease with precisely identifiable causes. Yet their persistent failure to come up with an all-embracing predictive theory of child abuse shows that the medical model is inappropriate. Indeed, it is in many ways implausible to expect that it ever could be.[8]

There is also a political point. Concentration on individual psychology may lead to neglect of the social preconditions of abuse. A society may be so keen to identify and debar individual bad parents as to fail to remedy the economic and social causes of child abuse. An emphasis on licensing would be at the expense of improvements in housing, education, health and childcare.

Even if there was a single predictive theory of child abuse in terms of individual psychopathology it could do no more than speak of 'risks' and 'probability'. It could not hope to establish a 100 per cent correlation between present traits and future abusive behaviour. If a successful licensing programme is one that prevents all potential abusers from becoming parents, then licensing can only succeed at the expense of denying perfectly fit parents the opportunity to rear their own children. When the detection of guilt is less than certain a number of 'innocents' must be caught up in the net to ensure all the guilty are included.

Society might calculate that such costs are acceptable, and claim a lower incidence of abuse among adoptive parents as evidence that children do benefit from a licensing procedure. Nevertheless, even if natural parents do not have a right to rear their own children, they do seem to have a claim to do so which is stronger than that of an adoptive parent to bring up *some* child. The interest of natural parents in rearing their own children, and the clear costs occasioned by their being prevented from doing so, cannot be discounted. At the very least, there seems to be a greater injustice in the screening of natural parents than of adoptive or foster parents.

The second practical objection to licensing is that its administration could not be fair or efficient. Unintended mistakes will be made, and the licensers may corruptly award licences to, or withhold them from, the wrong people. The defenders of the proposal may justifiably reply that these are possibilities which apply generally to any licence scheme, and that there are standard ways of reducing their occurrence to a minimum. Thus the performance of driving examiners can be independently and regularly audited to ensure consistency; the terms, conditions and place of examination can be arranged so as to diminish the opportunities and motive for corruption, and so on. The defender of parental licensing will conclude that such errors as will unavoidably still be made are a fair price to pay for the significant abatement of child abuse.

The third objection to licensing is how those who defy its terms are to be punished. What is to be done with the recidivist unlicensed begetter? Compulsory abortion or sterilisation suggest themselves but are extremely unpalatable solutions; the latter not least for its implication that a presently unfit parent will never be otherwise. It will be practically impossible to prevent all human beings who might be deemed unfit to bear children from having them. Even with lawful intentions mistakes are made.

Nevertheless, the problem can be exaggerated. A defender of licensing is presumably committed to removing children at birth from their unlicensed natural parents and reallocating them to licensed adoptive parents. Some individuals might continue to have child after child knowing in advance that they will not be able to keep them. There are those now who continue to have children despite being aware that they will be taken into care. But a society sufficiently concerned about the problem of child abuse to institute licensing is unlikely to fail in the provision of alternatives, such as licensed adoptive parents and residential institutions.

The knowledge that state agencies will, consistently and unfailingly, remove children from unlicensed parents should act as some kind of deterrent to those who might otherwise risk removal for the chance of an unapproved child. Indeed, only removal will work. If the law or policy is not prosecuted but merely serves an exhortatory or educational purpose it will probably not discourage bad parents from having children. After all, bad parents as much as good parents have very strong interests in having children. Financial disincentives – fines or the removal of benefits – are likely to be ineffective and to be seen by the well-off as merely the price that can be paid for having one's own child. The well-off can buy adoptive children; they can also pay to keep, and badly rear, their own. The removal of the child itself is certainly sufficient punishment of a palpably bad parent. An unlicensed driver should be punished for putting other road users at risk and prevented from continuing to do so. The purpose of licensing parents is to protect their children, and this purpose is served when the children are, through being removed, no longer at risk from their unlicensed parents.

The three objections to licensing discussed thus far are serious but perhaps not insuperable. The fourth objection is decisive. For there are less objectionable means of securing the ends which would justify licensing. Licensing as proposed is of *all* prospective parents. In this way, its defenders argue, the very bad ones will be excluded. But a great number of these may come to the attention of state agencies without a need to review every single possible parent. Thus those who have committed offences against children, or who have already shown themselves to be abusing parents, may reasonably be denied the opportunity to rear. Perhaps we might extend the category of debarred persons to include anyone who has been convicted of a crime of extreme violence. This is for society to judge. The fact remains that the state, without a universal licensing programme, may be able successfully to identify the worst potential abusers.

The point is that a licensing programme is proposed as a means of excluding *all* bad parents. The argument so far is that there can be no certain way to identify all bad parents, and that any licensing programme served by a theory that can necessarily speak only of probabilities and risks will almost certainly make serious mistakes, misidentifying both good and bad parents. However, when the category is restricted to the very bad parent and is based upon previous convictions then these kinds of risk are virtually eliminated.

There is a further point. Defenders of a licensing programme cannot remain content with licensing alone. They will be committed to an extensive and rigorous monitoring of a child's development after his birth. Any licence may be revoked upon evidence of incompetence in the activity for which the licence was originally granted. Thus, a licenser of parents would have to be assured that even licensed parents were still fit to care for their children. To presume that the acquisition of a licence guarantees non-malicious parenting thereafter is dangerously naive, and at odds with the scrupulous care for children which can be said to motivate the proposal for licensing.

Such extensive monitoring would detect the harms that would warrant removal of a child from her parents and thus, other things being equal, ensure the discontinuance of the abuse. Now, such monitoring is objectionable if parents are thought to have a right to privacy. Notwithstanding the arguments given in chapter 12 against such a right, its violation would clearly be less objectionable than the removal of children at birth from their natural parents – especially where, as is inevitable with the licensing programme, this is mistakenly done to fit parents. Thus, having already excluded those who can be confidently identified as very bad prospective parents, monitoring alone does all the work at less cost that the more cumbersome and contentious licensing scheme is designed to do.

It might be said that such monitoring only detects bad parents *after* harm has been done to their children. But chapter 12 argued that this was more aptly claimed of the kinds of monitoring allowed by the 'liberal standard'. The monitoring of parents envisaged in the example from that chapter would be far more extensive, and would consequently serve to prevent and deter a much greater amount of child abuse than is possible with the liberal standard.

A final brief point about the defence of licensing. Too easy use is made of the apparent asymmetry in licensing adoptive or foster parents but requiring nothing similar of natural parents. It is often said that there is something unjust or anomalous about licensing the former but not the latter, with the implication that either all parents should be licensed or there should be no licence needed for foster and adoptive parents. But if adoptive or foster parents are assessed it is not simply or solely to gauge whether they are fit parents as such. It is to evaluate whether or not they are well suited and situated to cope with children who, *because* they are being adopted or fostered, may present particular and possibly serious difficulties – those, for instance, arising from the fact that they have been rejected or abused by their natural parents. Adopted and fostered children differ from others in that they may be much harder to rear. These differences may thus provide some, even if not the whole, reason for exercising particular care in selecting their future guardians.

14

THE PROBLEM OF CHILD ABUSE

THE DISCOVERY OF ABUSE

The problem of child abuse presents a certain apparent paradox. Children have been cruelly treated for as long as there has been human society. Yet it is only in recent times, when arguably things are better for children, that there has been an almost obsessive social interest in how much children are abused. There is abundant evidence of past maltreatment. Children, throughout history and across cultures, have been the victims of practices of abandonment, infanticide, sacrifice, mutilation, slavery, excessive discipline and exploitation at work.[1]

However, an organised movement to protect children began, in both the USA and UK, only in the 1880s, and the first legislation to defend children's interests dates from the beginning of the twentieth century. The last thirty years alone have witnessed an extraordinary 'rediscovery' of child abuse which is now commonly represented as socially endemic. It was in 1962 that the 'battered child syndrome' was first formally described. In the 1980s the focus has been on sexual abuse with, in Britain, the events surrounding the Cleveland 'crisis' of 1987 stimulating intense and widespread public debate on the subject. Various accounts are offered to explain our current concern with child abuse. These include the influence of the women's movement in exposing intra-familial violence in general, the concern of elements within the medical profession to advance their own status by securing a socio-medical 'label' for abuse, and the creation of a 'moral panic' in response to broader worries about the apparent decline of the traditional family.[2]

What does seem clear is that, in all the talk of child abuse as a new problem, two related mistakes are often made. The first is to think that child abuse itself, rather than its recognition and description, is a modern phenomenon. The second is to believe that child abuse is more extensive than in the past, whereas what, in fact, has increased is the reporting of abuse. This in turn may be ascribed to the explicit acknowledgement by society that child abuse does exist and that an account of it can be rendered.

Nevertheless, the fact that child abuse is a modern discovery is significant for how we view the concept. First, long-established usage gives confidence in a concept's settled meaning. Where the provenance of a term is comparatively recent our command may be less secure. Second, the newness of the concept underlines its status as a 'human kind' rather than a 'natural kind'. Natural kind terms carve nature at its joints; the lines between them correspond to divisions of reality. By contrast, human kind terms are artifices, or constructions of human language and thought. A number of writers view 'child abuse' as being, in this sense, a social construction.[3] Third, in consequence of the first two considerations, 'child abuse' is a term whose meaning can be and is contested. Moreover, it is contested by groups interested in supplying a definitive account of the phenomenon. Each seeks to define child abuse, offer an aetiological account of it, and, crucially, lay claim to be uniquely or specially qualified to deal with it. Thus, whereas the early voluntary agencies such as the NSPCC and Barnardos strove to give themselves an officially sanctioned role in the detection and remedying of child cruelty, it was paediatricians who offered a medicalised account of the 'battered child' in 1962.[4] Again, it has been specialists in child *sexual* abuse who have pioneered and defended the use of particular (and often controversial) methods for its detection.

At each moment in the progressive modern uncovering of child abuse a new form of abuse has been specified. The philosopher and historian of ideas, Ian Hacking, comments on the concept of child abuse: 'Malleable and expansionist, it has gobbled up more and more kinds of bad acts'; '[N]o one had any glimmering, in 1960, of what was going to count as child abuse in 1990.'[5] Those unsympathetic to this expansionist development of the term can react in one of two very different ways. The first is to cease using the term 'child abuse', and to talk simply of a range of harms that can befall children through human action and inaction. Rather than singling out a particular class of harms as 'abuse', the harmfulness of *all* acts and omissions in respect of children would be graded. The second reaction to conceptual expansionism is conceptual conservatism. An orthodox, narrow definition of child abuse is agreed upon with any attempts to broaden the term strenuously resisted.

In favour of expansionism, albeit of a constrained kind, is the conviction that child abuse is a special sort of harm done to children and that we should not, by definitional fiat, settle the question of what forms of harm done to children are special. Caution in conceptual expansionism arises from recognition of the role of 'persuasive definition' in argument. A persuasive definition is one which gives a term a new meaning without any change in its evaluative or emotive force, thereby serving the purposes of changing people's attitudes towards a phenomenon.[6] Hence someone offering a persuasive definition of child abuse might seek to persuade people that something, not previously covered by the term, is nevertheless child abuse and should be viewed with the same disapproval that attaches to all other instances of abuse. The scope of the pejorative word is extended whilst its capacity to evoke the appropriate attitudes of disapproval is retained.

Terms such as 'real', 'genuine' or 'true' often accompany persuasive definitions. Thus, anti-abortionists often remark that abortion is the real abuse of children that disfigures our society. Persuasive definition is not of itself improper, although philosophers rightly view with suspicion any attempt to win a case or make a point simply by changing the meaning of words. Any change in the definition of a term needs to be supported by independent argument and evidence. Moreover, there is a reasonable fear that attempts at persuasive definition can backfire. If we do not feel the appropriate degree of revulsion for what is urged to fall under the extended category then we may doubt the legitimacy not only of the extension but also of the original term. Child abuse is not everything the persuasive definer says it is because not everything so defined does horrify us. But then – we may add – nothing is properly called 'child abuse', not even what was originally, and centrally, so termed. Everything turns then on how we choose to define 'child abuse'.

DEFINING ABUSE

What is required of an acceptable definition of 'child abuse'? Child abuse is, first and foremost, a special kind of wrong done to children. Things do and can go badly for children in a variety of ways and for a number of reasons. Children may suffer a large range of harms. Some, such as illness, disease, genuine accidents and disability, can occur naturally. Others may properly be attributed to the actions or inaction of human beings, individually and collectively. No one disagrees that 'child abuse' does not exhaustively capture all of the harms attributable to human agency. Child abuse is a particularly serious kind of harm. 'The two basic concepts underlying all definitions of abuse are harm and responsibility for that harm.'[7] In this spirit I offer the following as plausible criteria of any defensible definition of 'child abuse'.

First, the definition must be clear and unambiguous. It should not generate too many disagreements about what does and does not count as 'abuse'. Second, any definition of 'child abuse' must be substantive. It should not be truistic or tautological; it does not help to be told, for instance, that 'abuse' is 'behaviour injurious to a child's welfare'. Third, 'abuse' should surely be defined so as not to impose unreasonable demands on those who care for children. It will not do to understand 'abuse' in such a way that the vast majority of parents cannot avoid being abusers of their children. Note that the responsibility for serious harm being done to children need not be restricted to individuals such as parents. We want to allow for the possibility of 'collective abuse'.

Fourth, the definition of 'child abuse' should not be constitutively controversial, by, for instance, using elements that are open to evident and immediate disputes over meaning. A definition of child abuse should not be non-neutral, as the philosopher Gerald Dworkin defines it, where a non-neutral principle is one 'whose application to particular cases is a matter of controversy for the parties whose conduct is supposed to be regulated by the principle in question'.[8] Words such as 'proper' and 'adequate' invite controversy. Different parents will have different ideas as to the proper way to bring up children, or as to what counts as adequate care for them. It would be wrong for liberal legislators to impose one particular ideal or set of ideals upon all parents. Liberal society should and can be tolerant of diversity in modes of childrearing – subject, of course, to the protection of children from what can be agreed upon by all as 'abuse'.

Fifth, any definition of 'child abuse' should retain its strong negative evaluative connotations. Child abuse, however defined, is an evil to be detected, prevented and punished. This requirement was at the heart of the previously expressed concern about persuasive definition of the term. If child abuse is evil it must be stopped. Hence, 'abuse', as legally defined, will normally trigger state intervention. Since it is presumed that children in a liberal society will, normally and in the first instance, be brought up within families by their parents, such intervention will be into families and against the wishes of the parents. As we have seen, intervention can consequently be represented as violating parental and familial rights. 'Abuse' must thus be something serious enough to warrant such intervention. We might call this the 'threshold requirement'. Many things can be done to children which are not condoned or encouraged. But when a parent exceeds a certain point in their ill-treatment of their child the state may step over the family's threshold and protect the child. That point serves to separate bad parenting from parental 'abuse'.

In sum, the definition of 'abuse' must be clear, unambiguous and substantive. It must not make impossible demands on caretakers. It must be uncontroversial and function to define the threshold of justified legal intervention into family life. What definition of 'child abuse' satisfies these criteria?

There is an orthodox definition of child abuse which has four subcategories: physical abuse, physical neglect, sexual abuse and emotional abuse. Let me cite some good examples of straightforward definitions of each of these subcategories. Physical abuse is 'violence and other non-accidental, prohibited human actions that inflict pain on a child and are capable of causing injury or permanent impairment to development or functioning'.[9] Physical neglect is the 'persistent or severe neglect of a child (for example, by exposure to any kinds of danger, including cold and starvation) which results in serious impairment of the child's health or development, including non-organic failure to thrive'.[10] Sexual abuse is the 'involvement of dependent, developmentally immature children and adolescents in sexual activities that they do not fully comprehend, are unable to given informed consent to, and that violate the social taboos of family roles'.[11] Emotional abuse or psychological maltreatment is 'a concerted attack on a child's development of self and social competence, a *pattern* of psychically destructive behaviour, and it takes five forms: *Rejecting . . . Isolating . . . Terrorizing . . . Ignoring . . . Corrupting*'.[12]

The orthodox definition extends child abuse beyond mere physical cruelty. It is understandable why some would think of abuse as only palpable serious bodily harm. After all, we think of abuse in terms of its consequences and in the case of physical assaults these are evident and detectable. However, this would be a mistake for two reasons. In the first place, there is a danger of taking obviousness as a straightforward indication of seriousness. Thinking that an injury is the more serious the more obvious it is represents a big if understandable mistake. There is no doubt that physical injuries tend, on the whole, to be more evident, and their effects more public. Certainly this is so in comparison with emotional injuries. But there is no doubt that persons can suffer emotional damage which is long-lasting and serious. This is perhaps even more true of children who are vulnerable and not yet fully developed.

Take the case of sexual abuse. It is becoming clear that a major element in such abuse, and that perhaps which causes the greatest distress, is the betrayal of trust and responsibility involved. It thus affects children in the very core of their psychological being, and can leave them with abiding feelings of shame, guilt and self-hatred. The injury to sexually abused children is less palpable than bruising, fractures or burns. But it is certainly more enduring, deeper and more debilitating.

Second, it is a mistake to think that 'physical harm' is uncontroversial in a way that 'emotional harm' is not. In general, 'harm' must be understood in terms of detriment to well-being, and well-being in turn needs to be defined by reference to the normal functioning of the entity in question. Since we are

196

speaking of children we should add normal *development* to normal functioning. A child may be harmed both as a child *and* as a prospective adult. The adult of the future can be harmed by what is now done to the child.

As always, the problem with the use of 'normal' is that it uncomfortably straddles the senses of 'customary' or 'general', and 'prescribed'. It may be normal for a child to develop or function in certain kinds of way because that is how it does or indeed must happen in this particular society. It may not be normal in the sense of being the best way for the child to live and grow up. To know whether a child has been harmed we need to know how it is normal for the child to function and develop. But there simply is no universally agreed, transcultural and timeless norm of children's health and progress. There are differences between social norms, and between a social custom and a social ideal. What is customary in one society need not be so in another. What is seen as morally desirable in one society may not be so viewed in another. And, even within the same culture, there may be moral criticism of what many see merely as general practice.

Take, for instance, the custom of corporal punishment. There has been a persistent tendency in British and American society to view the hitting of a child by her parents in the interests of discipline as a legitimate and necessary part of the child's education. Indeed, law in our societies tends to characterise it as a protected right. Yet there seems to be clear merit in the view that to strike a child, for whatever reason, is to occasion him harm. Corporal punishment is, for its critics at least, an evident form of child abuse. The distinct claim that corporal punishment is a prelude to or is conducive to abuse is an empirical, and not obviously proven, one. The assertion that corporal punishment is on a continuum with physical abuse, and thus morally indistinguishable from it, is simply bad rhetoric. After all, by parity of reasoning, any disciplinary alternative to corporal punishment – such as, for instance, a withdrawal of privileges – is on a continuum with, and thus morally no different from, emotional abuse.

It is true that what is done to children with corporal punishment would be prosecuted as assault if done to an adult. But an appeal to the wrong of discrimination begs the question. Children are not allowed to do what adults are. Yet this amounts to a wrong only if children should enjoy the same liberty rights that adults have. It may be acceptable to do to a child what one may not do to an adult precisely because it is a child one is doing it to.

Some critics of corporal punishment would prefer to characterise it as seriously wrongful but not as abuse, as being instead 'subabusive'.[13] Unfortunately there does not seem as yet to be clear, unambiguous empirical support for the following three propositions that would need to be established: that corporal punishment has no beneficial effects on a child's development;

that it has serious harmful effects on a child's development; and that the feasible alternatives to corporal punishment are just as effective in disciplining children.

Such evidence may be seen as beside the point. Corporal punishment may be judged a violation of a child's rights, those that she enjoys under the CRC such as Article 19 which proscribes 'all forms of physical or mental violence, injury or abuse' of the child 'while in the care of parent(s), legal guardian(s) or any other person who has the care of the child'. A case can be made along these lines, and there is evidence that the Committee on the Rights of the Child, charged with overseeing the implementation of the CRC, views things in this way. However such an interpretation of what these rights amount to is bound to be controversial. Those who see no evidence that corporal punishment does occasion any serious harm to children will view any such critique of it as yet more evidence that rights statements can be interpreted to support whatever position one already endorses.

It may still be true that smacking children is wrong and that it is a poor parent who resorts to such measures in controlling her offspring. At the least it seems uncivilised to strike the young and defenceless. Furthermore, making corporal punishment illegal may serve an important exhortatory or pedagogic purpose. A law against corporal punishment – as there is currently in a number of European countries – may not be extensively or rigorously prosecuted. Yet it may still help to change attitudes, and persuade parents that there are so many better ways to discipline their children than hitting them. However, even if corporal punishment is wrong, and even if it merits legal proscription, it may be a serious mistake to view it as a form of child abuse or as a violation of a child's rights.

Cross-cultural evidence on abuse is illuminating.[14] Every society has a standard which identifies what is and is not abuse of children; there is always *some* limit set to acceptable rearing practices. Yet these standards and limits vary across cultures. What one society might view as abusive, another will see as perfectly normal. This is especially so when the contrast is drawn between Western and non-Western cultures. Let me cite some examples. Painful initiation ceremonies, practices of 'mutilation' or deliberately induced physiological 'deformations' in the service of some ideal of beauty, will probably be seen as seriously harmful in the West. They are not so characterised within the cultures where they occur. Moreover, these same cultures may see some Western childrearing practices as cruel – such as compelling the child to eat according to a strict regimen, or to sleep separately from its parents. It is also true that in these cultures what are seen in the West as paradigm acts of child abuse or neglect – physically beating a child or leaving it in conditions of serious risk to its health – are virtually unknown.

Now there are obvious twin dangers here: either adopting an ethnocentric standpoint whereby Western values and customs are assumed as the benchmark of what is best for all children; or of abandoning oneself to a form of moral relativism, where what each culture determines to be acceptable parenting *is* acceptable. There is no need to be reduced to either extreme if it is recognised that more general values do operate as a context within which 'harms' are inflicted on children. It is evident that what the West might regard as abusive behaviours may not be gratuitous. Initiation ceremonies are the means by which the young are formally accepted into the adult community and thereby acquire a value as full and equal members of their society. Analogous comments can be made of beautification practices.

Indeed, children who did *not* undergo these rites of passage would feel abused in so far as they were thereby excluded from their own culture. This suggests that the crucial context within which 'harms' to children must be evaluated are those beliefs which help determine the child's self-esteem and social identity. There are still problems. Many non-Western cultures disparage certain groups of children, those marked out at birth as different or 'inferior' – such as orphans and the handicapped. Again, their practices can be gender-specific. Initiation ceremonies differentially process boys and girls into adulthood, so that the latter find their social identity as subordinates of men. In this respect female circumcision is abusive to the extent that it both mutilates the girl and does so to give her an inferior sexual identity.

It is not enough then to excuse 'harmful' practices which nevertheless are necessary to a child's self-esteem and sense of identity. For the cultural beliefs which give meaning to these various practices may be deeply inegalitarian. And this suggests that one cannot be relativist about certain fundamental values, such as a commitment to the equality of all the members of a society. It may be judged ethnocentric to adopt such a commitment. But it is unacceptable to think that something as fundamental as human equality has value only relative to certain cultures.

There are difficult questions when it comes to the issue of cultural differences within one and the same society, especially when such differences correspond to structured ethnic and racial divisions. On the one hand a liberal society is required to be tolerant of diversity. Moreover, a principle of equality might seem to require that one group should have as much right to bring up its children in its ways as any other group. It would be wrong for society to expect every child to be reared as one particular group does simply because this group happens to be in a majority. Yet on the other hand, every child is entitled to the equal protection and promotion of his interests.

These two egalitarian requirements can conflict. Should a group's children be denied the same educational opportunities as other children within society because that group sees such education as incompatible with its own ideals? Should a group be permitted to betroth girls below the age of consent because that is how things have long been managed within the group? Should society be tolerant of excessive physical punishment of children when their parents claim to be acting in ways sanctioned by the cultural traditions of their group? These are hard issues to resolve and go to the heart of the relationship between cultural pluralism and democracy. Any satisfactory answer must attend to the question of a child's right to a certain cultural identity, that is to membership of some group, and its relation to her other rights. And this question can only properly be answered when the balance between these different claims has been resolved for adults within society.

I have argued that physical harm is not necessarily more serious than other kinds of harm. I have also argued that what counts as harm depends on norms of well-being which can vary culturally. However, there must be limits to the extent to which social context can be taken as excusing all 'harms', and the presumption that all children are equal forms an essential background to any consideration of what shall be thought of as 'harm'. The third point is that it would be a mistake to restrict the concept of 'harm' to the outcome of acts of commission. Standardly it is thought that a child is harmed when something is done to him by another person. But, of course, harm may result to a child from acts of omission, from the failure of others to do certain things. The category of 'neglect' is intended to cover those cases where a wilful disregard for a child's welfare is responsible for her suffering real harm.

Yet a case of neglect is normally taken to be one where gross harm results (or would have resulted) and where the negligence is palpable. More interesting is the suggestion that a child is harmed when his caretakers fail to fulfil certain specified duties in respect of him, duties whose discharge brings benefits to the child. In *On Liberty*, J. S. Mill understood the 'harm principle' – that an individual's liberty may only be limited to prevent harm to others – to license the compulsory performance of particular positive acts. The duties Mill chiefly had in mind are those he took to be required for successful social existence – such as jury service and assistance in defence of the realm.

Now it is arguable that children are owed certain duties, not because this is in the public interest (though it will probably be so) but in so far as they have rights. Children are harmed not simply when they are positively injured, nor even when, in addition, they are neglected. They can be harmed through a failure to act towards them as is required by their possession of certain rights. I have argued throughout that every child has the right to a minimally decent life, and that parents are obliged to ensure that there is every prospect of their children enjoying such a life. A much stronger position would hold

200

that every child is entitled to the best possible upbringing and, further, that any child who does not enjoy such a maximal prospect is abused.

David Gil is a prominent defender of just this view. He defines child abuse as 'inflicted gaps or deficits between circumstances of living which would facilitate the optimal development of children to which they should be entitled, and their actual circumstances, irrespective of the sources or agents of the deficit'.[15] The intention behind the definition is laudable but the result is unacceptable. *Any* failure to optimise a child's development will count, on this definition, as abuse. This seems to violate the requirement of a definition of abuse that it should not impose unreasonable demands on the child's caretaker. However good the parent, there must always be some conceivable improvement in the circumstances of its children's upbringing – for instance, a slightly better diet or slightly more access to physical exercise. Even if the 'possible' in 'best possible upbringing' is interpreted liberally to accommodate the practical realities of parenting and parental motives, it would still mean the imposition of an impossibly stringent condition. For any departure from feasibly good parenting, however small, would have to be understood as abuse.

Nevertheless, it would be a pity to dispense entirely with the thought that harm might usefully be understood as a falling short of some ideal of development. From economics we could borrow the distinction between 'optimising' and 'satisficing', that is, between securing the 'best possible' and 'good enough'. Abuse of or harm to a child could then be defined as the gap between actual circumstances and those which would be satisficing. Children are abused if they do not get an upbringing which is good enough.

That still leaves the question of how to specify this minimal standard of rearing. But that there should be such a standard is plausible. And we can imagine how we might begin to spell it out in terms of the following: adequate structured opportunities for physiological and cognitive development, a healthy environment with access to proper health care when appropriate, and relatively permanent, stable affective relationships with adult caretakers. Indeed, the CRC specifies a range of entitlements which each and every child should be guaranteed. The standard of minimal care can thus be defined in terms of these rights. A child who has no reasonable prospect of enjoying most of the rights listed in the CRC suffers a life that falls below the minimum standard of care which all children should enjoy.

Moreover, we can say the following things about a definition of abuse as what falls below a satisfying level of upbringing. The prevention of abuse corresponds to the guarantee of a child's basic rights. The definition is broader than one which encompasses only acts of physical injury and neglect. Yet it could not be said to impose unreasonable demands upon those responsible for the rearing of children. It supplies a substantive account of abuse, even if it has not been given clear and precise boundaries. It is controversial in that any attempt to fill out precisely what each and every right amounts to will be open to dispute. But there is general agreement that children do have the rights they are accorded by the CRC. Moreover, any legal definition or statute needs to be spelled out, and it is precisely the function of evolving law to give clarity and substance to the general forms of a covenant.

What of the 'threshold requirement'? Can the suggested definition be said to supply the point at which state intervention into family life is justified? This can only be answered by backtracking and challenging the pertinence of the requirement. For it presumes that the state's role in protecting children is limited to, or is primarily that of, an official caretaker in the last instance. When the state intervenes children are *already* being brought up within particular families which subsist within particular communities and classes, which, in further turn, form part of a broader set of social, political and economic arrangements. The circumstances of any one child are determined by how things are at a number of levels. What is thought of as statutory protection of the child, what is triggered by abuse over the threshold, is in fact action at the final level of determination.

Talk of different levels complements the criticisms made in chapter 11 of the presuppositions the 'liberal standard' makes about the state. The 'liberal standard' thinks of the state as a child's caretaker in the last instance because it ignores the extent to which the condition of any particular child is determined by 'public' considerations. A child's family is not a 'private' environment because the family is not in general immune from the influence of economic, legal and political factors. The state's 'public' role cannot, as the liberal believes, be impartial whilst significant social and economic inequalities are ignored. Let me now spell out the various levels in schematic fashion.

At a very fundamental level, a society has a particular socio-economic system, that is, an arrangement for the production and distribution of resources, goods and labour. This will play a major role in determining what kind of a life a child can hope to enjoy. Where there is a significant measure of socio-economic inequality this will significantly affect the life prospects of different children. A child who is brought up within a family occupying the lowest socio-economic position will enjoy poorer health, a lesser life expectancy, lower educational qualifications and a worse career than a child from the highest socio-economic position.

At another level a society's political and juridical institutions define the ways in which children are thought of, as for instance incapable of voting or responsible for their criminal actions. At yet another level a society makes explicit provision for its children through its healthcare, childcare and educational facilities. There is also a general cultural or ideological level wherein children are characterised in particular ways, given a value and distinguished from adults in certain ways.

At both the legal and cultural levels, different groups of children, for instance illegitimate children or the handicapped, may be characterised in particular ways. Differences at every level will significantly affect the kind of existence each child within society can expect to have: how they are cared for, what kinds of activities they will engage in and what sort of progress to maturity they will make.

The final level is that where the state explicitly takes on the role of guardian of society's children, intervening where appropriate into family life to protect those children it can reasonably deem to be at risk of serious harm from their caretakers. Within the liberal understanding of the state's role the definition of 'abuse' serves as a threshold beyond which such intervention is justified. A threshold is needed because it is thought that the family should be a protected private space within which the child is reared, and breaching this privacy requires a clear justification. I have already criticised the attribution to parents of a right of privacy, and the suggestion that state and family stand opposed to one another as 'public' to 'private'. Now I want to challenge the idea that somehow a child is abused only *within* the family and thus that the prevention of abuse must necessarily be limited to action at the final 'public' level.

I have argued that each child has a right to a minimally decent upbringing, and that a child is abused if her upbringing is not good enough. We need to give both of these assertions their full and proper egalitarian context. Each child has a right to a good enough upbringing, consistent with all other children being able to enjoy the same; a child is abused if her upbringing is not good enough, but could be without any other child thereby suffering a less than sufficient upbringing. Now it should be clear that a child can be the victim of abuse because of the way his particular circumstances have been determined at what have been called the first and second levels. A child from a poor socio-economic background is abused if he enjoys a less than adequate upbringing as a result of this background. A redistribution of social and economic resources could ensure that the child did enjoy a good enough upbringing without thereby jeopardising the chances of any other child having one.

A number of writers have, in this spirit, written of social and collective abuse. It should be noted that, following Gil, they tend to see such abuse as being done to any child whose right to an optimal upbringing is denied as a result of socio-economic circumstances. I have given reasons for thinking it a mistake to use an optimising definition of abuse. But this does not of course mean that significant inequalities affecting the life chances of children should not be reduced – even if it is not done in the name of preventing abuse. And, notwithstanding the narrower definition, 'collective abuse' remains a problem which should not be ignored. Indeed there are two reasons for thinking it should be given priority. In the first place, it is likely to be more extensive than the incidence of conventional intra-familial abuse. More children suffer significantly reduced life opportunities as a result of their socio-economic circumstances than are injured as a result of parental behaviour. This is especially true in a global context.

Second, there is a significant correlation between poverty and what is standardly understood as child abuse and neglect. Study after study has indicated that the preponderance of such abuse occurs within families at the lowest socio-economic levels. Attempts to dispute the significance of such findings by, for instance, an appeal to the disproportionate reporting of lower-class abuse can be shown to be ill-founded, and one is left with the suspicion that the failure to recognise the implications of the figures is self-interested.[16] On the one hand, there is a general political unwillingness to see that the elimination of child abuse requires a major egalitarian programme of social and economic reform. On the other hand, the agencies presently involved in the prevention of abuse have a stake in its continuing to be represented as something affecting individual families and which must be dealt with at that level.

Indeed, what can be called the 'disease' or 'medical' model of child abuse predominates. Child abuse is seen as pathological individual behaviour with a specific aetiology (and such as may even permit accurate prediction of its future occurrence) and remediable through appropriate forms of treatment. Such a model obscures both the abuse which is social and the social causes of even individual abuse. To speak of abuse as having predetermining socio-economic factors is not to say, it should be noted, that poor people have no choice but to be abusers. Nor is it to ignore the reasons why particular individuals should be disposed to abuse, whereas others of a similar social background are not.

SEXUAL ABUSE

Some comments are in order about sexual abuse, and these will form a coda to this chapter. They are needed not simply because a definition of abuse as an inadequate upbringing cannot capture the specific wrong of sexual abuse. It is also because sexual, unlike physical, abuse *does* appear to be classless.

It is thus a more prevalent problem, and one which raises separate issues. It might be possible to think of sexual abuse as having a collective form, if, for instance, one thought of social circumstances as leading children to develop an inadequate sexuality and sexual identity. For instance, the Dutch employ a category of cognitive abuse which, as one study notes, 'can . . . be extended to include family socialisation processes typified by extreme male sexist views which, in turn, constrain a female child's life experiences and opportunities'.[17] However, sexual abuse is most significant as something that normally takes place within the essentially private space of the home, possibly the child's own. Indeed, the protected privacy of the family may serve to cloak sexual abuse.

There are two dangers in using the adjective 'sexual'. The first is that it might lead one to think of it in narrow terms as sexual intercourse between adult and minor. Sexual abuse constitutes a continuum of activities which can range from flashing and exposure to pornographic material, through inappropriate fondling to anal or vaginal penetration. Second, just as feminists have sought to define rape as an act of violence, not a sexual act, it is right to remember that what is at stake in sexual abuse of a child is the expression of superior power rather than an inapposite sexual relationship. For, although sexual abuse is classless, it is nevertheless the expression of deep-structured inequalities – between men and women, and between adults and children.

The vast majority of sexual abuse is perpetrated by adult males on girls. It is thus proper that feminists, who have done most to expose the problem, should continue to urge its identification as one particular expression of masculinity and male violence against women. Not only does this claim constrain the possible acceptable explanations of sexual abuse; it also sets the agenda for any solution, especially in recommending long-term and radical changes in the respective status of men and women.

The inequality of the sexes compounds that between adult and child. This double inequality explains why sexual abuse is essentially wrong for being unconsenting. A standard definition of child sexual abuse is that it is 'the involvement of developmentally immature children and adolescents in sexual actions which they cannot fully comprehend, to which they cannot give informed consent, and which violate the taboos of social roles'.[18] The last part of this definition is dubious. It is somewhat redundant given what goes before, and it yokes abuse too closely to incest as traditionally understood. The key to the wrong of sexual abuse is that the child does not consent and does not because it *cannot*.

Of course, adult abusers can forcibly compel children to participate in sexual acts, and the children may be unwilling precisely because they know what is involved. But often children are simply uncomprehending of the nature and significance of the abuse. And it is important to note how adults may maintain children in their ignorance, or deliberately mislead them by, for instance, representing their abuse as 'normal' between parent and daughter. To that extent informed consent may be something that a child cannot give. However, to see sexual abuse as always wrong only because children are ignorant innocents can be dangerously oversimplified. Children can be the unwilling victims of sexual abuse even when they know what is happening to them. Moreover, we have seen how much the 'innocent incompetence' of childhood is an ideological construction. It is also one which may block – by representing as wrong or inappropriate – attempts to inform children about sex and sexuality.

Consent can be absent because children are powerless rather than unknowing. They need not be forcibly coerced to be unconsenting victims; their trust in, love of and reliance upon someone who is their parent, or just an adult, can be exploited. It is not inconsistent for a child to hate the abuse but not the abuser, and to fear the abuser's removal from the family home. Indeed, playing on just that fear can make a child an accomplice in the non-disclosure of the abuse.

Talk of the possibility of consent by children to their abuse is inappropriate if consent requires a comprehension of what is being consented to and a position of independence and power from which to consent or dissent. Children lack either understanding or equality with adults, or both. This suggests that any strategy to protect children from abuse will be inadequate if it maintains children in their ignorance and powerlessness.

This chapter began with an apparent paradox. Children are less abused than in previous times, yet child abuse is somehow seen as a contemporary problem. Discussion of how best to define abuse has revealed that what concerns present observers is a particular kind of abuse, that which takes place in families. Set in a wider context abuse raises fundamental issues about equality between children. Even when abuse is something that essentially takes place within families, as with sexual abuse, the issue of equality – that between the sexes, and between adult and child – is still pertinent. As long as the question of equality, in its various aspects, is not addressed the sad history of children's maltreatment at the hands of adults is unlikely to end.

15

CONCLUSION

A MODEST COLLECTIVIST PROPOSAL

How should a society think of its children, how should it care for them and what rights if any should it accord them? One immediate difficulty in answering these questions is the ambiguity of 'a society'. If we mean 'our' society, that is, a modern, capitalist, liberal democratic society then, arguably, the answers will be of one sort. But if we mean a society that conforms to our ideal – whether the vision is socialist, feminist, egalitarian, communitarian or whatever – then the answers will be different. A distinction familiar to critics of existing society is that between reform and radical replacement, between improving without altering the basic constitutive structures of society and instituting a new kind of society. So it might seem that we should distinguish between getting the best for children in *this* society and getting the best society for children (and everyone else).

The distinction can be overstated, especially if it envisages a consummate qualitative change from optimally reformed present society to future perfect. Many things we would wish for children could be implemented in most societies including our own. Others, perhaps, will require significant structural change. But the dangers of overdrawing the contrast between the reformable and the irreparable are twofold. First, it leads to a blanket criticism of everything done in the imperfect present. Second, it makes for agnosticism about the inexistent ideal or, worse, trusts to the deliverance of all things good by radical change alone.

Take the state's role in the provision of welfare and social services. It is reasonable to argue that the existence of some groups – the poor and the homeless, for instance – is due to the fact that our society is characterised by serious, structured economic inequalities, and that such groups would cease to exist or be radically reduced in number within a more equal society. To that extent, providing for these groups is an imperative only within our society, and one that would be unnecessary in a different one. It is quite another thing, and evidently false, to think that other groups – the sick, the

207

handicapped, the elderly and the very young – would disappear in the wake of radical social change. No revolution will abolish human mortality and biological development. In any society the state or official agencies must assume some measure of responsibility for the care of some of society's members, including the very young.

There is a related point. It is fair to criticise the ways in which the state, and its constituent agents, operate within a society marked by fundamental divisions – between classes, the sexes and ethnic groups. In chapter 11 the 'liberal standard' was accused of making the naive and implausible presumption that the state acts impartially to protect all children. There are serious inequalities in the childcare and protection policies of our society. But such criticism does not mean that in a different society the state would play no role in the care of children. Nor is the critic excused the important task of specifying what that role might be. Yet socialists, for instance, are notoriously vague about the precise lineaments of a socialist society, and this is especially true when it comes to social and welfare policy. It is not always possible to draw together a clear, consistent picture of what such policy would look like when its sources are critiques of the present, general theory and the practice of 'existing' socialist countries.[1]

The disappearance after 1989 of the principal orthodox socialist states has radically changed the terms of political debate. Variants of socialist theory and practice endure but their influence is significantly reduced. It would oversimplify to say that the ideological battle is now one between some version of social democratic liberalism and its various critics. Nevertheless it is true that those who defend collective action to reduce inequality or to protect children and limit parental autonomy need not do so from a classical socialist viewpoint. They could just as well be liberals or feminists.

In this concluding chapter I propose to offer some ideas for thinking about, caring for and empowering children. I leave it relatively open and undiscussed whether these can be realised within existing societies. But I do want first to state a principle and review three centrally relevant values. The principle is that the valuation and understanding of childhood and adulthood are mutually interdependent. What we see as childlike in children depends on what is viewed as adult in adults; what we value in maturity is depreciated for its absence in the young. Childhood is a preparation for adulthood but we can only know how to prepare the child if we know what is expected of the adult.

In saying this I do not forget Rousseau's admonition to understand childhood in its own right. We do and should not value childhood *only* as a preparation for adulthood, although it is at least that. Children do have interests that are not those of adults, or even of adults in the making. These need to be properly understood and appreciated. Yet doing so requires that we be clear what distinguishes a child from an adult, what interests an adult has that cannot be those of a child, and vice versa. It is also true that our valuations of adulthood and hence of childhood in its anticipation of or preparation for that state vary. Indeed, they are deeply and pervasively contested. We should thus not presume what it is that makes being an adult valuable. Liberals, for instance, are often criticised for appearing to think that the only thing worth having as an adult is autonomy. There may well be other virtues or valued capacities of maturity which the child should acquire.

It is self-evident that the character of adult society will derive from the ways in which its children are brought up, and that, in turn, the nature of childrearing will reflect the values and priorities of adult society. Yet political and social philosophy seems sometimes to have forgotten this fact, representing as merely natural development what is a choice of upbringing. States need citizens and societies need doctors, lawyers, soldiers and farmers. These are created, not born into their occupations. States, in particular, survive only if they have a citizenry adequate to their nature and ends. Citizens are the result of education. Plato's *Republic* has aptly been described as less a political than an educational treatise. But there is no conflict of purposes. Plato rightly saw his political community as only realised through, and as necessarily requiring, a systematic, structured nurtural and pedagogic programme. Moreover, an education in citizenship is always relative to the state for which it is intended. Aristotle correctly observed that, 'The citizen should be moulded to suit the form of government under which he lives'.[2]

It is a commonplace that every political theory presupposes an account of human nature. What is less often accepted is that human nature is not a given, and that its forms may, to a lesser or greater degree, be determined by historical and social circumstances. An adult nature owes much to nurture and education. According to Rousseau, the father, upon whom the tasks of rearing and teaching fall, 'owes to his species men; he owes to society sociable men; he owes to the state citizens'.[3] Locke recommended an education directed to the end of rational, autonomous independence because that is what characterises the ideal citizen of his liberal state. If Plato is vilified for his totalitarian indoctrination of the young we should remember that it may not be the act of moulding that is wrong so much as the mould in which they are cast.

What then are the values of adult society which should determine our thinking about childhood? Three are of especial importance: equality, democracy and collectivism. In respect of equality we must distinguish between the treatment of *children* as equals and the implications for our treatment of children that follow from our treatment of *adults* as equals. It is a matter of deep and enduring controversy what the ideal of equality requires. Much contemporary discussion has taken the fundamental question in need of answer to be 'Equality of what?' Even a radical libertarian who is prepared to countenance a large degree of social and economic inequality will insist upon an equality of basic liberty rights. So what should children enjoy an equality of?

Only liberationists demand that children should be equal to adults in their enjoyment of all their rights. Those who deny the liberationist claim will nevertheless acknowledge that if any child is entitled to the enjoyment of some right then all are equally. The CRC accords every child a range of fundamental rights. These, as we saw in chapter 4, comprise both liberty and welfare rights. A familiar socialist critique of equal liberty rights is that, set against a background of social and economic inequality, such an equality is merely formal and of little real value. All, for instance, may be formally free to express their views but only some have the resources others lack to make their views publicly known. Only very few can own newspapers and television stations. It is notable thus that the CRC does not just accord all children liberty rights but, for instance and crucially, a right 'to the enjoyment of the highest attainable standard of health' (Article 24) and 'to a standard of living adequate for the child's physical, mental, spiritual, moral and social development' (Article 27).

These latter welfare rights do have substantial and substantive egalitarian implications. A commitment to see that all children everywhere can enjoy just these rights would surely entail a massive global redistribution of resources. At the very least it is clear that very many children do not currently enjoy the second of these welfare rights, and that they fail to do so because of deep, structured inequalities. It needs to be added, not least because it is often forgotten, that many of the children in question live not in the developing world but in developed Western societies. They are brought up below the poverty line. A commitment to end child poverty is also a commitment to eradicate the poor circumstances of those adults who rear such children.

Correlatively, a commitment to treat adults as equals also has implications for how we treat children. A familiar egalitarian principle is that of equal life chances, by which it is understood that all adults should enjoy the same opportunity to lead lives of comparable value. Everyone should, as it were, line up without handicap and alongside one another at the starting gate of mature life. But it is clear that the family is a means, perhaps the principal means, by which advantage and disadvantage is passed onto the child. Parents transmit goods to their children – genetic traits, inheritable property, and the conditions under which they are brought up. If we really wanted to promote adult equality of opportunity then we would have to choose from a limited number of radical policies, including the involuntary abolition of the family and the transfer of genetically less favoured children to socially more favoured parents. Less radically, we should consider whether better-off parents should be permitted to favour their own children – educationally, by sending them to better schools, or economically by the bequest of money and other goods.

A further egalitarian issue is that of *sexual* equality and the part that childhood may play in the construction of sexual difference. Women's subordination to men and their occupation of stereotypical roles has already been criticised in the discussion of the traditional family. Male power over women has been criticised in so far as it helps to explain the sexual abuse of children. The crucial question is whether children can be reared so as to eliminate this kind of inequality.

This is a large and complex question and perhaps the best way to consider it is by sketching a simple if influential argument which can then be criticised. The argument rests on the familiar distinction between sex and gender. The former is a matter of biology, and its paired terms are 'male' and 'female'; the latter is a matter of psychology and culture, and its paired terms are 'masculine' and 'feminine'. The argument proceeds as follows. Whilst one's sexual identity is more or less given at birth and remains unchangeable, one's gender identity is due to the influence of social and psychological factors. One is born female, but made feminine.

Chief amongst the influences upon human beings is the family structure with its division of sexual labour, whereby the mother nurtures and the father is an independent provider. What goes with these basic roles are clusters of associated traits. To be feminine is to be passive, caring, emotional, loyal and so on; to be masculine is to be active, dispassionate, logical, independent and so on. The conclusion of the argument is that these gender differences can be abolished if society's practices, especially the way children are brought up, are fundamentally changed. Only a woman can bear children, but she does not have to be the only or primary nurturer. Thus, boys need not grow up to be masculine, and girls need not be made into feminine women.

This position, so important to the early women's movement, has been increasingly criticised over the last twenty years. The basic sex–gender distinction is, it has been alleged, overstated. Biology is not immutable in the way suggested; much also depends on the significance accorded to natural facts and distinctions. Correspondingly, it would be an oversimplification to think gender can be changed at will or through a simple alteration of social practices. Gender must have some relation to sex. Denying that it does is an over-reaction to the claim that sex entirely determines gender. Of course it remains controversial what kind of relation there is.[4]

The differences between men and women have social causes, of which the family is only one. Nonetheless it is an important factor. Hence any demand for *sexual* social equality or justice must surely accord great importance to childrearing within the family. The family, as we have seen, is the principal means by which social and economic advantage is passed on to the child. It is also the principal means by which the advantages and disadvantages of gender are transmitted to children. Or, more accurately, it is such a means to the extent that the family exemplifies a traditional, unfair division of gender roles. The family as such may not be at fault, only certain forms of it.

Moreover, sexual equality does not require the abolition of gender differences. It requires only that the distinction not be disadvantageous to either gender. Men and women can and do differ in ways that do not matter in terms of equality. What is important is that women should not, as a gender, be the subordinate and social inferior of men. Equality between distinct genders, and not androgyny, is the proper goal of reform.

The second value which should determine our thinking about children is democracy. If society is self-governing then its members must be able to take part in its collective self-management. This means more than simply acquiring rational autonomy, the ability to make up one's mind and exercise independent choice. It involves an appreciation of how others may differ in viewpoint, a tolerance of difference and a willingness to work together despite these differences. It requires an accommodation to the demands of collective decision-making, a willingness to accept those decisions with which one disagrees, and preparedness to play one's part in the execution of decisions. It requires an understanding of what is involved in making a democracy work, a commitment to defend its maintenance, to participate as fully as feasible and to assume the burdens that democratic administration imposes.

A citizen must be educated both to and in democracy. Education must have a certain content, comprising not just an introduction to the principles and practices of democratic government, but also an inculcation of the civic virtues – tolerance, respect for others' rights and non-violence, among others. At the same time children must learn democratic participation through practice. That practice should not simply commence at the age of majority and thereafter be only quinquennial. There is no reason why both the family and the school should not be the sites for exercises, even if limited, in self-government. Active democratic citizens are not born overnight when a certain age is reached. Moreover, as was argued in chapter 7, children can and should play a political role even while still lacking the vote. They can do so by participating in children's parliaments or similar bodies. Such participation is not only educative but motivational. It both gives practical experience of politics and displays the point of taking part.

The final value is collectivism. This is the most crucial, for here intersect a number of considerations having to do with the role of the family, the relationship between individuals and their society, the extent and character of social care provision for children, education and general political values. Several issues need to be separated. The first is the extent to which society, as opposed to individual parents, assumes responsibility for the rearing of children. In chapter 13 I specifically contrasted 'collectivist' to 'individualist' approaches to this question, citing Plato's as an extreme form of 'collectivism' and the 'liberal standard' as an individualist thesis. The same basic contrast is given elegant expression by Amy Gutman, who counterposes the ideal of the 'family state' to that of the 'state of families'.[5] The former is represented by Plato's Commonwealth; the latter, attributed to John Locke, sees parents as having an exclusive right to the upbringing of their offspring.

In much political and legal thinking this contrast is viewed as amounting to a pair of mutually exclusive alternatives: either children are entrusted to the care of their parents and brought up within families, or they become the charges of the state and are collectively reared. A great deal of influential American judicial thinking accepts the contrast, opposing the right of individuals to bring up their own children as they choose, to 'Platonic' collectivism.[6] The clear implication is that if parents do not have rights over their children then they must be for the state to rear as *it* chooses. The contrast is oversimplified and misleading, for there are other possibilities. Gutman herself favours what she calls 'democratic education', where a community prepares its young for their eventual participation in the running of their society. I will myself propose a modest collectivism.

In general terms, the stark contrast between Platonic collectivism and a state of families can be moderated through a distribution of responsibilities and a dilution of entitlements. Thus, in the first place, some rearing duties can be assumed by the state, such as, most obviously, education whilst others, such as feeding, housing and clothing the child, remain with the parents. Second, parental authority can be constrained and monitored by the state. A parent may have the authority to punish the child, for instance, but only within carefully specified bounds which if exceeded incur official sanctions.

The second issue is the extent to which the rearing and education of children is informed by a collectivist ethic, which accords primary importance to the collectivity, and understands individuals principally in terms of the groups to which they belong. The classic Soviet education, now defunct, and that in the People's Republic of China, itself now also changing, offer a good example of the inculcation of collectivist values. At its starkest this means that a child is brought up, to quote the Soviet educationalist A. S. Makarenko, 'in the collective, by the collective, and for the collective'.[7]

This is managed through both the form and the content of the teaching. As for its form, great stress is placed upon collective, cooperative activity. Competition between individual children is discouraged and group achievement through interdependent effort is encouraged. As for content, individuals are taught to set the judgment of the group above their own and to subordinate their interests to those of the collective. Both the Chinese and the Soviet educations emphasise 'character formation' in so far as this means becoming a good member of the community, a living exemplar of a new collective morality. At its most dramatic the Chinese employ the model of Lei Feng, celebrated for his self-sacrificial deeds in the service of the people.

It is noteworthy that the Soviet and Chinese systems of education are 'collectivist' in the sense that their ethic is group-based, but the manner of rearing children within these societies is not 'collectivist' in the Platonic sense. Indeed, the family plays a particularly important role in Chinese social life, and in both cultures the family's responsibility for children is complementary to that of the state. Significantly, both societies display consensus on what the child is and can become; there are shared conceptions of what the properly raised child should be like and on what her role as an adult ought to be. This owes much, perhaps, to the existence of a single official ideology, namely Marxism-Leninism.

I have already noted that a liberal democratic society is characterised by ideological pluralism, and that this conduces to a diversity in styles of parenting. It might be appropriate, consequently, to distinguish an education in the value of collectivity as such from one in the specific values of a particular collective. The liberal is worried by the idea of imbuing the minds of very young children with narrowly defined moral, religious, patriotic, civic or political precepts. Dogmatic Christianity is as much the liberal's target as Marxism-Leninism. Requiring nursery children to study Mao Zedong's thought is Jesuitical indoctrination in form at least. But an education based on a single collectivist ideology can be distinguished from one which emphasises the importance of cooperation, non-competitiveness, equality, and being part of a collective. It is not immediately self-evident that this kind of 'collectivist' education is incompatible with the aims of liberal democracy.

My own modest collectivism comprises not only a commitment to democratic, egalitarian and collectivist values in the rearing of children. It also comprises the fulfilment of four goals. These are a significant assumption of collective responsibility for childcare, a 'diffusion of parenting', a collective valuation of children and a significant extension of children's rights.

The most important measure of a modest collectivist childcare policy would be the universal provision of pre-school facilities. Every child should, from the earliest feasible opportunity, be given a place at a nursery or kindergarten. These should be properly housed, have qualified staff in sufficient numbers, fulfil a clear pedagogic purpose and be managed so as to permit full parental involvement. This ideal has been recognised in a number of countries but has yet to be fully realised in any. Provision across European countries, for instance, varies in terms of the age group served, the eligibility criteria (whether it is universal or for working parents only or for parents in receipt of welfare), and the extent of a parental fee, if any.

Historically, pre-school facilities arose out of a need for women to be freed from their traditionally constraining domestic role of childcarer. They continue to be defended in these terms. In socialist countries the provision of childcare has been seen as important for enabling women to fulfil a productive role alongside men. It thus had both economic and political value.

Notwithstanding its importance for women, childcare is fully consonant with the right of every child to a minimally decent upbringing. There is increasing evidence that a child's intellectual and cognitive development benefits enormously from the kind of structured learning environment that a nursery or kindergarten can provide. Children are better prepared for their later primary education. Their need to develop linguistic skills is met. They can be actively creative and independent, whilst at the same time developing important non-familial affective ties in an atmosphere of cooperation with other children.

The universal provision of pre-schooling is merited on egalitarian grounds. Given the foundational importance of the child's pre-school years for its later educational attainment, such provision can help to ensure that all children get off to the same start. Pre-schooling may supply a site for the provision of primary health care to children, as well as services designed for the detection and prevention of abuse. In general there is a need for 'collective uniformity', that is, for a coherent 'nesting' of agencies concerned with children and their well-being, and a clear coordination of the functions of family, school, health and welfare services.

There is a general point of importance concerning the role of the state in respect of children. It would be a mistake to see the state in merely 'negative' child protectionist terms as only a guardian of the child against abuse, which acts by intervening into the family and removing the child from any detected abusive situation. The state should also always serve as a 'positive' guarantor that every child within its jurisdiction enjoys a minimally decent upbringing. This requirement reinforces what we might term the 'holistic' approach to children: child protection cannot be separated or insulated from more general official efforts to promote the welfare of children. Such holism is best served by 'joined up' law and policy on children, including, most centrally, coordinated cooperation between the various agencies – educational, welfare and health – that deal with them.

By the 'diffusion of parenting' I mean four interrelated things. In the first place, society should encourage a diversity of familial forms. Children should be able to recognise that the classic nuclear family is not the only possible or necessarily most ideal way to be brought up. Long-term changes in Western society are starting to give effect to this. The important causal elements in these changes are the following. First, the new reproductive technology has allowed those incapable of conceiving naturally to have children. It has also allowed those – such as single-sex couples – who would wish not to conceive naturally to have children. Second, there has been a slow but steady increase in recognition – legal, social and economic – of single-sex couples and of their parental rights over children. Third, marriage has been declining in popularity. Divorce rates have risen, so that a greater percentage of children now reside with single parents or with a step-parent. Fourth, more women work full-time or part-time. This has put pressure on, though it has far from abolished, a traditional gender-based division of domestic labour. It is certainly no longer possible when we speak of children reared within families simply to assume that the family will be a married heterosexual couple who are the child's biological or 'causal' parents.

By the 'diffusion of parenting' I mean, second, that children should have available to them feasible alternatives to their parents. The child liberationist, Richard Farson, defends this as a means of realising the child's right to choose its own home environment.[8] Even if one does not recognise that children *do* have such a right it may be important that there is as wide a range as is practicable of adequate nurtural choices. A child's strong interest in not staying with its present parents is of diminished weight when no less detrimental alternative is possible.

A key imperative of childcare policy is 'permanency planning', that is, securing an alternative permanent home for those children whose relationship with their parents has, for whatever reason, irretrievably broken down. Unfortunately, far too many children suffer the fate of being moved from one temporary placement to another until they are too old to think of in terms of permanency. Children with special needs and disabilities may fail to find a home. Hence an adequate network of good foster and prospective adoptive parents is essential. Moreover, society should strive to supply well-funded and imaginative residential schemes. In Britain at present children's homes are stigmatised, poorly staffed and insufficiently funded. That needs to change.

The 'diffusion of parenting' means, third, that, even where the family still retains its social role as the main form of childrearing, responsibility for upbringing should not continually and exclusively fall upon the parents.

Parenting may be 'embedded' in a network of kin and community, who can assume – occasionally and to varying degrees – parental responsibility. There are cultures where children unhappy with their parents or whose parents find themselves under too much pressure simply move to another family and are temporarily adopted. In China, complementary to the extensive public provision of childcare is the extended family and the neighbourhood. Grandparents will often care for young children whilst their parents are at work; neighbours will assume responsibility for collecting children from school, feeding and looking after them when their parents cannot.

Diffusion of parenting means, fourth and finally, that it is seen as appropriate for any adult within a society to act in a parental role towards any child. In many cultures it is accepted that an adult may discipline a child who is not his own for some transgressions, or attend to a child in distress. This compares unfavourably with the distancing Western respect shown for what are seen as the rights of the child's actual parents. One depressing aspect of the Bulger case, discussed briefly in chapter 9, was that adult passers-by observed a clearly upset child being dragged unwillingly through the streets by the two older boys and did nothing. Generally, individuals are unwilling to intervene publicly in what is seen as none of their business. The explanation for this unwillingness is often a sound, prudential fear of suffering harms or serious embarrassment. However, a bad reason in the case of children would be the thought that nobody but a child's parents has any duties of care towards her.

The collective valuation of children is expressed in the general cultural attitude towards them. It is important that children be seen as valuable – even if, as in some societies, this is for straightforward economic reasons. In such a context, it is just not seen as appropriate to subject them to cruel treatment or to neglect them. It is recognised that society has a responsibility to ensure that they receive a decent upbringing. Children may be formally acknowledged as a valued section of society, with their own needs and interests, by various institutional means. The UN Convention on the Rights of the Child (CRC) is obviously the most salient legal instrument codifying the many proper entitlements of children everywhere. A step beyond ratification would be its incorporation into domestic law. This would make legally effective the obligation of government to conform all its laws and policies to the terms of the CRC. It would also allow children, and their advocates, to make legal challenges in the domestic courts for any failure to respect their rights.

A government could appoint a children's minister with executive status. Some countries have opted for a children's ombudsman.[9] A children's commissioner, independent of the government but empowered to monitor its childcare law and policy, is a similar idea. In chapter 7 I discussed the idea of children's parliaments, general or specific assemblies of young people who can make their views known. Every institutional means should be devised to ensure that children have a voice and that in every material area of their lives that voice is heard and, where appropriate, heeded.

It is important to add that children can be valued in the wrong way and for the wrong reasons. The modern conception of children views them as incompetent innocents. But we should be suspicious of continuing to 'infantilise' children, that is, have a regard for them as cute, lovable creatures but, above all, weak, vulnerable and dependent. In this respect the child liberationists are right to object when we make of children what we want them to be for the satisfaction of our needs: lovable so that they can be loved, frail and feeble so that we can protect them. In similar fashion 'respect' for the 'weaker sex' constructs a femininity whose powerlessness serves a male desire for domination.

The liberationist is wrong to conclude that *all* children should have all of the rights currently possessed by adults. But reasons have been given for thinking that older children are wrongly denied them. A start could be made by lowering the age at which individuals can, amongst other things, vote and exercise sexual choice. Of course the possession of rights is not a cure-all. Any expansion of children's entitlements must form part of a more general empowerment. However, rights are now an established and central part of our moral and political discourse. Moreover, the CRC is the unavoidable contemporary context for thinking about the status of children. The CRC is a public and palpable affirmation of the standing and worth of children.

The implication of my modest collectivism would be that children are brought more into the public domain and out of the private shades of the family. This would make it easier for them to be monitored for their physical and psychological progress. It is modest in that it falls far short of Plato's scheme; yet it is collectivist in that it represents a significant abridgment of liberal rights to parental privacy and autonomy. It is appropriate here to say something about child abuse. It would be utopian to think that child abuse is a 'disease' which preventive social medicine could finally cause to disappear. Yet there are reasons to believe that the modest collectivism proposed would make a significant difference.

A more equal society would help to reduce the 'collective abuse' of children who are victims of poor circumstances and the predisposing social causes of much physical abuse. Recognition of sexual abuse as part of a more general male domination of women makes the demand for full and real equality between the sexes all the more pressing. Children, empowered by knowledge and a sense of their own independence, are more capable of resisting their exploitation by adults. Evidence also suggests that a high cultural valuation of children and the embeddedness of parenting in an extended network are two major factors in a low societal incidence of child abuse.[10] The modest collectivist is also a 'holist' recognising that the detection and prevention of abuse cannot be separated from a broader social and political concern to safeguard and promote the welfare of all children.

As for the detection of abuse, the modest collectivism envisaged would ensure a greater public space within which children's development could be monitored. It is evident that the 'liberal standard' presently disposes professionals concerned with children's welfare not to see abuse. An excellent study of the operation of child-welfare agencies within the UK, *The Protection of Children*,[11] clearly shows how their structure and the thinking of their members are such that the maltreatment of children is recognised only in the most extreme and obvious cases. Unwilling to intervene, fearing that intervention is illiberal, professionals succumb to the 'liberal compromise': they make the best of what they do find. The authors of the study speak of a 'rule of optimism' which, trusting to 'natural love' and reasoning that abusive behaviours are justified by different cultural standards, explains away any parental misconduct.

The modest collectivist, on the other hand, is deeply sceptical of natural parental rights and denies that the family is entitled to protected privacy. Not only will a modest collectivism present a wide range of professionals with the opportunity to recognise the abuse of children when it occurs. It will predispose them to accept that it does occur and to act accordingly.

The remaining worry about any collectivism is that it conflicts with the liberal commitment to pluralism. So long as we cannot agree on how best to rear children, it will be best to trust to plural parenting. And the historical evidence shows a long sequence of abandoned proposals for childrearing remarkable for their diversity and mutual inconsistency.[12] However, a modest collectivism does not insist upon a single nurtural blueprint for all society's children. It stipulates only that all children merit a decent upbringing, presumes that some ways of bringing up children are better than others, and thinks that this necessitates a measure of collectivism. It *is* undoubtedly true that, in the last analysis, no answer can be given to the question of how we should understand and behave towards children without broaching the issues of what adulthood is, what makes it valuable and what would make for a better community of adults. To that extent the oft-repeated claim that its treatment of children says most about a society expresses a deep truth.

NOTES

1 JOHN LOCKE'S CHILDREN

1 There is a full critical edition of the *Thoughts* and other relevant educational essays in *The Educational Writings of John Locke*, edited by J. L. Axtell, Cambridge, Cambridge University Press, 1960, but there is also a very usefully abridged edition with commentary by F. W. Garforth, *Locke's Thoughts Concerning Education*, London, Heinemann, 1964. Hereafter referred to as *Thoughts*.

2 Jean-Jacques Rousseau, *Émile or On Education*, translated with introduction and notes by Allan Bloom, Harmondsworth, Penguin, 1991. Hereafter referred to as *Émile*.

3 Christina Hardyment, *Dream Babies: Childcare from Locke to Spock*, London, Jonathan Cape, 1983.

4 *Of the Conduct of the Understanding in The Works of John Locke*, Vol. 1, edited by J. A. St. John Freeport, New York, Books for Libraries Press, 1969.

5 Edited with a foreword by Peter H. Nidditch, Oxford, Oxford University Press, 1975. Hereafter referred to as the *Essay*.

6 A critical edition with an introduction and *apparatus criticus* by Peter Laslett, revised edition, Cambridge, Cambridge University Press, 1963. Hereafter referred to as the *Treatises*.

7 J. C. Stewart-Robertson, 'The Well-Principled Savage, Or the Child of the Scottish Enlightenment,' *Journal of the History of Ideas*, 42(3), July–September 1981, pp. 503–25.

8 Aristotle, *The Politics*, Chapter V, §9.

9 Robert Nozick, *Anarchy, State, and Utopia*, Oxford, Basil Blackwell, 1974, pp. 287–9.

10 Lawrence C. Becker, *Property Rights: Philosophic Foundations*, London, Routledge & Kegan Paul, 1977, pp. 37–9.

11 R. W. K. Hinton, 'Husbands, Fathers and Conquerors: I', *Political Studies*, 15(3), 1967, p. 294.

12 Richard Allen Chapman, '*Leviathan* Writ Small: Thomas Hobbes on the Family', *American Political Science Review*, 69(1), March 1975, pp. 76–90.

2 THE CONCEPT OF CHILDHOOD

1 Philippe Ariès, *L'Enfant et la vie familiale sous l'ancien régime*, Paris, Libraire Plon, 1960. Translated from the French by Robert Baldick as *Centuries of Childhood*, London, Jonathan Cape, 1962.
2 Ariès, *Centuries of Childhood*, p. 125.
3 See Linda Pollock's *Forgotten Children: Parent–Child Relations from 1500 to 1900*, Cambridge, Cambridge University Press, 1983.
4 Daniel Farson, *Birthrights*, London, Collier Macmillan, 1974; another child liberationist, John Holt, similarly speaks of an *Escape from Childhood*, Harmondsworth, Penguin, 1975.
5 N. Postman, *The Disappearance of Childhood*, New York, Vintage Books, 1994, p. xi.
6 *A Theory of Justice*, Oxford, Oxford University Press, 1972, p. 5.
7 T. E. James, 'The Age of Majority', *The American Journal of Legal History*, 4, 1960, pp. 22–33.

3 THE MODERN CONCEPTION OF CHILDHOOD

1 Quoted in the Introduction to Margaret Mead and Martha Wolfenstein (eds), *Childhood in Contemporary Cultures*, Chicago, University of Chicago Press, 1955.
2 The CRC is available in a number of places, but a good web site is that of UNICEF: http://www.unicef.org/crc/crc.htm
3 'Understanding Child Labour', Special Issue of *Childhood*, 6(1), February 1999.
4 'The Subjection of Women' (1869), in *Collected Works of John Stuart Mill*, vol. XXI, London, Routledge & Kegan Paul, 1984, pp. 270, 305.
5 For full bibliographical details of work by G. S. Hall and other pioneers of child psychology see Wayne Dennis, 'Historical Beginnings of Child Psychology', *Psychological Bulletin*, 46, 1949, pp. 224–35.
6 Harry Hendrick, *Children, Childhood and English Society 1880–1990*, Cambridge, Cambridge University Press, 1997, pp. 3–4.
7 See for instance his 'From Is to Ought: How to Commit the Naturalistic Fallacy and Get Away with It in the Study of Moral Development', in Theodore Mischel (ed.), *Cognitive Development and Epistemology*, New York, Academic Press, 1971, pp. 151–235.
8 This distinction is suggested by William J. Bouwsma in an excellent article, 'Christian Adulthood', in *Daedalus*, 105(2), Spring 1976, pp. 77–92. Bouwsma describes the distinction as one between 'adulthood' and 'manhood'. Further articles in what is a special issue of *Daedalus* explore the non-Western understanding of adulthood: Tu Wei-Ming, 'The Confucian Perception of Adulthood', pp. 109–23, and Thomas P. Rohlen, 'The Promise of Adulthood in Japanese Spiritualism', pp. 125–43.

9 Quoted in John Cleverley and D. C. Phillips, *From Locke to Spock: Influential Models of the Child in Modern Western Thought*, Melbourne, Melbourne University Press, 1976, p. 30.

10 Behn is quoted in Lawrence Stone, *The Family, Sex and Marriage in England 1500–1800*, abridged edition, Harmondsworth, Penguin, 1979, pp. 255–6; *Émile*, Harmondsworth, Penguin, 1991, p. 37.

11 The following paragraphs largely summarise Peter Coveney, *Poor Monkey, The Child in Literature*, London, Rockliff, 1957.

12 J. M. Barrie, *Peter Pan and Other Plays*, edited with an Introduction by Peter Hollindale, Oxford, Oxford University Press, 1995.

13 Michel Foucault, *Histoire de la sexualité, 1, La Volonté de savoir*, Paris, Gallimard, 1976, esp. pp. 38–42; translated by Robert Hurley as *The History of Sexuality, An Introduction*, Harmondsworth, Penguin, 1981, esp. pp. 27–30.

14 For an interesting discussion of these issues, see Jenny Kitzinger, 'Defending Innocence: Ideologies of Childhood', *Feminist Review*, 28, January 1988, pp. 77–87.

4 CHILDREN'S RIGHTS: MORAL AND LEGAL

1 Neil MacCormick, 'Children's Rights: A Test-Case for Theories of Rights', *Archiv für Rechts und Sozialphilosophie*, 62(3), 1976, pp. 305–17.

2 H. L. A. Hart, 'Bentham on Rights', in A. W. Simpson (ed.), *Oxford Essays in Jurisprudence*, Oxford, Oxford University Press, 1973, p. 184, fn. 86.

3 Joel Feinberg, 'The Child's Right to an Open Future', in *Whose Child? Parental Rights, Parental Authority and State Power*, edited by W. Aiken and H. LaFollette, Totowa, NJ, Rowman & Littlefield, 1980, pp. 124–53.

4 John Eekelaar, 1986. 'The Emergence of Children's Rights, *Oxford Journal of Legal Studies*, 6, 1986, pp. 161–82.

5 R. H. Mnookin, 'Foster Care – In Whose Best Interests?' in *Having Children: Philosophical and Legal Reflections on Parenthood*, edited by O. O'Neill and W. Ruddick, Oxford, Oxford University Press, 1979, pp. 179–213; Jon Elster, *Solomonic Judgements, Studies in the Limitations of Rationality*, Cambridge, Cambridge University Press, 1989.

6 P. Alston (ed.), *The Best Interests of the Child: Reconciling Culture and Human Rights*, Oxford, Clarendon Press, 1994.

7 *Gillick v. West Norfolk and Wisbech Health Authority* (1985) 3 All ER, pp. 188–9.

5 LIBERATION OR CARETAKING?

1 Richard Farson, *Birthrights*, London, Collier Macmillan, 1974; John Holt, *Escape From Childhood, The Needs and Rights of Children*, Harmondsworth, Penguin, 1974.

2 Shulamith Firestone, *The Dialectic of Sex, The Case for Feminist Revolution*, London, Jonathan Cape, 1970, p. 81.

3 Holt, *Escape From Childhood*, p. 28.
4 See, for example, Holt, *Escape From Childhood*, pp. 120, 131 and 203; Farson, *Birthrights*, p. 31. My emphases.
5 Farson, *Birthrights*, respectively pp. 172 and 185.
6 Howard Cohen, *Equal Rights for Children*, Totowa, NJ, Littlefield, Adams & Co., 1980.
7 Holt, *Escape from Childhood*, p. 15; emphasis in original.
8 Farson, *Birthrights*, p. 11.
9 Ibid., p. 27.
10 *On Liberty*, Harmondsworth, Penguin, 1974, p. 166.
11 See Connie K. Beck, Greta Glavis, Susan A. Glover, Mary Barnes Jenkins and Richard A. Nardi, 'The Rights of Children: A Trust Model', *Fordham Law Review*, 46(4), March 1978, pp. 669–780.
12 L. M. Purdy, *In Their Best Interest? The Case Against Equal Rights for Children*, Ithaca NY, Cornell University Press, 1992.
13 Ibid., p. 217.
14 Ibid., p. 113.
15 Joel Feinberg, 'The Child's Right to an Open Future', in William Aiken and Hugh La Follette (eds), *Whose Child? Children's Rights, Parental Authority and State Power*, Totowa, NJ, Rowman & Littlefield, 1980, pp. 124–53.
16 Eamonn Callan, 'Autonomy, Childrearing, and Good Lives', in D. Archard and C. Macleod (eds), *The Moral and Political Status of Children*, Oxford, Oxford University Press, 2002, pp. 118–41.
17 S. Burtt, 'In Defense of *Yoder*: Parental Authority and the Public Schools', in I. Shapiro and R. Hardin (eds.), *Political Order*, Nomos XXXVIII, New York, New York University Press, pp. 412–37.
18 See, for instance, Will Kymlicka, *Liberalism, Community, and Culture*, Oxford, Clarendon Press, 1989.

6 ARBITRARINESS AND INCOMPETENCE

1 Richard Farson, *Birthrights*, London, Collier Macmillan, 1974, pp. 172 and 185.
2 John Kleinig, 'Mill, Children, and Rights', *Educational Philosophy and Theory*, 8(1), 1976, p. 7.
3 See, for instance, Margaret Donaldson, *Children's Minds*, Glasgow, Fontana, 1978.
4 Immanuel Kant, *The Philosophy of Law: An Exposition of the Fundamental Principles of Jurisprudence as the Science of Right*, translated by W. Hastie, Edinburgh, T. & T. Clark, 1887, p. 118.

7 CHILDREN'S RIGHTS TO VOTE AND SEXUAL CHOICE

1 For an excellent discussion of this issue see Michael Walzer, *Spheres of Justice: A Defence of Pluralism and Equality*, Oxford, Basil Blackwell, 1983, Chapter 2.

2 For UK studies of involving young people in politics see Vicki Combe, *Up For It: Getting Young People Involved in Local Government*, The National Youth Agency for the Joseph Rowntree Foundation, 2002, and Clarissa White, Sarah Bruce and Jane Ritchie, *Young People's Politics: Political Interest and Engagement Amongst 14 to 24-year-olds*, York, York Publishing Services, 2000.

3 Speech in the House of Commons, 11 November 1947.

4 Olive Stevens, *Children Talking Politics: Political Learning in Childhood*, Oxford, Martin Robertson, 1982, p. 148.

5 For a good example of an outline and defence of a model civic education, see Final Report of the Advisory Group on Citizenship, *Education for Citizenship and the Teaching of Democracy in Schools*, London, Qualifications and Curriculum Authority, 1998.

6 Jenny Kitzinger, 'Defending Innocence: Ideologies of Childhood,' *Feminist Review*, 28, 1988, pp. 77–87.

7 The following paragraphs summarise the findings of Ronald and Juliette Goldman, *Sexual Thinking: A Comparative Study of Children Aged 5 to 15 Years in Australia, North America, Britain and Sweden*, London, Routledge & Kegan Paul, 1982.

8 See Michèle Elliott, *Preventing Child Sexual Assault: A Practical Guide to Talking with Children*, London, Bedford Square Press/NCVO, 1985.

9 John Stuart Mill, *On Liberty*, edited by Gertrude Himmelfarb, Harmondsworth, Penguin, 1974, p. 69.

10 Wolfenden quoted in Policy Advisory Committee on Sexual Offences, *Report on the Age of Consent in Relation to Sexual Offences*, London, HMSO, April 1981, §35.

11 See, for instance, Tom O'Carroll, *Paedophilia: The Radical Case*, London, Peter Own, 1980, and the contributions by Jamie Gough, 'Childhood, Sexuality, and Pedophilia' and Pat Califia, 'Man/Boy Love and the Lesbian/Gay Movement', to Daniel Tsang (ed.), *The Age Taboo: Gay Male Sexuality, Power, and Consent*, London, Gay Man's Press, 1981, pp. 65–71 and pp. 133–46.

8 THE WRONGS OF CHILDREN'S RIGHTS

1 For an extensive list of the legal rights of children in Britain, see Michael Freeman, 'Coming of Age', *Legal Action Group Bulletin*, June 1977, pp. 137–8.

2 C. M. Rogers and L. S. Wrightsman, 'Attitudes Towards Children's Rights: Nurturance or Self-Determination?', *Journal of Social Issues*, 34(2), 1978, pp. 59, 61.

3 For a classic statement of this view see Joel Feinberg, 'The Nature and Value of Rights', *The Journal of Value Inquiry*, 4, 1970, pp. 243–61.

4 *Community and Association (Gemeinschaft und Gesellschaft)*, translated and supplemented by Charles P. Loomis, London, Routledge & Kegan Paul, 1955.
5 The most central and relevant 'communitarian' text is Michael Sandel, *Liberalism and the Limits of Justice*, Cambridge, Cambridge University Press, 1982.
6 Carol Gilligan, *In a Different Voice, Psychological Theory and Women's Development*, Cambridge, MA, Harvard University Press, 1982.
7 Sarah Ruddick, 'Maternal Thinking', *Feminist Studies*, 6(2), Summer 1980, pp. 342–67.
8 Michael Ignatieff argues for something like this in his *The Needs of Strangers*, London, Chatto & Windus, 1984.
9 Sandel, *Liberalism and the Limits of Justice*, pp. 34–5.
10 *Being and Nothingness, An Essay on Phenomenological Ontology*, translated and with an introduction by Hazel E. Barnes, London, Methuen, 1957, p. 367.
11 'When Justice Replaces Affection: The Need for Rights', *Harvard Journal of Law and Public Policy*, 11(3), 1988, pp. 625–47.
12 Onora O'Neill, 'Children's Rights and Children's Lives,' *Ethics*, 98, 1988, pp. 445–63.

9 CHILDREN UNDER THE LAW

1 Lord Kilbrandon, *The Kilbrandon Report: Children and Young Persons, Scotland*, 3rd edition, London: The Stationery Office, 1995.
2 See, for instance, evidence cited in Paul Cavadino, 'Children Who Kill: a European Perspective', *New Law Journal*, 13 September 1996, p. 1,325.

10 BEARING AND REARING

1 http://www.hmso.gov.uk/acts/acts1998/19980042.htm
2 P. Singer and D. Wells, *The Reproduction Revolution: New Ways of Making Babies*, Oxford, Oxford University Press, 1984.
3 Justine C. Burley, 'The Price of Eggs: Who Should Bear the Costs of Fertility Treatment?' in J. Harris and S. Holms (eds.), *The Future of Human Reproduction: Ethics, Choice, and Regulation*, Oxford, Clarendon Press, 1998, pp. 127–49.
4 Quoted in A. Honneth, *The Struggle for Recognition: The Moral Grammar of Social Conflict*, translated by J. Anderson, Cambridge, Polity Press, 1995.
5 A good separation and discussion of the issues is provided by John Harris in his 'The Right to Found a Family', in Geoffrey Scarre (ed.), *Children, Parents and Politics*, Cambridge, Cambridge University Press, 1989, pp. 133–53.
6 *Émile*, Harmondsworth, Penguin, 1991, p. 49.
7 The classic statement and discussion of the 'non-identity' puzzle is Derek Parfit, *Reasons and Persons*, Oxford, Clarendon Press, 1984, pp. 357–66.
8 John Robertson, *Children of Choice: Freedom and the New Reproductive Technologies*, Princeton, NJ, Princeton University Press, 1994; John Harris, *Wonderwoman and Superman: The Ethics of Human Biotechnology*, Oxford, Oxford University Press,

1993; Melinda Roberts, *Child Versus Childmaker: Future Persons and Present Duties in Ethics and the Law*, Boulder, Rowman & Littlefield, 1998.

9 See Onora O'Neill, *Autonomy and Trust in Bioethics*, Cambridge, Cambridge University Press, 2002, pp. 60–3.

10 *Nichomachean Ethics*, translated by W. D. Ross, revised by J. O. Urmson, Oxford, Oxford University Press, 1975, Book VIII.12, 20–5.

11 *Right and Wrong*, Cambridge, MA, Harvard University Press, 1978, p. 152.

12 *The Examined Life: Philosophical Meditations*, New York, Simon and Schuster, 1989, p. 28.

13 *On Liberty*, Harmondsworth, Penguin, 1974, p. 175.

14 'Are There Any Natural Rights?', in Anthony Quinton (ed.), *Political Philosophy*, Oxford, Oxford University Press, 1967, p. 63.

15 John Bowlby's ideas are to be found in his three-volume *Attachment and Loss*, London, Hogarth Press, 1965, 1973 and 1980. The important 'revisionist' works are A. M. and C. B. Clarke (eds), *Early Experience: Myth and Evidence*, London, Open Books, 1976; M. Rutter, *Maternal Deprivation Reassessed*, Harmondsworth, Penguin, 1972, 2nd edition, 1981; and J. Kagan, R. B. Kearsley and P. R. Zelazo, *Infancy: Its Place in Human Development*, Cambridge, MA, Harvard University Press, 1978.

16 Anna Freud and Dorothy Burlingham, *Young Children in War Time: A Year's Work in a Residential Nursery*, London, Allen & Unwin, 1944; Anna Freud and Dorothy Burlingham, *Infants Without Families: The Case For and Against Residential Nurseries*, London, Allen & Unwin, 1944.

17 I. Kant, *The Metaphysics of Morals*, translated and edited by Mary Gregor, with an Introduction by Roger J. Sullivan, Cambridge: Cambridge University Press, 1996, pp. 64–5.

18 P. Montague, 'The Myth of Parental Rights', *Social Theory and Practice*, 26, 2000, pp. 47–68.

11 FAMILY AND STATE

1 Christopher Lasch, *Haven in a Heartless World: The Family Besieged*, New York, Basic Books, 1977; Jacques Donzelot, *La Police des familles*, Paris, Les Editions de Minuit, 1977, translated by Robert Hurley as *The Policing of Families: Welfare Versus the State*, London, Hutchinson, 1980.

2 The following paragraphs summarise points made at greater length in two admirable articles: Frances E. Olsen, 'The Myth of State Intervention in the Family', *University of Michigan Journal of Law Reform*, 18(4), 1985, pp. 835–64, and M. D. A. Freeman, 'Towards a Critical Theory of Family Law', *Current Legal Problems*, 38, 1985, pp. 153–85.

3 The classic statement of the idea of the family as a school of injustice is to be found in J. S. Mill, *The Subjection of Women* [1869], in J. M. Robson (ed.), *Collected Works of John Stuart Mill*, Toronto, Toronto University Press, Volume XXI, 1984, pp. 294–5.

4 What James Fishkin calls a 'trilemma' in his excellent *Justice, Equal Opportunity, and the Family*, New Haven, CT, Yale University Press, 1983.
5 The problem is raised by Sue Himmelweit in 'Abortion: Individual and Social Control', *Feminist Review*, 5, 1980, p. 66, and discussed by Christopher Berry in his *The Idea of a Democratic Community*, Hemel Hempstead, Harvester Wheatsheaf, 1989, pp. 31–3.
6 See, for instance, Elizabeth Wilson, 'Women, the "Community" and the "Family"', in Alan Walker (ed.), *Community Care: The Family, the State and Social Policy*, Oxford, Basil Blackwell and Martin Robertson, 1982, pp. 40–55.

12 PARENTAL RIGHTS TO PRIVACY AND AUTONOMY

1 Quoted in M. D. A. Freeman, 'Freedom and the Welfare State: Childrearing, Parental Autonomy and State Intervention', *Journal of Social Welfare Law*, March 1983, p. 71.
2 Joseph Goldstein, Anna Freud and Albert J. Solnit, *Before the Best Interests of the Child*, New York, Free Press, 1979, p. 9.
3 The most notable defence of privacy in terms of intimacy is by Charles Fried, 'Privacy', *Yale Law Journal*, 77, 1968, pp. 475–93.
4 This is argued by Richard Wasserstrom in his 'Privacy: Some Arguments and Assumptions' in Richard Bronaugh (ed.), *Philosophical Law*, Westport, CT, Greenwood Press, 1978, pp. 148–66.
5 A useful survey of various cultural practices is provided in Irwin Altman, 'Privacy Regulation: Culturally Universal or Culturally Specific?' *Journal of Social Issues*, 33(3), 1977, pp. 66–84.
6 For an elegant and influential defence of this view see Ronald Dworkin's 'Liberalism' in his *A Matter of Principle*, Oxford, Clarendon Press, 1986, pp. 181–204.

13 COLLECTIVISM

1 The quotations from the *Republic* come from the Francis Cornford translation, Oxford, Oxford University Press, 1941; those from the other dialogues are to be found in *The Collected Dialogues of Plato*, edited by Edith Hamilton and Huntington Cairns, Princeton, NJ, Princeton University Press, 1961.
2 See Julia Annas, 'Plato's *Republic* and Feminism', *Philosophy*, 51, 1976, pp. 307–21.
3 The criticisms are to be found in Book II, Chapters I to IV of his *Politics*. The best edition of this is *The Politics of Aristotle*, translated and with an introduction by Ernest Barker, Oxford, Oxford University Press, 1946.
4 Ibid. p. 47.
5 Ibid. p. 43.
6 See Bruno Bettelheim, *The Children of the Dream*, London, Thames & Hudson, 1969.

7 This is the main argument of Hugh LaFollette, 'Licensing Parents', *Philosophy & Public Affairs*, 9(2), 1980, pp. 182–97.

8 For a brief but excellent critique of the medical model, see Stuart Montgomery, 'Problems in the Perinatal Prediction of Child Abuse', *British Journal of Social Work*, 12, 1982, pp. 189–96. See also Robert Dingwall, 'Some Problems about Predicting Child Abuse and Neglect', in Olive Stevenson (ed.), *Child Abuse: Professional Practice and Public Policy*, London, Harvester Wheatsheaf, 1989, pp. 28–53.

14 THE PROBLEM OF CHILD ABUSE

1 For a standard account see Samuel X. Radbill, 'A History of Child Abuse and Infanticide', in R. E. Helfer and C. H. Kempe (eds), *The Battered Child*, Chicago, University of Chicago Press, 1974, pp. 3–21.

2 These can be found in, respectively, the writings of Linda Gordon, *Heroes of Their Own Lives: The Politics and History of Family Violence, Boston 1880–1960*, London, Virago, 1989, and 'Feminism and Social Control: The Case of Child Abuse and Neglect', in Juliet Mitchell and Ann Oakley (eds), *What is Feminism?*, Oxford, Basil Blackwell, 1986, pp. 63–84; Stephen J. Pfohl, 'The "Discovery" of Child Abuse', *Social Problems*, 24(3), 1977, pp. 310–23; and Nigel Parton, *The Politics of Child Abuse*, London, Macmillan, 1985.

3 R. J. Gelles, 'The Social Construction of Child Abuse,' *American Journal of Orthopsychiatry*, 45, 1975, pp. 363–71; Pfohl, 'The "Discovery" of Child Abuse'.

4 G. K. Behlmer, *Child Abuse and Moral Reform in England, 1870–1908*, Stanford, CA, Stanford University Press, 1982; H. C. Kempe *et al.*, 'The Battered Child Syndrome', *Journal of the American Medical Association*, 181, 1962, pp. 17–24.

5 I. Hacking, 'The Sociology of Knowledge About Child Abuse', *Nous*, 22, 1988, p. 54 and I. Hacking, 'The Making and Molding of Child Abuse', *Critical Inquiry*, 17, 1991, p. 257.

6 C. L. Stevenson, 'Persuasive Definitions', *Mind*, 47, 1938, pp. 331–50.

7 D. Gough, 'Defining the Problem', *Child Abuse and Neglect*, 20, 1996, p. 996.

8 'Non-Neutral Principles', *The Journal of Philosophy*, 71(14), 15 August 1974, p. 492.

9 D. Finkelhor and J. Korbin, 'Child Abuse as an International Issue', *Child Abuse and Neglect*, 12, 1988, p. 8.

10 Department of Health and Social Services, *Working Together: a Guide to Interagency Co-operation for the Protection of Children from Abuse*, London, HMSO, 1991.

11 M. Schechter and L. Roberge, 'Sexual Exploitation', in R. Helfer and C. Kempe (eds), *Child Abuse and Neglect: The Family and Community*, Cambridge, MA: Ballinger Publishing, 1976, p. 129.

12 J. Garbarino, E. Guttman and J. Shelley, *The Psychologically Battered Child*, San Francisco: Jossey-Bass, 1986, p. 8.

13 Susan H. Bitkensy, 'Spare the Rod, Embrace Our Humanity: Toward a New Legal

Regime Prohibiting Corporal Punishment of Children', *University of Michigan Journal of Law Reform*, 31, 1998, pp. 353–474. This is a comprehensive statement of the case against corporal punishment.

14 What follows relies on the useful and interesting *Child Abuse and Neglect: Cross Cultural Perspectives*, edited by Jill E. Korbin, with forewords by Robert B. Edgerton and C. Henry Kempe, Berkeley, University of California Press, 1981.

15 'Unraveling Child Abuse', *American Journal of Orthopsychiatry*, 45(3), April 1975, pp. 346–7; see also his *Violence Against Children: Physical Abuse in the United States*, Cambridge, MA, Harvard University Press, 1970.

16 For a crisp and concise statement of this view, see the excellent article by Leroy H. Pelton, 'Child Abuse and Neglect: The Myth of Classlessness', *American Journal of Orthopsychiatry*, 48(4), October 1978, pp. 608–17; reprinted in *idem* (ed.), *The Social Context of Child Abuse and Neglect*, New York, Human Sciences Press, 1981, pp. 23–38.

17 Colin Findlay, 'Child Abuse: The Dutch Response', *Practice*, 1(4), 1987–8, p. 380.

18 Ruth S. Kempe and C. Henry Kempe, *The Common Secret*, New York, Freeman, 1984, p. 9.

15 CONCLUSION: A MODEST COLLECTIVIST PROPOSAL

1 For an interesting general discussion of these issues, see Bob Deacon, 'Social Administration, Social Policy and Socialism', *Critical Social Policy*, 1(1), Summer 1981, pp. 43–66.

2 Aristotle, *The Politics*, 1337ª, 10–19.

3 Jean-Jacques Rousseau, *Émile or On Education*, Harmondsworth, Penguin, 1991, p. 49.

4 For a good introduction to the sex–gender distinction, discussion of its nature and significance for feminism, and a guide to writing on the topic, see Linda Nicholson, 'Gender', in *A Companion to Feminist Philosophy*, edited by Alison M. Jaggar and Iris Marion Young, Oxford, Basil Blackwell, 1998, pp. 289–97.

5 *Democratic Education*, Princeton, NJ, Princeton University Press, 1987, Chapter 1.

6 See, for instance, the quotes from Justice McReynolds in *Meyer* v. *Nebraska* (1923) and *Pierce* v. *Society of Sisters* (1925) which serve as a preface to David Richard's 'The Individual, the Family, and the Constitution: A Jurisprudential Perspective', *New York University Law Review*, 55(1), April 1980, pp. 1–2.

7 Quoted in Urie Bronfenbrenner, *Two Worlds of Childhood: U.S. and U.S.S.R.*, London, George Allen & Unwin, 1971, p. 51.

8 Farson, *Birthrights*, London, Collier Macmillan, 1974, Chapter 4.

9 For an interesting account of the Norwegian experiment with an ombudsman see Målfrid Grude Flekkøy, *A Voice for Children: Speaking Out as Their Ombudsman*, London, Jessica Kingsley Publishers, 1991.

10 See Jill E. Korbin (ed.), *Child Abuse and Neglect: Cross Cultural Perspectives*, esp. 'Conclusions' by Jill E. Korbin.

11 Robert Dingwall, John Eekelaar and Topsy Murray, *The Protection of Children: State Intervention and Family Life*, Oxford, Basil Blackwell, 1983.
12 A fascinating study which makes precisely this point is Christina Hardyment, *Dream Babies: Childcare from Locke to Spock*, London, Jonathan Cape, 1983.

BIBLIOGRAPHICAL ESSAY

There is evidence of a renewed interest by anglophone philosophers in childhood in recent years. An early classic philosophical study of the family is Jeffrey Blustein, *Parents and Children: The Ethics of the Family*, Oxford, Oxford University Press, 1982. Classic early collections are: Onora O'Neill and William Ruddock (eds), *Having Children: Philosophical and Legal Reflections on Parenthood*, Oxford, Oxford University Press, 1979; William Aiken and Hugh LaFollette, *Whose Child? Children's Rights, Parental Authority, and State Power*, Totowa, NJ, Rowman & Littlefield, 1980; and Geoffrey Scarre (ed.), *Children, Parents and Politics*, Cambridge, Cambridge University Press, 1989. A good collection whose focus is the CRC is Philip Alston, Stephen Parker and John Seymour (eds), *Children, Rights, and the Law*, Oxford, Oxford University Press, 1992. David Archard and Colin Macleod (eds) *The Moral and Political Status of Children*, Oxford, Oxford University Press, 2002, is a recent collection of articles addressing the questions of children's rights, their education, and the family and justice. Susan M. Turner and Gareth B. Matthews (eds), *The Philosopher's Child, Critical Essays in the Western Tradition*, Rochester, NY, University of Rochester Press, 1998, collects a number of studies of various great philosophers – from Socrates to Rawls – on children.

The websites of two major international organisations devoted to the welfare of children globally are: Unicef (www.unicef.org) and Save the Children (www.save thechildren.org).

M. V. C. Jeffreys, *John Locke: Prophet of Common Sense*, London, Methuen, 1967, supplies a straightforward if unilluminating commentary on Locke's educational writings, whilst Edmund Leites's 'Locke's Liberal Theory of Parenthood', in Onora O'Neill and William Ruddock (eds), *Having Children*, pp. 306–18, offers an interesting analysis of Locke's ideas, drawing on both the *Thoughts* and the *Two Treatises*. For interesting discussions of Locke's views on patriarchy and the family, see Melissa A. Butler, 'Early Liberal Roots of Feminism: John Locke and the Attack on Patriarchy', *The American Political Science Review*, 72(1), 1978, pp. 135–50, and Linda J. Nicholson, *Gender and History: The Limits of Social Theory in the Age of the Family*, New York, Columbia University Press, 1986, Chapter 5, 'John Locke: The Theoretical Separation of the Family and the State'.

Two examples of accounts of the history of childhood which use Ariès's thesis to draw political conclusions for the present are Pat Thane, 'Childhood in History', in

Michael King (ed.), *Childhood, Welfare and Justice*, London, Batsford, 1981, pp. 6–25, and Martin Hoyles, 'Childhood in Historical Perspective', in Martin Hoyles (ed.), *Changing Childhood*, London, Writers and Readers Publishing Cooperative, 1979, pp. 16–29. Two good reviews of Ariès's book, which usefully summarise the main criticisms of it since publication are Adrian Wilson, 'The Infancy of the History of Childhood', *History and Theory*, 19, 1980, pp. 132–53 and Richard T. Vann, 'The Youth of *Centuries of Childhood*', *History and Theory*, 21, 1982, pp. 279–97. Jerome Kroll's 'The Concept of Childhood in the Middle Ages', *Journal of the History of the Behavioral Sciences*, 13, 1977, pp. 384–93 offers a direct rebuttal of Ariès's thesis about medieval society's lack of a concept of childhood. Linda Pollock's *Forgotten Children: Parent–Child Relations from 1500–1900*, Cambridge, Cambridge University Press, 1983, uses evidence from diaries, autobiographies and press reports to show that, *pace* Ariès, parents and society in general have treated children in a remarkably consistent way over the last five centuries.

Good sources for the social constructionist theory of childhood are Chris Jenks, *Childhood*, London, Routledge, 1996, the editors' first chapter 'A New Paradigm for the Sociology of Childhood' in Allison James and Alan Prout (eds), *Constructing and Reconstructing Contemporary Issues in the Sociological Study of Childhood*, London, The Falmer Press, 1990, pp. 7–34, and Barry Goldson '"Childhood": An Introduction to Historical and Theoretical Analyses', in Phil Scraton (ed.), *'Childhood' in 'Crisis'*, London, UCL Press, 1997, pp. 1–27.

A rare philosophical treatment of the concept of childhood which treats the status of the child from a Kantian perspective is Tamar Schapiro, 'What is a Child?', *Ethics* 109(4), 1999, pp. 715–738.

The standard commentaries on Rousseau's *Émile* are provided by Peter Jimack, *La genèse et la redaction de l'Émile de J.-J. Rousseau*', in *Studies on Voltaire and the Eighteenth Century*, vol. 13, Geneva: Institut et Musé Voltaire, 1960, and *Rousseau, 'Émile'*, London, Grant and Cutler, 1983. For an appreciation of Rousseau within the history of educational thought see G. H. Bantock, *Studies in the History of Educational Theory*, Vol. I: Artifice and Nature, 1350–1705, Chapter 12, and Vol. II: The Minds and the Masses, 1760–980, Chapter 1. Chapter 10 of Volume I discusses Locke. Timothy O'Hagan's *Rousseau*, London, Routledge, 1999, is a good, substantial, recent critical study of Rousseau's work as a whole. Chapter III discusses *Émile*.

The main sources for the view that, in the past, children were habitually treated with indifference or cruelty are Lloyd de Mause, 'The Evolution of Childhood' in *idem* (ed.), *The History of Childhood*, London, Souvenir Press, 1976, pp. 1–73, and Lawrence Stone, *The Family: Sex and Marriage in England 1500–1800*, London, Weidenfeld & Nicolson, 1977.

The standard history of English childhood is Ivy Pinchbeck and Margaret Hewitt, *Children in English Society*, London, Routledge & Kegan Paul, vol. 1, 1969, and vol. 2, 1973. For histories of Western theories of child-rearing see Christina Hardyment, *Dream Babies: Child Care from Locke to Spock*, London, Jonathan Cape, 1983; also John and Elizabeth Newson, 'Cultural Aspects of Childrearing in the English-Speaking World', in Martin P. M. Richards (ed.), *The Integration of a Child into a Social World*, Cambridge, Cambridge University Press, 1974, pp. 53–81.

For useful evidence of childhood in non-Western cultures see Beatrice B. Whiting (ed.), *Six Cultures: Studies of Child Rearing*, New York, John Wiley & Sons, 1963; Margaret Mead and Martha Wolfenstein (eds), *Childhood in Contemporary Cultures*, Chicago, University of Chicago Press, 1955, Part II on Bali; and Richard B. Lee and Irven DeVore (eds), *Kalahari Hunter-Gatherers: Studies of the !Kung San and Their Neighbours*, Cambridge, MA, Harvard University Press, 1976, Part III, 'Childhood'.

John Cleverley and D. C. Phillips, *From Locke to Spock: Influential Models of the Child in Modern Western Thought*, Melbourne, Melbourne University Press, 1976, is a good general survey of modern thinking about childhood. George Boas, *The Cult of Childhood*, London, Warburg Institute, 1966, examines the use of the child as a metaphor for the primitive in art and religion. Peter Coveney's *Poor Monkey: The Child in Literature*, London, Rockcliff, 1957, is the classic study of the subject.

Wayne Dennis, 'Historical Beginnings of Child Psychology', *Psychological Bulletin*, 46, 1949, pp. 224–35, supplies an informative chronology and bibliography of the first psychological studies of children. Arlene Sklonik, 'The Limits of Childhood: Conceptions of Child Development and Social Context', *Law and Contemporary Problems*, 39(3), Summer 1975, pp. 38–77, critically summarises the main developmental accounts of childhood in their relation to policy-making.

The main relevant works of Piaget are his *The Language and Thought of the Child*, translated by Marjorie Gabain, London, Routledge & Kegan Paul, 1932 and *The Child's Conception of the World*, translated by Joan and Andrew Tomlinson, London, Routledge & Kegan Paul, 1929. The main relevant writings of Freud are *Three Essays on the Theory of Sexuality* (1905) and the case study, 'Analysis of a Phobia in a Five-Year-Old Boy' ('Little Hans') (1909). These may be found in *Standard Edition of the Complete Psychological Works of Sigmund Freud*, translated from the German under the general editorship of James Strachey in collaboration with Anna Freud, assisted by Alix Strachey and Alan Tyson, London, The Hogarth Press, 1953–74, respectively vol. 7, pp. 125–248 and vol. 10, pp. 3–152. Excellent critical introductions to the work of each can be found in, respectively, Margaret Boden, *Piaget*, Glasgow, Fontana, 1979, and Richard Wollheim, *Freud*, Glasgow, Fontana, 1971.

A good critique of Piaget's theories and defence of the view that children are cognitively competent at an early age is Margaret Donaldson's *Children's Minds*, Glasgow, Fontana, 1978. Further discussion, with useful references, of children's mental abilities can be found in Richard L. Gregory (ed.), *The Oxford Companion to the Mind*, Oxford, Oxford University Press, 1987, under the entries for 'Children's Understanding of the Mental World', 'Mind in Infancy' and 'Reasoning: Development in Children'. Jerome Kagan's *The Nature of the Child*, New York, Basic Books, 1986, is a masterful review of the major themes in modern child psychology by one of its most distinguished modern practitioners.

Kohlberg's ideas are also outlined in L. Kohlberg and R. Kramer, 'Continuities and Discontinuities in Childhood and Adult Moral Development', *Human Development*, 12, 1969, pp. 93–120.

Philosophical introductions to the topic of rights range from the technically difficult, L. W. Sumner, *The Moral Foundation of Rights*, Oxford, Clarendon Press, 1987, which mentions the problem of 'rights inflation', to the accessible introduction by Jeremy

Waldron to *idem* (ed.), *Theories of Rights*, Oxford, Oxford University Press, 1984, or his 'Rights' in R. E. Goodin and P. Pettit (eds), *A Companion to Contemporary Political Philosophy*, Oxford, Blackwell, 1993. Rex Martin and James W. Nickel, 'Recent Work on the Concept of Rights', *American Philosophical Quarterly*, 17(3), July 1980, pp. 165–80, is a somewhat dated but useful bibliographical survey. Another is Tibor R. Machan, 'Some Recent Work in Human Rights Theory', *American Philosophical Quarterly*, 17(2), April 1980, pp. 103–15.

Prominent defenders of the 'will theory' of rights are H. L. A. Hart, 'Bentham on Legal Rights', in A. W. Simpson (ed.), *Oxford Essays in Jurisprudence*, Oxford, Oxford University Press, pp. 171–201, L. W. Sumner, *The Moral Foundation of Rights*, and H. Steiner, *An Essay on Rights*, Oxford, Blackwell, 1994. Prominent defenders of the 'interest theory' of rights are Neil MacCormick's 'Children's Rights: A Test-Case for Theories of Rights', *Archiv für Rechts und Sozialphilosophie*, 62(3), 1976, pp. 305–17, J. Raz, 'Legal Rights', *Oxford Journal of Legal Studies*, 4(1), 1984, pp. 1–21, and N. H. Kramer, 'Rights Without Trimmings', in *idem*, N. E. Simmonds and H. Steiner (eds), *A Debate Over Rights, Philosophical Enquiries*, Oxford, Clarendon Press, 1998.

Besides the books by Holt, Farson and Firestone, Howard Cohen, *Equal Rights for Children*, Totowa, NJ, Littlefield, Adams & Co., 1980, is relevant, and *Children's Rights: Towards the Liberation of the Child*, by Paul Adams, Leila Berg, Nan Berger, Michael Duane, A. S. Neill and Robert Ollendorff, London, Panther, 1972, is a useful representative collection of 'liberationist' pieces. Contemporaneous influential radical accounts of education were to be found in Paul Goodman's *Growing Up Absurd: Problems of Youth in the Organised Society*, New York, Vintage Books, 1960; A. S. Neill's *Summerhill*, Harmondsworth, Penguin, 1968; and Leila Berg's *Risinghill: Death of a Comprehensive School*, Harmondsworth, Penguin, 1968.

A standard and influential liberal discussion of paternalism is Gerald Dworkin's 'Paternalism', in *Morality and the Law*, edited by Richard Wasserstrom, Belmont, Wadsworth, 1971, pp. 107–26. Dworkin has also provided an excellent discussion of autonomy in his *The Theory and Practice of Autonomy*, Cambridge, Cambridge University Press, 1988. Richard Lindley's *Autonomy*, Basingstoke, Macmillan, 1986, is a good introduction to the idea, and contains a chapter specifically on children.

Articles defending some version of the 'caretaker thesis' are Jeffrey Blustein, 'Parents, Paternalism, and Children's Rights', *Journal of Critical Analysis*, 8(2), Summer/Fall 1980, pp. 89–98; Joel Feinberg, 'The Child's Right to an Open Future', in William Aiken and Hugh LaFollette (eds), *Whose Child? Children's Rights, Parental Authority and State Power*, pp. 89–98; Amy Gutman, 'Children, Paternalism and Education: A Liberal Argument', *Philosophy & Public Affairs*, 9(4), Summer 1980, pp. 338–58; Peter Hobson, 'Paternalism and the Justification of Compulsory Education', *The Australasian Journal of Education*, 27(2), 1983, pp. 136–50; and Geoffrey Scarre, 'Children and Paternalism', *Philosophy*, 55, 1980, pp. 117–24.

There are a number of general discussions of children's rights which cover the questions of arbitrariness and incompetence, for instance M. D. A. Freeman's *The Rights and the Wrongs of Children*, London and Dover, NH, Frances Pinter, 1983, esp. Chapter 2, and Colin Wringe's *Children's Rights*, London, Routledge & Kegan Paul, 1981. Bertram Bandman, 'Do Children Have Any Natural Rights? A Look at Rights and Claims in Legal, Moral and Educational Discourse', *Proceedings of the 29th Annual Meeting of the Philosophy of Education Society*, 1973, pp. 234–46, also looks at children's rights in the context of a general analysis of rights. Other pieces that do this are: James Griffin, 'Do Children Have Rights?', Harry Brighouse, 'What Rights (if any) do Children Have?', Samantha Brennan, 'Children's Choices or Children's Interests: Which do their Rights Protect?' all in D. Archard and C. Macleod (eds), *The Moral and Political Status of Children*, Oxford, Oxford University Press, 2002, S. Brennan and R. Noggle, 'The Moral Status of Children: Children's Rights, Parents' Rights, and Family Justice', *Social Theory and Practice*, 23(1), 1995, pp. 1–26.

Attacks on the arbitrariness or inadequacy of any distinction between children and adults for the purpose of denying the former rights can be found in John Kleining, 'Mill, Children and Rights', *Educational Philosophy and Theory*, 8(1), 1976, pp. 1–16; Francis Schrag, 'The Child in the Moral Order', *Philosophy*, 52, 1977, pp. 167–77; and Victor L. Worsfold, 'A Philosophical Justification for Children's Rights', *Harvard Educational Review*, 44(1), February 1974, pp. 142–57.

Amongst many discussions of children's actual legal rights the following are useful for exploring historical developments and the thinking underlying the changes: John Eekelaar, 'The Emergence of Children's Rights', *Oxford Journal of Legal Studies*, 6(2), 1986, pp. 161–82; M. D. A. Freeman, 'The Rights of Children in the International Year of the Child', *Current Legal Problems*, 33, 1980, pp. 1–31; Robert L. Geiser, 'The Rights of Children', *The Hastings Law Journal*, 28, 1977, pp. 1027–51; Laurence D. Houlgate, 'The Child as a Person: Recent Supreme Court Decisions', in William Aiken and Hugh LaFollette (eds), *Whose Child? Children's Rights, Parental Authority and State Power*, pp. 221–36; and Arthur Landever, 'The Rights of Children in America: The Differing Perceptions', *Poly Law Review*, 5, 1979, pp. 19–28. Bob Franklin, 'Children's Rights; Developments and Prospects', *Children and Society*, 3(1), 1989, pp. 50–66 reviews possible legal and institutional improvements.

The United Nations Convention on the Rights of the Child is available in a wide range of places, but a good place to read about it, its implementation, and related issues is the website of UNICEF: http://www.unicef.org/crc/crc.htm. Lawrence J. LeBlanc, *The Convention on the Rights of the Child: United Nations Lawmaking on Human Rights*, Lincoln, University of Nebraska Press, 1995, is a fine, comprehensive study of the origins of the Convention and its drafting. The impact of the CRC on UK law is outlined in Jane Fortin, *Children's Rights and the Developing Law*, 2nd edition, London, Butterworths, 2003.

Philip Alston (ed.) *The Best Interests of the Child: Reconciling Culture and Human Rights*, Oxford, Clarendon Press, 1994 is a useful collection of pieces addressing the relationship between a core CRC principle and the facts of cultural difference. More on the idea of best interests exposing the difficulties in understanding what it might mean can be found in Robert H. Mnookin, 'Foster Care – In Whose Best Interests?' in O. O'Neill and W. Ruddick (eds), *Having Children: Philosophical and Legal Reflections on Parenthood* (Oxford: Oxford University Press, 1979), pp. 179–213, and Jon Elster, in his *Solomonic Judgements, Studies in the limitations of rationality* (Cambridge: Cambridge University Press, 1989), III 'Solomonic Judgements: Against the Best Interests of the Child'.

An excellent study of the age of the age of criminal responsibility is provided by the Scottish Law Commission, *Report on the Age of Criminal Responsibility*, Edinburgh: The Stationery Office, 2002. Another similar official report which nevertheless provides an interesting comparison with the Scottish report is The Law Reform Commission of Hong Kong, *Report on The Age of Criminal Responsibility in Hong Kong* (http://www.info,gov.hk/hkreform). Julia Fionda (ed.), *Legal Concepts of Childhood*, Oxford, Hart Publishing 2001, offers a good collection of different perspectives on childhood as well as studies of various aspects of the child in law. A very good study of operation of the Scottish Children's Hearing System is A. Lockyer and F. H. Stone (eds), *Juvenile Justice in Scotland: Twenty-Five Years of the Welfare Approach*, London, Butterworths, 1998. An interesting essay on the Hearing System in relation to the justice and welfare models provided by a distinguished jurisprudential theorist is Neil MacCormick, 'A Special Conception of Juvenile Justice: Kilbrandon's Legacy' (the 2001 Killbrandon Lecture) (http://www.scotland.giv.uk/library5/education/ch30-00.asp).

There are a number of articles which have outlined a decline in parental rights correlative with an increase in the rights of children. Amongst these are John Eekelaar, 'What are Parental Rights?', *Law Quarterly Review*, 89, April 1973, pp. 210–34; Susan Maidment, 'The Fragmentation of Parental Rights', *Cambridge Law Journal*, 40(1), April 1981, pp. 135–58.

Olive Stevens's work apart, Fred I. Greenstein's *Children and Politics*, New Haven, Conn., Yale University Press, 1965, is an earlier, classic study of American school-children's political socialisation. Defences of children's suffrage may be found in John Harris's 'The Political Status of Children' in Keith Graham (ed.), *Contemporary Political Philosophy: Radical Studies*, Cambridge, Cambridge University Press, 1982, pp. 35–55, and Bob Franklin, 'Children's Political Rights', in Bob Franklin (ed.), *The Rights of Children*, Oxford, Basil Blackwell, 1986, pp. 24–53. An interesting and cautious defence of the adult vote is to be found in Francis Schrag's 'The Child's Status in the Democratic State', *Political Theory*, 3(4), November 1975, pp. 441–57; it is criticised by Carl Cohen in his 'On the Child's Status in the Democratic State: A Response to Mr. Schrag', in the same issue of *Political Theory*, pp. 458–63. Andrew Lockyer's chapter 'The Political Status of Children and Young People' in Lockyer, A., Crick, B. and Annette, J. (eds), *Education for Democratic Citizenship: Issues of Theory and Practice* (Aldershot: Ashgate, 2003), pp. 120–38 is a very good analysis of children and their proper citizenship status. Studies and research findings relevant to children and politics in the United Kingdom can be found at the following web sites: Children and Young Persons's Unit: www.cypu.gov.uk; Children's Rights Alliance for England: www.crights.org.uk; Joseph Rowntree Foundation: www.jrf.org.uk

Stevi Jackson's *Childhood and Sexuality*, Oxford, Basil Blackwell, 1982, is an admirably clear and thoughtful defence of the need for enlightened and early sex education. J. Mark Halstead and Michael J. Reiss, *Values in Sex Education: From Principles to Practice*, London, Routledge, 2003 is a good thoughtful exploration of the role of values in sex education, and a well informed guide to the forms that such an education can take. Ronald and Juliette Goldman's *Sexual Thinking: A Comparative Study of Children Aged 5 to 15 years in Australia, North America, Britain and Sweden*, London, Routledge & Kegan Paul, 1982, provides the empirical evidence for the need for such education. Michèle Elliott, *Preventing Child Sexual Assault: A Practical Guide to Talking with Children*, London, Bedford Square Press/NCVO, 1985, is one of the best examples of what such an education should be like. David Finkelhor's 'What's Wrong with Sex between Adults and Children: Ethics and the Problem of Sexual Abuse', *American Journal of Orthopsychiatry*, 49(4), October 1979, pp. 692–7, is a much quoted defence of the view that consent is the key criterion of permissible sex. Richard Ives's 'Children's Sexual Rights', in Bob Franklin (ed.), *The Rights of Children*, defends children's rights from sexual exploitation, and to both sexual expression and sex education. Judith Ennew, *The Sexual Exploitation of Children*, Cambridge, Polity Press, 1986, is a judicious if depressing survey of the subject.

David Archard's *Sexual Consent*, Boulder, Westview, 1998, is an overview of the topic and includes a chapter on the age of sexual consent. Igor Primoratz's *Ethics and Sex*, London, Routledge, 1999, has a chapter on pedophilia. Alan Soble (ed.) *The Philosophy of Sex, Contemporary Readings*, 3rd edition, Oxford, Rowman & Littlefield, 1997 is an excellent collection of philosophical pieces, both classic and more recent, on sex.

Following Tönnies, Lon Fuller distinguishes 'Two Principles of Human Association', *Nomos XI: Voluntary Associations*, Yearbook of the American Society for Political and Legal Philosophy, edited by J. Roland Pennock and John W. Chapman, New York, Atherton Press, 1969, pp. 3–23, one of shared commitment and one of legal principle. A recent critique of philosophy's obsession with rights is Robert B. Louden, 'Rights Infatuation and the Impoverishment of Moral Theory', *Journal of Value Inquiry*, 17, 1983, pp. 87–102, and a concise defence of the view that moral philosophy could do without rights is Robert Young, 'Dispensing with Moral Rights', *Political Theory*, 6(1), February 1978, pp. 63–74.

Relevant in addition to Gilligan is Nel Noddings, *Caring: A Feminine Approach to Ethics and Moral Education*, Berkeley, University of California Press, 1984. See also John Hardwig, 'Should Women Think in Terms of Rights?', *Ethics*, 94, April 1984, pp. 441–55. Gilligan and Noddings are both helpfully discussed in Jean Grimshaw, *Feminist Philosophers: Women's Perspectives on Philosophical Traditions*, Brighton, Wheatsheaf, 1986, Chapters 7 and 8. Andrea Maihofer's 'Care' in Alison M. Jaggar and Iris Marion Young (eds) *A Companion to Feminist Philosophy* (Oxford: Blackwell, 1998), pp. 383–92 provides a guide to the feminist debates about the ethic of care provoked initially by Gilligan's work.

Defences of the view that talk of children having rights is incompatible with the affective nature of the family can be found in Francis Schrag, 'Children: Their Rights and Needs', in William Aiken and Hugh LaFollette (eds), *Whose Child? Children's Rights, Parental Authority and State Power*, pp. 237–53, and Ferdinand Schoeman, 'Rights of Children, Rights of Parents, and the Moral Basis of the Family', *Ethics*, 91, October 1980, pp. 6–19. Schoeman is criticised by Iris Marion Young, 'Rights to Intimacy in a Complex Society', *Journal of Social Philosophy*, 14, May 1982, pp. 47–52; and Jeremy Waldron, 'When Justice Replaces Affection: The Need for Rights', *Harvard Journal of Law & Public Policy*, 11(3), 1988, pp. 625–47. Interestingly, an earlier article by Francis Schrag, 'Rights Over Children', *Journal of Value Inquiry*, 7, 1973, pp. 96–105 provides a nuanced defence of the rights of parents to act as their children's guardians.

Classic critical discussions of Locke's proprietarian argument are J. P. Day, 'Locke on Property' *Philosophical Quarterly*, 16, 1966, pp. 207–20, and Robert Nozick, *Anarchy, State, and Utopia*, Oxford: Blackwell, 1974, pp. 174–8. L. C. Becker, *Property Rights, Philosophic Foundations*, London, Routledge & Kegan Paul, 1977, pp. 38–9 offers an argument as to why self-owning children cannot be owned by their parents.

An article which sees features of the parent–child relationship as giving credence to a proprietarian explanation is J. Bigelow, J. Campbell, S. M. Dodds, R. Pargetter, E. W. Prior and R. young, 'Parental Autonomy,' *Journal of Applied Philosophy*, 5:2. 1988, pp. 183–96. A libertarian who does think parents have property rights over their children but that there is a public interest constraint on their exercise is Jan Narveson, *The Libertarian Idea*, Philadelphia, Temple University Press, 1998, pp. 272–4. Barbara Hall, 'The Origin of Parental Rights', *Public Affairs Quarterly*, 13(1), 1999, pp. 73–8, argues that parents own their genetic material, whereas Hillel Steiner, a contemporary Lockean, argues that parents do *not* own their genetic material, *An Essay on Rights*, Oxford, Blackwell, 1998, pp. 237–48. Both draw appropriate conclusions for parental rights over their children. Edgar Page defends a quasi-proprietarian argument to the conclusion that parents have a great interest in shaping the lives of their own children in his 'Parental Rights,' *Journal of Applied Philosophy*, 1(2), 1984, pp. 187–203. A piece sceptical of the idea of parental rights is P. Montague, 'The Myth of Parental Rights', *Social Theory and Practice* 26(1), 2000, pp. 47–68.

There are interesting discussions of *patria potestas* in W. K. Lacey, '*Patria potestas*', in Beryl Rawson (ed.), *The Family in Ancient Rome: New Perspectives*, London, Croom Helm, 1986, pp. 120–44, B. Nicholas, *An Introduction to Roman Law*, Oxford, Clarendon Press, 1962, pp. 65–8, Lord MacKenzie, *Studies in Roman Law*, Edinburgh, Wm. Blackwood & Sons, 1862, Chapter IX, and John Boswell, *The Kindness of Strangers: The Abandonment of Children in Western Europe from Late Antiquity to the Renaissance*, New York, Random House, 1988, pp. 58–75. Thomas Hobbes held a view close to *patria potestas*. It is stated in *Leviathan*, Chapter XX, 'Of Dominion Paternall, and Despotical', and discussed by M. M. Goldsmith, *Hobbes's Science of Politics*, New York, Columbia University Press, 1966, pp. 166–74, and David P. Gauthier, *The Logic of* Leviathan: *The Moral and Political Theory of Thomas Hobbes*, Oxford, Clarendon Press, 1969, pp. 117–19.

A contemporary defence of the 'priority thesis' is provided by J. Blustein, *Parents and Children: The Ethics of the Family*, Oxford, Oxford University Press, 1982. Thomas H. Murray, *The Worth of a Child*, Berkeley: University of California Press, 1996, criticises the idea that parents either own their children or are pure paternalists devoted exclusively to their children's good. The title of Julian Savulescu's 'Procreative Beneficence: Why We Should Select the Best Children', *Bioethics*, 15(5–6), 2001, pp. 413–26 is self-explanatory and the article itself is a short, provocative defence of the claim.

Whether parents should pay for or be subsidised in the exercise of their procreative liberty is discussed in P. Casal and A. Williams, 'Rights, Equality and Procreation', *Analyse & Kritik* 17, 1995, pp. 93–116, and in two articles by R. George: 'Who Should Bear the Cost of Children?' *Public Affairs Quarterly* 1, 1987, pp. 1–42 and 'On the External Benefits of Children' in D. Meyers, K. Kipnis and C.F. Murphy, Jr. (eds), *Kindred Matters:*

Rethinking the Philosophy of the Family, Ithaca, NY, Cornell University Press, 1994, pp. 209–17.

Discussion of the possibly objectionable role that the family can play in the transmission of ideas of injustice can be found in S. M. Okin, *Justice, Gender, and the Family*, New York, Basic Books, 1994, J. Exdell, 'Feminism, Fundamentalism, and Liberal Legitimacy,' *Canadian Journal of Philosophy*, 24, 1994, pp. 441–64, and S. A. Lloyd, 'Family Justice and Social Justice,' *Pacific Philosophical Quarterly*, 75, 1994, pp. 353–71. For differing views on whether family autonomy should be limited in the name of social justice see: James Fishkin, *Justice, Equal Opportunity, and the Family*, New Haven, CT, Yale University Press, 1983, Jeffrey Blustein, *Parents and Children: The Ethics of the Family*, Oxford, Oxford University Press, 1982, Chapter 4, P. Vallentyne and M. Lipson, 'Equal Opportunity and the Family,' *Public Affairs Quarterly*, 3 (4), 1989, pp. 39–45, C.M. Macleod, 'Liberal Equality and the Affective Family,' in D. Archard and C. Macleod (eds) *The Moral and Political status of Children*, Oxford, Oxford University Press, 2002, pp. 212–30, and V. Munoz-Dardé, 'Rawls, Justice in the Family and Justice of the Family,' *Philosophical Quarterly*, 48, 1998, pp. 335–52 and 'Is the Family to be Abolished Then?', *Proceedings of the Aristotelian Society*, 99, 1999, pp. 37–56.

Standard histories of the family are Lawrence Stone's *The Family, Sex and Marriage in England, 1500–1800*, Harmondsworth, Penguin, 1979, and Jean-Louis Flandrin, *Families in Former Times: Kinship, Household and Sexuality*, translated by Richard Southern, Cambridge, Cambridge University Press, 1979. A very relevant classic text is Peter Laslett, *The World We Have Lost*, London, Methuen, 1965. A useful brief historical survey of the modern family is Barbara Laslett, 'The Family as a Public and Private Institution: An Historical Perspective', *Journal of Marriage and the Family*, 35, August 1973, pp. 480–92.

A spirited right-wing defence of the family is Ferdinand Mount, *The Subversive Family*, London, Jonathan Cape, 1982; and an excellent introduction to socialist and feminist thinking about the family is Michèle Barrett and Mary McIntosh, *The Anti-Social Family*, 2nd edition, London, Verso, 1991.

Philosophical collections of articles on the family include Diana Tietjens Meyers, Kenneth Kipnis, and Cornelius F. Murphy, Jr. (eds), *Kindred Matters, Rethinking the Philosophy of the Family*, Ithaca, NY, Cornell University Press, 1993, and Uma Narayn and Julia J. Batkowiak (eds) *Having and Raising Children: Unconventional Families, Hard Choices, and the Social Good*, University Park, PA, Pennsylvania State University Press, 1999. An uneven collection which looks, *inter alia*, at adoption and race, education and parental authority, and same-sex families, is Stephen Macedo and Iris Marion Young (eds) *Child, Family, and State*, Nomos XLIV, New York, New York University Press, 2003. A collection addressing the relationship between feminism and the family is Hilde Lindemann Nelson (ed.), *Feminism and Families*, London, Routledge, 1997. A collection that specifically address the implications of the new reproductive technologies for our philosophical and legal understanding of the family is Carole Ulanowsky (ed.), *The Family in the Age of Biotechnology*, Aldershot, Avebury, 1995.

A revealing historical study of the beginnings of English childcare law is George K. Behlmer, *Child Abuse and Moral Reform in England, 1870–1908*, Stanford, CT,

Stanford University Press, 1982. Lionel Rose, *The Erosion of Childhood: Child Oppression in Britain 1860–1918*, London, Routledge, 1991, offers a comprehensive historical survey of the various respects in which children were oppressed and abused on the eve of the first children's legislation.

An excellent critical survey of the various strands of thinking underlying present-day child-care policy is Lorraine Fox Harding, *Perspectives in Child Care Policy*, London, Longman, 1991. Nigel Thomas, *Children, Family and the State: Decision-making and Child Participation*, Bristol, The Policy Press, 2002, also looks at the relationship between children, family and the state in the care system with interesting research on children's own views on these matters. A flavour of legal thinking about the relationship between state and family is given in M. D. A. Freeman (ed.), *State, Law and the Family: Critical Perspectives*, London, Tavistock, 1984. Brenda M. Hoggett and David S. Pearl, *The Family, Law and Society: Cases and Materials*, London, Butterworth, 3rd edition, 1991, is a standard legal source-book. In the UK the 1989 Children Act is the principal legal instrument, and Andrew Bainham, *Children – The New Law. The Children Act 1989*, Bristol, Family Law, 1990 is a standard guide.

The classic and very influential statement of the 'liberal standard' is in the two texts by Joseph Goldstein, Anna Freud and Albert J. Solnit, *Beyond the Best Interests of the Child*, New York, Free Press, 1973, and *Before the Best Interests of the Child*, New York, Free Press, 1979. Representative discussions of the 'liberal standard' can be found in Richard Bourne and Eli H. Newberger, '"Family Autonomy" or "Coercive Intervention"? Ambiguity and Conflict in the Proposed Standards for Child Abuse and Neglect', *Boston University Law Review*, 57, 1977, pp. 670–706; M. D. A. Freeman, 'Freedom and the Welfare State: Child-Rearing, Parental Autonomy and State Intervention', *Journal of Social Welfare Law*, 1983, pp. 70–91; and Michael Wald, 'State Intervention on Behalf of "Neglected" Children: A Search for Realistic Standards', *Stanford Law Review*, 27(4), April 1975, pp. 985–1040.

For an indication of radical and feminist thinking about state intervention in family life see Carol Smart, 'Regulating Families or Legitimating Patriarchy? Family Law in Britain', *International Journal of the Sociology of Law*, 10, 1982, pp. 129–47; and Nikolas Rose, 'Beyond the Public/Private Division: Law, Power and the Family', *Journal of Law and Society*, 14(1), Spring 1987, pp. 61–76.

Robert Dingwall, John Eekelaar and Topsy Murray, *The Protection of Children: State Intervention and Family Life*, Oxford, Basil Blackwell, 1983, remains the best study of how the 'liberal standard' works in practice.

For an excellent website providing comparative information on child care and family policies see The Clearinghouse on International Developments in Child, Youth and Family Policies at Columbia University: http://www.childpolicyintl.org/

A defence of privacy similar to Fried's can be found in Robert S. Gerstein, 'Intimacy and Privacy', *Ethics*, 89, 1978, pp. 76–81 and James Rachels, 'Why Privacy is Important', *Philosophy & Public Affairs*, 4(4), Summer 1975, pp. 323–33. The view is subjected to excellent criticism by Jeffrey H. Reiman, 'Privacy, Intimacy, and Personhood', *Philosophy & Public Affairs*, 6(1), Fall 1976, pp. 26–44. All of these and other useful philosophical articles on privacy can be found in the collection, *Philosophical Dimensions of Privacy: An Anthology*, edited by Ferdinand D. Schoeman, Cambridge, Cambridge University

Press, 1984. An illuminating historical study of privacy is Barrington Moore, *Privacy: Studies in Social and Cultural History*, London, Pantheon, 1984. A good article attacking privacy, especially in the context of the family, is Lorenne M. G. Clark, 'Privacy, Property, and the Family', in Richard Bronaugh (ed.), *Philosophical Law*, Westport, CT, Greenwood Press, 1978, pp. 167–87.

Hugh LaFollette, 'Licensing Parents', *Philosophy & Public Affairs*, 9(2), 1980, pp. 183–197, is an excellent and spirited philosophical defence of licensing; it is criticised by Lawrence E. Frisch, 'On Licentious Licensing: A Reply to Hugh LaFollette', *Philosophy & Public Affairs*, 11(2), 1981, pp. 173–80, and LaFollette responds in the same issue, pp. 181–3. The separation of family and marriage is defended by Margaret Mead, 'Marriage in Two Steps', in Herbert A. Otto (ed.), *The Family in Search of a Future: Alternate Models for Moderns*, New York, Appleton-Century-Crofts, 1970, pp. 75–84; also Joseph and Clorinda Margolis, 'The Separation of Marriage and Family', in Mary Vetterling-Braggin, F. Ellison and J. English (eds), *Feminism and Philosophy*, Totowa, NJ, Littlefield, Adams & Co., 1977, pp. 291–301.

Apart from Bruno Bettelheim's *Children of the Dream*, London, Thames & Hudson, 1969, other relevant studies of the kibbutz are Melford E. Spiro, *Kibbutz: Venture in Utopia*, Cambridge, MA, Harvard University Press, 1956 and *Children of the Kibbutz*, New York, Schocken, 1965, also by Spiro. See also Benjamin Beit-Hallahmi and Albert I. Rabin, 'Family and Communally Raised (Kibbutz) Children 20 Years Later: Biographical Data', *International Journal of Psychology*, 14, 1979, pp. 215–23.

For a brief survey of socialist childcare with recommendations see *Changing Childcare: Cuba, China and the Challenging of Our Own Values*, by The Socialist Childcare Collective, London, Writers and Readers Publishing Collective, 1973. Useful studies of Chinese childcare, although dating from the 1970s, can be found in Ruth Sidel, *Women and Child Care in China: A Firsthand Report*, London, Sheldon Press, 1972, and William Kessen (ed.), *Childhood in China*, New Haven, CT, Yale University Press, 1975. A classic comparison of childrearing in the Soviet Union and America is Urie Bronfenbrenner, *Two Worlds of Childhood: U.S. and U.S.S.R.*, London, George Allen & Unwin, 1971.

Huge amounts have been written on the subject of child abuse since the 1970s. Brian Corby, *Child Abuse: Towards a Knowledge Basis*, 2nd edition, Buckingham, Open University Press, 2000, is a comprehensive and up-to-date guide to the history, definitions, nature, causes, consequences and child protection implications of child abuse. In addition to the works cited in the footnotes to chapter 14, Nigel Parton, *The Politics of Child Abuse*, London, Macmillan, 1985, is a good left-wing study of how child abuse has been defined and dealt with in the UK; The Violence Against Children Study Group, *Taking Child Abuse Seriously: Contemporary Issues in Child Protection Theory and Practice*, London, Unwin Hyman, 1990, is a useful collection of articles from a socialist and feminist perspective. Cyril Greenland, *Preventing CAN Deaths: An International Study of Deaths Due to Child Abuse and Neglect*, London, Tavistock, 1987, is a much-quoted defence of the view that the characteristics of abusing parents conform to a high-risk check-list. Gay Search, *The Last Taboo: Sexual Abuse of Children*, Harmondsworth, Penguin, 1988, is an accessible journalistic account of the subject. C. Henry Kempe and Patricia Beezley Mrazek (eds), *Sexually Abused Children and their*

Families, Oxford, Pergamon Press, 1987, is a collection of interdisciplinary essays which shows current thinking about the subject. The Special Issue of *Feminist Review*, 28, January 1988, 'Family Secrets: Child Sexual Abuse Today', is a useful representative selection of feminist articles; and Bea Campbell's *Unofficial Secrets: Child Sexual Abuse – The Cleveland Case*, London, Virago, 1988, is an interesting polemic in response to the Cleveland events. Natalie Abrams, 'Problems in Defining Child Abuse and Neglect', in Onora O'Neill and William Ruddick (eds), *Having Children*, pp. 156–63, is a rare attempt by a philosopher to explore the problem.

A balanced consideration of the arguments for and against corporal punishment from a number of different backgrounds is the Special Issue, 'Corporal Punishment', of *Children's Legal Rights Journal*, 17(4), Fall 1997.

INDEX